The Way of Love

The Battle for Inner Transformation

Ronda Chervin, Ph.D.

Cover Art & Text Design
Benedict J. Longenecker

Cover Artwork
"The Journey to Emmaus" by Robert Zund

Printed and Bound in the USA
CreateSpace

ISBN: 1482569833
ISBN-13: 978-1482569834

INTRODUCTION
by
Ronda Chervin

The year 1958 when I was 21, turned out to be the greatest turning point of my life. I went from thinking that there was no truth and no real love to finding that Truth was a Person: Jesus, the Christ; and that Love was the source of all reality, abundantly gifting me through the sacraments of the Church.

Eventually I would become a wife, a mother, a professor of philosophy, a writer, a speaker, a grandmother, a TV presenter, and a widow dedicated to the Lord. All this time I have been striving, with many set-backs, to follow the *Way of Love*. The personal insights I gained from set-backs and repentance you can read about in my books. (See www.rondachervin.com)

In this book *The Way of Love: the Battle for Inner Transformation*, I am putting together four different short books about love into one. Each of these books is interactive with questions for personal response and group sharing. I have used them in classes and also in workshops and retreats.

Book One: The Way of Love: What is Love? is the most philosophical. It is a mixture of the concepts of Dietrich Von Hildebrand, my professor of philosophy in graduate school; C.S. Lewis, one of my all time favorite thinkers; and my own ideas.

Book Two: The Way of Love: Overcoming Negative Emotions is a study of the bad emotions we need to battle with to become more loving.

Book Three: The Way of Love: Making Loving Moral Decisions is a reprint of a book I wrote in the '70's on ethics previously entitled: Living in Love: About Christian Ethics.

Book Four: The Way of Love: A Spiritual Marathon: 100 Steps
is my latest writing – is a blog published by Watershed
(ccwatershed.org/100Steps), presented on EWTN, and being
used in parishes throughout the world.

Of course you can read more scholarly and deeper books about
love, but I am praying that these booklets, by being so simple,
will open you to receive swift blessing from our God who went to
great lengths to prove to us that He is the Way of Love.

CONTENTS

VOLUME 1: WHAT IS LOVE?

VOLUME 2: OVERCOMING OBSTACLES TO LOVE

Volume 3: Making Loving Moral Decisions

Specific Controversial Moral Teachings:

VOLUME 4: THE WAY OF LOVE: STEP BY STEP

VOLUME 1
WHAT IS LOVE?

INTRODUCTION

When I ask students, or participants in my workshops, "what is love?" they come up with many different answers. Mostly they reply with one word such as "caring," "sacrifice," "self-giving."

They are surprised to learn that there are many definitions of love, not one. They find that learning about types of love is helpful in growing in love. For example, if you have never thought about "delight love", you will be happy to see that showing delight in others goes a long way to making others happier. Sometimes, only doing favors for others but never telling them you delight in them can even be a downer!

Read on. You will learn a lot.

SESSION

1

WHAT IS LOVE?

"You are called by name…" (Isaiah 43:1)

On a separate sheet of paper make a list of all the persons and things you have loved or now love.

Now write the words you think define the concept of love.

A great philosopher of the 20th century, Dietrich Von Hildebrand, defined love as "a response to the unique preciousness of another." In Biblical language, God has called each one of us by name when He created us in our mother's womb.

In a different perspective, St. Thomas Aquinas defines love as an appetite for the good. Love includes being pleased with something, desiring it, and taking joy in it. When a beloved person becomes a part of oneself this is called union. Such union can take place with God, who is a person in the sense of being conscious, choosing, and thinking, This level of love includes intimate closeness through knowledge of the other, feeling what the other feels, leading to doing good things for the other. It is ecstatic, drawing one out of oneself and zealous – withstanding all opposition.

The great 20th century writer, C.S. Lewis, thought that there was not one definition of love but rather 4 types of love. (In parenthesis are the Greek names for these 4 loves):

Passionate Love (Eros) – passion can be lust but it can also be intense love for a beloved person, for beauty, truth, or God.

Friendship Love (Philia) – this forms a "we" bond based on common values ranging from football to the rosary.

Affectionate Love (Storge) – this is found in families, but also for pets, or for people we see often in the workplace, parish, or gym. It comes from familiarity.

Caring-Serving Love (Agape) – in this love we help others because they are in need even if we don't know them.

More about each of these types of love in sessions to follow.

Now mark your list of persons and things according to the type of love that fits best (P for passion, F for friendship, A for affection, C for caring.)

Spiritual Exercises:

1. That "the eyes are the windows of the soul" is an image found in a poem of Yeats. Look into the eyes of the person sitting next to you for 5 minutes. "Soften" your own eyes to receive the other so that your look is not like a cold staring. When you can see the unique preciousness of him or her, smile.

2. Scorecard: Carry a file card or a sheet of paper for a whole week making notes of loving thoughts, words and deeds vs. unloving thoughts words and deeds. For example, in the loving column could be: brushed my teeth (self-love); said hello or asked "how are you?" of someone with real affection and care in your heart. In the unloving column could be cursing another driver or telling a third person something bad about someone you dislike so that he or she will dislike that person also.

For Personal Reflection and Group Sharing:

(If you are working on your *Way of Love* with a group, the questions below can be answered during each session.)

1. How did you define love before this session? Did you find the definition of love as a response to the unique preciousness of another thought-provoking? What about the description of Thomas Aquinas?

2. What did you learn from looking into someone's eyes?

If you wish, write your own teaching for a class for children, teens or adults, or a homily you might give in the future? You could include a song, a drawing, or dance? If you so choose, you can share what you create with the group at the beginning of some other session of the Way of Love.

SESSION

2

LOVE: A MATTER OF THE WILL OR OF THE HEART?

"You shall love the Lord your God with all your heart, and with all your soul, and with all your mind... you shall love your neighbor as yourself." (Matthew 22:37-39)

(Before Session 2 begins, you could share insights from your scorecard experience with a few people sitting near you.)

"Love is not a matter of feeling but of the will," we are often told. This sounds as if it contradicts the famous words of Our Lord in the passage quoted above about loving God with your whole heart. Confusing!

Let's look at a few examples:

Alicia is the mother of a new-born baby. She feels delight in her little child, but she doesn't feel happy when she's changing diapers. A more seasoned mother tells her: "Look, love isn't a feeling. It's a matter of will. If you love your baby you have to do things you don't feel like doing."

Clear enough!

But, look at another example. John works at a job he hates because he loves his wife and children and wants to bring home the pay check that feeds, clothes and houses them. However, when he walks in the door each evening he fails to smile at his wife or children. For dinner he grabs his plate and strides into the family room where he spends the whole evening drinking a 6 pack of beer while watching sports. He has used his will to do the loving thing by working at his job, but since he doesn't feel love in his heart when he is home, the wife and kids, though grateful for his support, don't feel very loved on a day to day basis.

Could it be that love is both an act of the will and also a feeling?

In his book *The Heart*, Dietrich Von Hildebrand, throws light on the way the heart and the will need to work together for love to be complete.

Von Hildebrand teaches that it is out of the heart that love is expressed. In his book *The Heart* he shows how some thinkers over-emphasize the intellect and the will over the heart because of false ideas about our emotions. Some feelings are not in our direct control such as feeling blue on a grey day or tired because of not enough sleep. Sometimes we give into irrational bad moods or, worse, into extreme feelings of rage or despair. But we also have feelings in our hearts which are neither out of control or irrational such as joy, peace, hopefulness, gratitude and … deep, authentic love.

The *Way of Love* involves growing in the right kind of emotions. Such emotions are described by Von Hildebrand as responses to genuine values. How so? Consider the joy you have in your faith that there is a God of love who cares for you. The feeling of joy is a response to your faith in this great truth and reality. Consider the grief you experience when a beloved person leaves this world. The feeling of sadness is a response to your experience of loss because even though you believe his or her soul still exists, this person will be, outside of a supernatural vision, invisible to you until the Day of Judgment.

When God teaches us to love Him and each other with all our hearts He surely hopes that we will experience this love more and more as an emotion based on gratitude for His gifts of our creation and redemption. He does not command us to act "as if" we loved God and neighbor, but to really love Him and our neighbor.

Does Von Hildebrand mean it is wrong to do loving things such as changing diapers, working at a job we hate, or going to Holy Mass on Sunday when we don't feel like it? Of course not!

The key concepts here are what Von Hildebrand calls *sanction* and *disavowal*. To sanction something is to affirm it. To disavow something is to reject it. These are decisions that include acts of the intellect and the will. Let me explain.

The mother of the baby, in the example given above, feels joy (in her heart) as she gazes upon her child. She might *think* (an act of the mind) to herself: how happy I am to have my little darling. Then she might decide (an act of the *will*) to thank God for this great gift. That is to *sanction* (affirm) her joy. When she *thinks* of the unpleasant chore of changing diapers she might *disavow* (reject) her feeling of disgust by *thinking* to herself: well, diapers are yucky but my baby is surely worth it. She might make a decision (an act of *will*) in the future to sing a little song when she is changing diapers.

The father who hates his job may use his will-power to overcome the bad mood he has after work. He might *disavow* (reject) his usual grumpy ways because he thinks about how sad his family is that he is so unfriendly. He can *sanction* (affirm) himself whenever he succeeds in being more friendly to his wife and family and spending more time with them.

Over time the heart can grow in loving feelings through the help of the intellect and will's sanctions and disavowals.

Spiritual Exercises:

1. Watch yourself tonight and tomorrow and make a list on paper or in your head of loving thoughts, words and deeds that come from the heart and those that come more from the will in the form of sanctioning or disavowing some of them.

   For example: you gave a newcomer at the *Way of Love* session a smile, a handshake or a hug as he or she was leaving. This was a spontaneous little deed of love. You sanctioned it. Later, you failed to greet someone you live with because you didn't feel like talking to anyone. Then you disavowed this neglect and, in a loving act of will, you sat down next to him or her and asked "How was your day?"

For Personal Reflection and Group Sharing:

1. On average how much comparative time in your life do you give to:

   thinking, as in analyzing things such as news items, work projects, personal problems (the intellect);

   deciding, as in planning for the short or long term future (the will);

feeling, not as a matter of good or bad moods but as in genuine value response (the heart).

If you wish, write a percentage next to each of the above categories. You might write a prayer for growth in one of these areas that you think you need to be better at.

2. Do you try to get away from feelings because they sometimes seem to you to be uncontrollable or irrational or painful?

3. Do you think you might experience more love of God and others in your life if you were willing to risk more?

4. How do you think the relationship between the will and the heart should be understood?

The will tries to overcome deficiencies of the wounded heart.

If you wish, write your own teaching about the heart and the will for a class for children, teens or adults, or a homily you might give in the future? You could include a song, a drawing, or dance? If you so choose, you can share what you create with the group at the beginning of some other session of the *Way of Love*.

SESSION

3

PASSIONATE LOVE

"I came to cast fire upon the earth; and would that it was already kindled." (Luke 12:49)

(If you wish, share with those sitting next to you your experience of sanction (affirmation of good impulses) and disavowal (rejection of bad impulses) since the last session).

What are you passionate about? Make a list all the way from, say, ice-cream to God.

In Plato's philosophy what is called eros or passionate love is broad. We tend to use the word eros or erotic only for sexual passion. The term Platonic love is used to describe love for others that is without any sexual passion. For Plato eros also includes love for beauty, truth, and the ideal. He calls love a divine madness, giving wings to the soul.

If you have ever been in love, and I've only met one or two people in my seventy-two years of life who have never been in love, you know how passionate is the joy just in knowing so precious a person. As Von Hildebrand explains, you are enchanted with the beauty of the entire personality of the beloved.

Passionate love is, therefore, often good. Think of ecstatic feelings when listening to beautiful music or watching sun rays on the ocean. Think of the unceasing energy of those working for justice, for example in pro-life work. Think of the fiery love of mystical saints for God. Do you realize that God is happy when you appreciate His creation?

In the sensory sphere, however, passion becomes disordered when eros dominates, leading to sinful exploitation. In addictive behaviors passion leads to destructive compulsions. The problem with such passions is that we want to grasp goods lower than God, our highest good. In the process we sacrifice God's will to our other desires. In his book *Four Loves*, C. S. Lewis describes how such passion love can become demonic as it seeks to justify even violence in the pursuit of its goals

There will be more about liberation through grace from such patterns later on in the *Way of Love*.

Because of the bad kind of enslaving passion, some think that a Christian should avoid all strong emotions. A 20th century theologian, Martin D'Arcy, in *The Mind and Heart of Love* explains that even though God loves us with tender caring love and we are to love our neighbor in this way, we also are to passionately desire union with God. We are to simultaneously desire to enjoy all created things but also sacrifice them to a higher call. Passionately yearning to be filled with God's love should overflow in us so that we can, in turn, love those who need us.

Let's look at good and bad features of passionate love:

Good: delight, appreciation, happiness in closeness to whatever we desire with passion, whether it be persons, beauty, truth or God, Himself.

Bad: inordinate idol worship of creatures who cannot deliver the happiness we seek, possessiveness, co-dependency, sin.

Spiritual Exercises:

1. Look at your list of passions. What have been good and bad sides of each? Write a prayer to God to take away the bad part and leave you the good part.

2. Go to the Adoration Chapel and surrender your bad passions to God. Let the soothing peace of His love fill you so that you are less desperately attached to your desires.

For Personal Reflection and Group Sharing:

1. Can you write a short history of the passions that have dominated your life from childhood onward?

2. What ideas of philosophers, works of literature or music expresses good and bad sides of passion love?

3. Ask for others to pray over you for whatever makes your passion love too desperate or compulsive.

If you wish, write your own teaching about passionate love for a class for children, teens or adults, or a homily you might give in the future? You could include a song, a drawing, or dance? If you so choose, you can share what you create with the group at the beginning of some other session of the *Way of Love*.

SESSION

4

FRIENDSHIP LOVE

"Behold, how good and pleasant it is when brethren dwell in unity...." (Psalm 133, 1)

(If you wish, share with those around you any thoughts you had about passionate love from the spiritual exercises and reflections from Session 3)

√ **Friendship can be defined as a bond with those we like to be with.**

Make a list of the friendships you have had in the past and in the present all the way from kids you played with in the neighborhood or at school to deep spiritual friendships.

Aristotle, the great Greek philosopher, writing before the birth of Christ, taught that there we had three types of friends: useful friends, pleasurable friends, and friendships based on the goodness of each one's character.

We become friendly with people we find useful for obvious reasons. Then, when that usefulness if over we usually don't stay close. I need a ride to work. A friendly co-worker picks me up each morning. We chat in the car about office politics. Then my friend moves to another state. At first I e-mail him or her with tit-bits of gossip, but after awhile the friend becomes more of a memory than a living friend for me. Some people call such friends contacts rather than real friends. But, consider, there are people we call contacts who we don't consider to be friends at all. The difference, I believe, is that we don't particularly like such contacts. We are only interested in their temporary usefulness to us.

Look down your list of past and present friends and, in your mind, check off those who have been or now are mostly utility friendships.

Aristotle described friendships of pleasure as those we love to be with because they are enjoyable. I would list here people who made me laugh or those who liked to play the same games with me. I thank God for such friends of the past or present. However, if one of these ceases to be pleasurable because he or she is going through a long, miserable, crisis, I may sympathize and try to help that person, but no longer want to be with that person in the same fun situations as before.

Look down your list of past and present friends and, in your mind, check off those who have been or now are friends for pleasure.

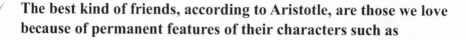

The best kind of friends, according to Aristotle, are those we love because of permanent features of their characters such as generosity, compassion, and deep shared values such as love of music, art, nature, God. Such qualities exist even when, because of distance or illness there is no usefulness for us in being close to them. Such qualities bring us joy even if there few pleasurable occasions to enjoy together.

Look down your list of past and present friends and, in your mind, check off those who have been or now are friends of goodness. Thank God for the gift of each one of them.

A category of friendship we read about often in the lives of the saints is that called "spiritual friendship." Think of Mary and Joseph, Teresa of Avila and John of the Cross, Jane of Chantal and Francis de Sales. There is a classic about spiritual friendship going back to the 12th century by a French Abbot, St. Aelred of Rievaulx.

What characterizes a spiritual friendship is that it is rooted in God. It is a gift of God and is nourished by the grace of God for the purpose of the sanctification of each of the friends. St. Aelred believed that such friendships can be foretastes of heaven as we share our yearning for God and encourage each other in our battles with evils without and within. However, we must be sure we are not attracted to another for the wrong reasons. Spiritual friendships need to be tested for even monks might have unholy motives.

In my book, *Spiritual Friendship: The Darkness and the Light,* I describe four stages: attraction, rejection or mutuality, enchantment, unity. The first stage comes with admiration of the character of a person who appears to have holy virtues.

However, one can be a disciple of someone who is holy without it being a true friendship, for the relationship has to pass through a time of seeing if the love is mutual. All friendship is a gift not a right. The admired one might not feel an inclination to bond with me. Then I can suffer feelings of rejection. A future session of the *Way of Love* provides some insights into coping with rejection.

Enchantment is the stage of spiritual friendship where each friend is delighted with the other seen as a wonderful mirror of their common yearnings for holiness. We help each other through prayer and counsel. Especially we experience the love of God for ourselves through the love in the eyes of the friend.

Here there can come a special type of darkness. Some spiritual friends become co-dependent, substituting the friend for Jesus. Love of God, and love of neighbor are neglected in favor of constant thinking of and talking to the beloved friend. When this takes place there can be danger of sexual sin, or break up of commitments of marriage, parenting, or of religious vows. In such cases friendship has become a kind of idol-worship. Fear of loss of the friend or actual loss can throw people into despair. To avoid such darkness it is imperative to have a counselor or spiritual director other than the friend.

Spiritual friendships that pass through the stages of attraction, mutuality, and overcome the wrong kind of enchantment, move into a wonderful, tender, steady stage of union, truly a foretaste of heaven.

Look over your list of friends. Have any been spiritual friendships?

Spiritual Exercises:

1. Write a letter of gratitude to friends letting them know all the qualities you love about them and how you thank God for their part in your life.

2. Affirmation Circle: If you are in a group setting, form circles of 4 to 5 people. Think about what you like best about a

quality of personality of each one. Then think of what you like best about how each one looks (for example, I like your curly hair or I like the way you walk.) Now go around the circle. Start with one person and everyone in the circle tells that person what they like best about him or her in character and looks. Then go to the next person until you complete the circle.

FOR PERSONAL REFLECTION AND GROUP SHARING:

1. How would you define friendship? What ideas of Aristotle, Aelred or Chervin do you agree with? What ideas do you question?

2. Do you have any friends who fit more than one of the categories: utility, pleasure, goodness, spiritual bonding?

3. Have any of your friendships moved from one category to another?

4. Can you write a prayer concerning the friends you have had or hope to have in the future?

If you wish, write your own teaching about friendship love for a class for children, teens or adults, or a homily you might give in the future? You could include a song, a drawing, or dance? If you so choose, you can share what you create with the group at the beginning of some other session of the *Way of Love*.

SESSION

5

AFFECTIONATE LOVE

"Your wife will be like a fruitful vine within your house; your children will be like olive shoots around your table. Lo, thus shall the man be blessed who fears the Lord." (Psalm 128: 3-4)

(If you wish, share your reflections from the last session about friendship love with others.)

Write a few paragraphs about the family you grew up in (biological or adoptive), or the institution, including the names of the members and the adjectives you would use to describe the atmosphere of your home, such as big/small/medium-sized, full of laughter/full of conflict, etc. If you are now a parent in a family you brought into being, also write some paragraphs about this family. (Note: marriage will be a separate topic for Session 7) If you are living in a community setting write about this experience.

In our times because of the number of children born outside of marriage and of divorces, many Christians no longer think of family life as a blessing. Some children, far from learning affection in family life, have found it to be frightening. Later in the *Way of Life Series* there will be healing prayers for those victimized by such experiences. In this session the focus will be on the nature of the love that ought to be prevalent in family life.

By affectionate love, of course, is meant touching, but its wider meaning is a kind of coziness and security that comes with familiarity. Someone once said that home is where they have to take you in.

In his Encyclical Familiaris Consortio, John Paul the Great, after writing about all the conflicts and problems of the family in our times, gives this positive description:

"The family, which is founded and given life by love, is a community of persons: of husband and wife, of parents and children, of relatives. Its first task is to live with fidelity the reality of communion in a constant effort to develop an authentic community of persons...."

"The inner principle of that task, its permanent power and its final goal is love: without love the family is not a community of persons and, in the same way, without love the family cannot live, grow and perfect itself as a community of persons... "Man cannot live without love. He remains a being that is incomprehensible for himself, his life is senseless, if love is not revealed to him, if he does not encounter love, if he does not experience it and make it his own, if he does not participate intimately in it....

"The love between husband and wife and, in a derivatory and broader way, the love between members of the same family-between parents and children, brothers and sisters and relatives and members of the household-is given life and sustenance by an unceasing inner dynamism leading the family to ever deeper and more intense communion, which is the foundation and soul of the community of marriage and the family." (Familiaris Consortio, #18)

In the Catechism of the Catholic Church there is a direct *should be* reference to affectionate love: The family is "a community of faith, hope and charity…a communion of persons….The relationships within the family bring an affinity of feelings, affections and interests, arising above all from the members' respect for one another" (#2204-2206)

In simpler terms a child needs to feel sheltered in the family. The home needs to be a refuge from problems outside. Because of the closeness of being together so much of the day and night, in spite of the inevitable conflicts of personality that arise in every human situation, each member should feel understood and cherished.

SPIRITUAL EXERCISES:

Contemplative Photography:

Consider the difference between an expensive portrait photo and a hastily drawn caricature. The portrait photographer watches carefully to see the most beautiful or strongest expression on the face of the one sitting for the portrait. The caricaturist swiftly sketches the worst features and exaggerates them.

Here's the analogy. When you think of each member of your family, do you look for the best features of character of each one? Instead, do you tend to think of each person at their worst?

Right now, make a list of the closest members of your family or community. Then write about each one's best traits and, if you have time, write about an incident where that trait was displayed.

Here is a second exercise you might choose: read the challenging passage below called "Family" and pray about whatever pertains to your family of origin or present family circumstances:

(The following is from a locution allegedly given by the Trinity to an anonymous recipient)

Family

"You would like it to be all the good part: the long understandings from proximity through the generations; the physical closeness; the built-up gratitude for all the helps. We understand that. After all, We (the Trinity) created the family.

But, then, there are the swift judgments born of long knowledge; the resistance to compromise as each digs in with prideful self-defense; the love dished out in spoonfuls that more be not demanded.

And from this family love you flee back to friendship love, lighter, less painful but less primordial, less of the gut. We understand, We created friendship.

You hope your own marriage and children would have all the best of family and friendship; in the image and likeness of what was best in your past families, but free from all the tangled grief and disappointments.

We don't dash your hope. We wanted, by our grace, to transform everything natural, through supernatural virtues and gifts, into its best form.

Each time anyone in the family opens to grace there is more love, more joy, more peace. Each time one in the family closes the heart to the others and to us, there is less love, joy and peace.

We urge you into the arms of forgiveness, to heal the rifts, and to make new beginnings. Even when on earth the bonds break, we aim for final restoration in Our home, which is called heaven.

FOR PERSONAL REFLECTION AND GROUP SHARING:

1. What families have you known personally or from the media that you most admire? What quality of the way they related to each other delighted you or touched your heart?

2. What do you think blocks affection in family and community?

3. Do you think there is hope for family life in our culture at this time?

If you wish, write your own teaching about affectionate love for a class for children, teens or adults, or a homily you might give in the future? You could include a song, a drawing, or dance? If you so choose, you can share what you create with the group at the beginning of some other session of the *Way of Love*.

SESSION

6

CARING, SERVING LOVE

"Love your neighbor as yourself." (Matthew 19:19)

"He who has two coats, let him share with him who has none; and he who has food, let him do likewise."(Luke 3:11)

More sharing with the group about affectionate love?

There is much talk these days about people not having enough self-love. If the Lord tells us to love our neighbors as ourselves, surely it is important that we actually do love ourselves. What is self-love? Von Hildebrand says that we have a solidarity with ourselves in our daily life that is basic. Under usual conditions it is up to us to brush our teeth, eat enough, get dressed, and sally forth into the world to try to do the best with our day. Our neighbors are not only those who live next door but also anyone who comes into our lives in a state of need, as in the parable of the Good Samaritan.

Von Hildebrand thought that the first meaning of loving our neighbor as ourselves is that we should move out of our self-centered preoccupations to feel solidarity with others in their daily needs. An obvious example could be the way parents of small children get up earlier on the weekend than before they had children. Because they care for their little ones they make the sacrifice of the pleasure of sleeping in to make sure the children are fed.

St. Thomas Aquinas has a beautiful insight concerning self-love. He thought that one can only love oneself loving! In other words we cannot love ourselves when we are being hateful. But when we are being caring we are happy to be ourselves as instruments of love.

Make a list on paper or in your head of all the caring/serving things you do for others on a typical weekday and then on a typical Saturday or Sunday.

Tolstoy, the great 19th century Russian novelist, claimed that the world is a terrible place for one simple reason: people think there is something more important than love. By this he meant that they value things like money or power or success more than Christian love.

Some of you do think that caring/serving love is the most important thing and spend all your days proving that. For example, a man or woman might begin the day taking care of the children. One or both may do work for pay that helps others such as health-care, keeping a food store, building homes, teaching, driving needed items from place to place. Those with sufficient income for a simple and wholesome life-style may choose to donate money to the poor.

Priests, brothers, sisters and consecrated lay people may devote their whole lives to caring/serving love. Others may work at home and/or volunteer part-time or full-time in the community or the Church.

Much of this is a matter of fixed commitments. In our free time there is more of a fresh choice about whether to do something pleasurable to us that doesn't benefit others, or to sacrifice enjoyment for the sake of a fulfilling the need of another. Of course, most of us have to have some times of relaxation and recreation, if only to have the strength to serve during the rest of the time.

If we look at the life of the holy family, Jesus, Mary, and Joseph, we see hearts dedicated to caring and serving. Followers of Christ throughout the centuries are known for pouring themselves out in service, including, of course, the love of neighbor expressed in prayer for others.

Spiritual Exercises:

1. Ask the Holy Spirit to show you where gratitude should be expressed for the way others have cared for and served you.

2. Ask God to help you see what your areas of failure might be in love of the caring/serving type.

3. Do you wish to write a prayer that Jesus may expand your heart to lovingly serve more in those areas where you tend to fail?

For Personal Reflection and Group Sharing:

1. In what areas of the past or present do you care and serve?

2. At what times past or present do others care for and serve you?

3. Can you trace failures in caring/serving love to over-valuing things like money, power, success, etc.? If you are in a group you might ask others to pray with you about such choices.

If you wish, write your own teaching about caring/serving love for a class for children, teens or adults, or a homily you might give in the future? You could include a song, a drawing, or dance? If you so choose, you can share what you create with the group at the beginning of some other session of the *Way of Love*.

SESSION

7

MARRIAGE

"For they are no longer two, but one." (Matthew 19:6)

If you wish share with a group studying the *Way of Love* anything you learned from last week's session on serving/caring love.

Alas! Some of you when you read the title of this session will feel sadness or even dread! Some think of the marriage of their parents with horror. Some came into the world outside of marriage. Some are longing to be married but can't seem to find the right person. Some have been unhappily married, separated or divorced.

Blessed are those of you who are happily enough married to consider it a great source of love, even the greatest of human loves! You would consider it strange, indeed, to have a booklet entitled the *Way of Love* without a chapter on marriage.

In our times we have an array of concepts of marriage: a breakable contract; a covenant commitment that is nonetheless breakable; a vow: 'til death do us part'; indissoluble unless it is annulled (on the basis that it was not a true marriage).

In former times if you asked someone what the purpose of marriage was many would say to bring babies into the world. Others would say to help each other through life. Others would think helping each other get into heaven is the highest purpose.

Catholic teaching is that one of the main purposes of marriage is procreation. So couples should be open to children even if they don't receive this gift. Participating in God's creation of new life is an incredible experience. Each child, in a certain sense, makes the love of the couple visible. The meaning of marriage is not only procreation but also includes helping each other in life and toward eternity. Marriage consists of an intimate union of a man and a woman based on mutual love, consummated by bodily union, with a promise of fidelity and commitment until the death of one or both of the partners.

Although most marriages in our part of the world begin with falling in love, the Church does not include this as part of its definition. After all, for centuries marriages were arranged for couples without reference to passionate delight. Falling out of love is also not a reason to split a marriage. I am convinced that, in marriage, the loss of the vision of the unique preciousness of the other comes not from falling out of love but from unforgiveness. Living together in peace and harmony requires virtue and hard work. To the extent that couples fail in virtue they become each other's victims. Disappointment, anger, and bitterness cloud the vision of the beauty of the beloved seen in an inter-penetrating gaze when we are in love. <u>Forgiveness based on</u> <u>Christian love, and attempts to act more lovingly in the future,</u> remove that veil and allow us to see that preciousness of the spouse once again.

In his book *Marriage*, Dietrich Von Hildebrand teaches married couples never to let busyness dull the love for the spouse. Even more than in other relationships <u>it is so important to show love</u> <u>by affection and care.</u>

But what if a spouse is unfaithful or cruel?

The Church has procedures for judging whether in some cases one or both of the spouses was not able to live out the sacrament of marriage in a Christian way for reasons such as mental illness or other conditions. In these cases an annulment is declared and the party who was the victim can re-marry in the Church.

In many marital situations there are conflicts and sins, but <u>change is possible. With God's grace</u> couples can learn how to compromise and how to repent and forgive. Indissolubility of marriage would indeed be for many a terrible burden were it not for faith and prayer.

Spiritual Exercises:

1. If you are a married person, reread the above teaching and highlight sentences that could cause you to examine your conscience (going to sacramental confession?) or to pray for greater love of your spouse. What are areas where you need to forgive even if the spouse has not repented?

2. Write a letter to God about the history of your marriage, begging him to heal any areas of conflict.

3. **If you are separated or divorced bring your broken-heart to the Sacred Heart of Jesus and ask Him for healing, and forgiveness. Is the Holy Spirit urging you to ask forgiveness also in sacramental confession or in other ways?**

4. **If you are single not by choice, pray for God to send you a spouse or ask Him to show you why He has given you a single life.**

FOR PERSONAL REFLECTION AND GROUP SHARING:

1. **Were your parents married? If so, what features of their marriage did you think were loving, and what unloving? How have these qualities affected your understanding of marriage now? If they were not married, or married in a civil ceremony but not married in the Church, what impact did that have on you as a child?**

2. **What is your philosophy of marriage?**

3. **If it is not too personal, what about marriage do you struggle with in your own married or single life?**

If you wish, write your own teaching about marriage for a class for children, teens or adults, or a homily you might give in the future? You could include a song, a drawing, or dance? If you so choose, you can share what you create with the group at the beginning of some other session of the *Way of Love*.

SESSION

8

VIRTUES: MORAL RESPONSES OF LOVE

"Make every effort to supplement your faith with virtue, and virtue with knowledge, ..." (2 Peter: 5)

If you are in a group, you may wish to share with others insights into marriage that came to you during the time between sessions.

What does it mean when someone tells you over and over again how much he or she loves you but then treats you badly, not just under severe pressure, but most of the time? Examples might be never coming on time to appointments, not paying back borrowed money, avoiding necessary chores in a family or community, or talking to you in a rude manner.

I don't think that it means that such persons are lying when they tell you they love you. I think they feel what is called delight love, but are lacking in what is called donation love. Following on the concepts in Session 1 about types of love, it could be said that some people are stronger on passion love, friendship love, and affectionate love, but weak on serving/caring love.

Many times unloving daily words and actions are hasty, not at all thought out. We can go about our business and pay little attention to the personal hopes and needs of others even in family, at work, or in church community.

Our session is entitled: "Virtues as Moral Responses of Love." At first sight the word "moral" with regard to virtue may seem surprising. We may think of morality as involving big, terrible, crimes or toxic vices rather than everyday "dull" sounding virtues such as honesty, patience, or even goodness.

Let's look at these three virtues to see how they are responses of love.

Take honesty. Being a liar means failing to respond to the great value of truth. Honesty is a moral response demonstrating love of truth. The virtue of honesty also manifests a love of others in the form of wanting to have trust between people rather than suspicious wariness. Clearly, no one trusts a liar.

Take patience vs. impatience. The impatient person unlovingly tries to hurry everyone else to further his or her own time-table. "Faster, faster!" would be such a person's domineering wish in interactions with anyone or even any machine that is not up to speed! A patient person lovingly accepts the slow processes of daily existence, careful never to make others feel stupid or inadequate.

Goodness? This virtue seems too general to even describe. Nonetheless it is an unmistakable quality of love highly valued by us whenever we find it. A good person appears to be 24/7 eager to help with whatever need arises. With someone lacking in this virtue, we sometimes walk on egg-shells before asking him or her for the slightest favor.

When you think of Jesus, Mary, Joseph and other saints, don't you always picture them as full of the virtues of love? Could you ever think of them as liars, fierce impatient bossy people, or mean-spirited and self-centered?

In the next series of sessions *Obstacles to Love* you will get a chance to examine yourself concerning many a fault and get insight into the beautiful qualities of various virtues.

Spiritual Exercises:

1. Go through a day watching how loving attitudes fluctuate with unloving attitudes. For example, I woke up grumpy and hoped I wouldn't have to talk to anyone before noon. At 10 AM a fellow-worker asked me for a favor and I quickly agreed with a loving smile.

2. Check out the people around you. What do you see of loving virtues? What do you see of unloving faults?

3. Can you write a prayer about a specific pattern you exhibit that is unloving and/or one to increase in a virtue you wish you had in greater abundance?

For Personal Reflection and Group Sharing:

1. Describe some of the virtues you admire the most in others and analyze them in terms of the love manifest in them.

2. **What specific virtues do you love that you find in the lives of the saints?**

3. **What lines from Scripture about specific virtues do you find challenging?**

If you wish, write your own teaching about virtues and love for a class for children, teens or adults, or a homily you might give in the future? You could include a song, a drawing, or dance? If you so choose, you can share what you create with the group at the beginning of some other session of the *Way of Love*.

SESSION

9

EXCUSES: FAILURES TO LOVE

"What good is it for a man to gain the whole world, yet forfeit his soul?" (Mark 8:36)

Any thoughts to share about the last session on virtue as a loving response?

In my book, *Living in Love: Christian Ethics for Everyday Life*, I have a section about excuses. Most of us don't outright say that in order to gain the whole world we are ready to forfeit our souls. No. Instead we fail in love by making excuses for many an unloving choice.

In *Living in Love* I gave as an example an unmarried couple trying to decide whether to keep their baby or abort that child. Eventually they keep the baby, but they first try to find excuses to get rid of the baby. I will use their example here. (If are reading this account and you have had an abortion, do not shut the book for fear of condemnation. We all know that many women make such decisions out of panic. Priests are waiting to give you the forgiveness of Jesus in confession. There are groups of women ready to bring you healing.)

A common excuse used for making an unloving choice is, "I gotta survive!" The use of this phrase takes it for granted that "survival" is more important than love. In fact the couple considering abortion would survive keeping the baby, giving him or her up for adoption, or keeping the baby. See how slippery this excuse is? What "survive" usually means is not life and death for those choosing but rather a comfortable life without interruption of their agendas vs. a life that includes big loving sacrifices.

Another excuse can be "My conscience doesn't bother me." Most of us feel relieved making any decision. So the couple choosing abortion might feel good at the moment, happy to be free of a burden. But, consider huge examples where wrong-doers didn't feel bad at the time of doing something evil. Hitler exterminated Jews by the millions and felt good about it. Slave-holders were blind to the value of freedom. Have some of us been blinded to the humanity of the tiny child in the body of the mother?

"Nobody will be hurt," is another excuse often heard. But some victims don't scream. An employer who underpays his/her workers may never see the pain they face because of lack of money for themselves and their families. Many would never have abortions if they could see the baby being chopped up in the womb.

"Everybody's doing it," is another handy excuse. We don't think that because many abuse children that it is okay? Shouldn't we choose what is most loving over what is most common? Does the frequency of abortion make it right?

A final excuse is "Nobody's perfect, I'm not a saint." Would you accept that excuse from a drunk driver who killed your brother or sister in an accident? Don't we need to always try to be loving even if we sometimes fail? Maybe it would help us to become saints to lovingly take care for a baby conceived out of wedlock.

Perhaps listing these excuses seems itself harsh to you. "Hate the sin, love the sinner," proclaimed St. Augustine. We must be full of forgiving compassion for others and ourselves, but we must not cover-up lack of love with excuses.

Spiritual Exercises:

1. Make a list of times you have made unloving choices. Think about whether you used any of the excuses described above when making those decisions.

2. Bring to confession, or to prayer, if you are not a Catholic, any guilt that came up during exercise 1.

For Personal Reflection and Group Sharing:

1. Which of the excuses listed do you see used most often in our society today?

2. If it is not too personal, describe an instance of using excuses to make an unloving choice.

3. Can you describe a breakthrough you have made, or that you have seen others make in life or in fiction, that involves

getting away from the deceit of making excuses for unloving choices.

If you wish, write your own teaching about excuses for a class for children, teens or adults, or a homily you might give in the future? You could include a song, a drawing, or dance? If you so choose, you can share what you create with the group at the beginning of some other session of the *Way of Love*.

SESSION

10

LOVING AND UNLOVING CHOICES

"...their god is the belly...with minds set on earthly things." (Philippians 3: 19)

If you wish, share any new insights you got about excuses since the last session.

Let's take an example of how minds set on earthly things can lead to unloving choices.

A relatively rich owner of a large farm hires undocumented migrant workers during the harvest season. He pays them minimum wages and supplies them minimal housing and food. He is a regular attendant at church. One day he hears that a friend on a neighboring farm has called in the border patrol to pick up the workers and send them back to Mexico just before their monthly pay-day! At first he is horrified, but then he thinks about how his neighbor will be able to sell the crop cheaper and beat him out. He considers having the border patrol take off his workers also.

Obviously calling the border patrol is an unloving decision. It is based on what Von Hildebrand calls desire for the subjectively satisfying. Many times, when making choices, we look to see what will be the most pleasurable outcome for ourselves. This is perfectly legitimate when choosing between chocolate or vanilla ice cream. Most Christians don't believe that we have to sacrifice our own preferences every minute of the day. But when it is a choice between something loving and something wrong we should always give up the wrong choice in favor of the loving one.

In our example, the farmer thinks about it and decides that he should not call the border patrol and that he ought to pay his workers the wage that is due. In making this decision he is choosing what is called an intrinsic value over something subjectively satisfying. The intrinsic value would be justice – that is, giving people their due. Justice is a minimum of love.

An even more loving choice would be to increase the salaries or improve the living conditions of the workers. This would involve sacrificing more of what is subjectively satisfying to him. For instance, he might have to live with moderate vs. huge profits.

Clearly, a lover of Jesus should wish always to make loving decisions. This doesn't mean never enjoying any of the good things of life, but it does mean, out of love for God, to avoid harming others and often to choose what is most loving, even at a cost.

SPIRITUAL EXERCISES:

1. What is an ethical decision that you have to make at this time, or have made in the past?

2. Analyze what elements in the choice involve the subjectively satisfying such as pleasures and advantages.

3. What are or were intrinsic values at stake such as the dignity of another person, fulfilling a promise, paying back a debt, helping someone in need?

FOR PERSONAL REFLECTION AND GROUP SHARING:

1. Describe instances in society, church or work situations where unloving choices are being made.

2. What would be intrinsic values to which a Christian should be responding in these situations?

3. Can you remember key choices in the lives of the saints where great sacrifices were made out of love for God or for others?

If you wish, write your own teaching about loving and unloving choices for a class for children, teens or adults, or a homily you might give in the future? You could include a song, a drawing, or dance? If you so choose, you can share what you create with the group at the beginning of some other session of the *Way of Love*.

SESSION

11

FEMININE AND MASCULINE LOVING AND UNLOVING TRAITS

"God created them, male and female, he created them" (Genesis 1:27)

If you are in a group can you share any insights on loving and unloving choices you had after the last session?

Do women and men show love differently? Do they fail to love in different ways? Even if you don't think so, it can be good to read about what most people think if only to formulate your own ideas more sharply.

Years ago I wrote a book called *Feminine, Free and Faithful*, (the masculine equivalent would be *Masculine, Loving and Faithful*). In the course of my research I discovered that many who think that men and women are very different don't focus much on how traits can also be divided as positive and negative. To clarify this I constructed a description of the stereo-type most of us have in mind if we talk about feminine and masculine separating out positive and negative traits. During the next session you will get a chance to consider a few contrasting theories about feminine and masculine.

As you look through the categories I have presented as part of the spiritual exercise for this session, it is easy to see that the positive traits for each sex are loving and the negative ones very unloving.

SPIRITUAL EXERCISES:

Go through the entire list of traits. *If you are a woman also go through the masculine traits. If you are a man also go through the feminine traits.* Put a circle around traits you have or many others say you have. For example, even if you feel weak, if everyone says you are strong circle that trait.

Now go through the lists again and put a square around traits you wish you had more of.

Positive Feminine Traits:

affectionate, caring, charming, compassionate, considerate, delicate, diplomatic, empathetic, enduring, expressive, faithful, friendly, gentle, gracious, hospitable, intuitive, kind, nurturing, perceptive, polite, pure, quiet, sincere, soft, supportive, sweet, tender, trusting, warm.

Negative Feminine Traits:

catty, chatter-box, complaining, (overly) curious), (overly) dependent, (overly) emotional, fearful, flirtatious, gossipy, grudging, hysterical, jumpy, manipulative, mean, moody, nagging, naive, passive, petty, pouty, prudish, seductive, (overly) sensitive, silly, slavish, smothering, spiteful, vain, weak, weepy, wishy-washy.

Positive Masculine Traits:

adventuresome, assertive, authoritative, brave, chivalrous, daring, decisive, determined, driving, firm, focused, forceful, initiating, just, leading, logical, objective, protective, prudent, self-controlled, sporty, steady, straightforward, strong, valiant.

Negative Masculine Traits:

(overly) ambitious, argumentative, blunt, brutal, callous, cold, (overly) competitive, condescending, dare-devil, domineering, hiding of feelings, inconsiderate, insensitive, isolated, lustful, plotting, proud, rude, ruthless, sarcastic, self-centered, smugness, task-oriented, territorial, uncaring.

FOR PERSONAL REFLECTION AND GROUP SHARING:

1. Were there any names of traits you didn't know the meaning of? If so, look them up or ask other participants for rough definitions.

2. Were there any traits listed that you don't think of as general to all people rather than being more masculine or more feminine?

3. Try to analyze the nature of any negative traits you listed yourself as having. For example, a woman might be overly curious because she feels insecure and, therefore, wants to be in the know all the time to protect herself. Or a man might be

dare-devil in his driving because his work is not challenging and dangerous stunts relieve boredom.

4. With positive traits you wish you had, try to analyze them to see why they are so desirable. For example, sweetness is good as an opposite to bitterness or sourness. Assertiveness is good as a contrast to being afraid to make waves or lacking the courage of one's convictions.

5. Write a prayer to ask God for specific traits you wish you had and to overcome ones that you want to get away from.

If you wish, write your own teaching about loving and unloving choices for a class for children, teens or adults, or a homily you might give in the future? You could include a song, a drawing, or dance? If you so choose, you can share what you create with the group at the beginning of some other session of the *Way of Love*.

SESSION

12

THEORIES ABOUT HOW WOMEN AND MEN SHOULD RELATE

"For as many of you as were baptized into Christ have put on Christ. There is neither Jew nor Greek, there is neither slave nor free, there is neither male nor female; for you are all one in Christ." (Galatians 3:27-28)

Do you want to share insights about the traits list you worked on during the last session with others?

One modern theory about how women and men should relate is that what counts is that we are human persons. What sex we are is not fundamentally important! What about biological differences? "Biology is not destiny!" is the battle cry of some such thinkers. In other words, by means of contraception and abortion, no woman should think she has to be a mother if she wants sex! No man should think that he can't be a nurse or a house-husband just because he has large muscles!

Most feminists believe that divisions of traits in the manner presented in the last session are misguided and harmful. They point to the way in which brutal men justify such practices as sexual harassment or battering on the basis that women are weak and stupid and need "to be kept in line." Or how some women manipulate men by pretending to be weak so that they don't have to work up the courage to work in the outside world. Men and women will only be able to love each other authentically, some believe, until we get rid of fixed gender images and roles.

An opposite theory, complementarity, upholds the idea that it is good that men and women are different. They fit well together because they have different traits: men should be bosses because they are more logical and strong – with women secretaries because they do best when taking direction; men should do outdoor labor such as hunting or construction since they are physically stronger – with women at home breast-feeding babies. We love best, they believe, when we do what we are made for.

In my book, *Feminine, Free and Faithful*, I explain that none of these theories is adequate for a Christian philosophy of woman and man. For instance, most feminists justify terribly unloving choices such as abortion and no-fault divorce.

Many holding to complementary views, especially in the past, unlovingly restricted women from using talents that didn't fit the traditional image of woman such as being leaders or competing in strenuous sports. They also restricted men from using talents that didn't fit the traditional image of man such as being poets or artists or working in child-care. They justified unequal salaries for the same work.

Christian philosophies of gender aim to avoid the pitfalls of the other two main theories to construct a realistic and positively loving way for women and men to relate to each other. We believe that it was God the Creator who wished to have a 2 sexed humanity. After the Fall of Adam and Eve, we see the negative traits sabotaging love. The Old Testament does depict some holy loving men and women but it is also full of examples of cruel, domineering , cold men and sly, seductive and naive women. With the redemption offered us by the sacrifice of Christ on the cross, the goal for both women and men is love. In this they are not male or female, but simply Christian. However, in the saints we see beautiful examples of whole and holy men who can be poets and nurses and philosophers and leaders at the same time. We see whole and holy women who can be soldiers, orators, prophetesses at the same time that they are gentle and compassionate.

Behind such issues as inclusive language and women in the priesthood are sometimes grievances that reflect one-sided theories. In my writings I try to cut through the layers of argumentation with easy to understand images. To those who think we should call God Our Mother I ask fathers, "Even if you want your children to think of you as tender in a motherly way, would you like them to call you Mommy?" To those who think that women should be priests if they are equally well educated and spiritual as men, I ask, "If you were putting on a Nativity play at Christmas and you happened to have a famous male actor in the parish would you choose him for the part of Mary? I bet you'd rather choose any woman for that role. By analogy, the priest plays the role of Jesus, who was a male, when he presides at the altar. Shouldn't he then also be a male?" Are such choices really unloving or more just fitting?

Spiritual Exercises:

1. Do you disagree with any ideas presented in the teaching for this session?

2. When you grew up which of the theories described above fit with the way men and women related in your family, neighborhood, church?

3. Bring to consciousness any bad experiences you have had or now undergo in male/female relationships. Do you need healing from any of the destructive patterns described in these teachings? If so, write a prayer for healing and forgiveness based on your experience. Could you benefit from sacramental confession?

For Personal Reflection and Group Sharing:

1. Decide if you want to share anything that emerged in the spiritual exercises above with others in a group or in conversation with people whose wisdom and love you trust.

2. What is your own theory about how women and men should relate based on experience or reading?

3. Describe saints you admire in terms of liberation from rigid societal gender expectations or, positively in terms of holy complementary friendships with those of the opposite sex.

If you wish, write your own teaching about theories of male/female relationships for a class for children, teens or adults, or a homily you might give in the future? You could include a song, a drawing, or dance? If you so choose, you can share what you create with the group at the beginning of some other session of the *Way of Love*.

SESSION

13

MINISTRIES OF LOVE

"Now there are a variety of gifts, but the same Spirit, and there are varieties of service, but the same Lord…To each is given the manifestation of the Spirit for the common good." (1 Corinthians 12: 4-7)

Do you wish to share thoughts that came to you about theories of how women and men relate since the last session?

As Christians we minister to others in love in many circumstances. Some are life-long, others temporary to meet a specific need. In the widest sense all our occupations from doing dishes to inventing a space shuttle can be seen as callings or ministries to building a loving community.

In this session, however, we will be considering how loving ministries *within* the Church fit with our own personalities and characters. Religious psychologists think it is helpful to pinpoint the type of ministry you feel most called to. This can be useful in preventing barking up the wrong tree and then, eventually, feeling resentful at being trapped in activities we are unsuited for.

In my booklet *Freed to Love: Healing for Catholic Women*, I adapted a topology devised by followers of Carl Jung for use in workshops with Catholics. Here it is adapted once more to fit men as well as women.

Four Types of Ministry:

> **Motherly/Fatherly**
>
> **Prophetic**
>
> **Creative**
>
> ✓ **Contemplative**

Motherly/Fatherly

Clearly the most obvious motherly and fatherly roles are caring for one's own children (birth or adoptive). This a 24/7 job. It is especially appealing to those whose love for those in need transcends love for themselves. No matter how great or small the need of the child, a motherly or fatherly person is ready to provide.

Similar motherly and fatherly roles involving caring for the needs of others are to be found in society in day-care, schools, and hospitals, for instance. In the Church priests are called Father and are called to be willing to sacrifice themselves at all times to provide sacraments and counsel. Sisters and brothers in religious orders were usually motherly and fatherly in this way. Lots of other Church ministries usually conducted by lay people involve motherly and fatherly love, such as soup-kitchen, parish receptionist, pro-life centers for pregnant women, or being an extraordinary minister of Holy Communion at Masses, ministry to the homebound or to the sick, or running bake sales. Administering finances in a just and protective way can be seen as extensions of a basic motherly or fatherly character.

a. Prophetic Roles

When you can see around you grave evils due to actions of others of bad motivation, or due to false philosophies of life, do you shrink back and wish it would all go away, retreat into prayer, or do you rush to try to bring change through crusading actions or direct verbal challenging of those at fault?

Those with a prophetic vocation, like the prophets in the Old and New Testament and those we read about in the history of the Church, out of love for the good and desire to bring about Christ's kingdom "on earth as it is in heaven" feel impelled to take a stand and try to make things better.

Some exercise a prophetic role in direct confrontation with evil as did St. Joan of Arc, but other examples less dramatic abound such as charismatic prophecy before thousands of listeners, pro-life or peace activism, counter-cultural public speaking, teaching unpopular truths, street evangelism, missionary work, advocacy, writing the truth even when others might object.

Creative Roles

Are you an artist, a sculptor, a musician, an actor or actress, a writer, a member of the choir, a dancer, photographer, architect, film maker, web-master, donating your talents to benefit the

Church? Or, do you express your creativity in other ways such as gardening, cooking, decoration, hosting, or devising new ways to improve parish ministry such as having greeters at the Masses to welcome newcomers and visitors.

Sometimes these gifts given with so much love and care are not as valued as motherly/fatherly roles because they seem less necessary. But, think, doesn't God, the creator of everything beautiful in nature, want us to show our love for Him and for His creation through the arts? What would it be like if there was no music and no art in the Church? How bleak and unloving the atmosphere would seem?

Contemplative Roles

Do you feel most loving of God and others in the interior of your own heart and soul expressed through prayer? Does your experience of God's love overflow in prayer for others and supporting initiatives in the Church such as daily Mass, Eucharistic Adoration, spiritual reading, leading prayer groups, conducting healing services or offering spiritual direction?

This role can also be underrated. How often do you hear the priest commending the rosary group for pouring out their hearts in prayer for the priest and the parishioners?

Spiritual Exercises:

1. Do you identify with one of these types of ministries the most? Maybe with several or all of them?

2. To check if you feel called to a motherly or fatherly ministry you could ask yourself: "When there are needs in situations am I the first to respond or do I hope that someone else will take care of it so that I can get on with more important work?"

3. To check if you feel called to a prophetic ministry you could ask yourself: "When I see an injustice in my personal life, society or Church, do I get a surge of energy to come against it, or do I hope someone else will lead the battle?

4. To check if you feel called to a creative ministry consider whether you feel uplifted when engaged in the arts or in other creative plans. Might you be called to give even more time than at present to these roles?

5. To check if you feel called to contemplative ministry ask yourself if you experience God's presence more and more at Mass and in different forms of prayer. Do you wish others had the same kind of peace you get from drawing closer to God?

FOR PERSONAL REFLECTION AND GROUP SHARING:

1. Can you think of other types of ministry not mentioned above?

2. Instead of fitting into a type of role, do you think it can be better just to do what is needed regardless of your own personality and preferences?

3. Which of the 4 ministries, (motherly/fatherly, prophetic, creative, or contemplative) have you found most satisfying? Describe your efforts in that type of ministry.

4. Which of the 4 ministries have you found most difficult?

5. Describe some of your problems. Do you think you need to stretch by continuing in difficult ministries or that you might need a change?

6. Think of favorite saints who fit each of the 4 ministries.

If you wish, write your own teaching about theories of ministry roles for a class for children, teens or adults, or a homily you might give in the future? You could include a song, a drawing, or dance? If you so choose, you can share what you create with the group at the beginning of some other session of the *Way of Love*.

SESSION

14

LOVE OF BEAUTY

"The Mighty One, God the Lord, speaks and summons the earth from the rising of the sun to its setting. Out of Zion, the perfection of beauty, God shines forth." (Psalm 50:1-2)

Anything to share with the group that came to you after the last session?

When I think of beauty I picture the ocean, the faces of my beloved family members and friends, great music, noble high vaulted Churches, and finally the beauty of the face of Jesus as portrayed by artists such as El Greco and Rembrandt. But I also have tears of joy at the beauty of some unbelievable sacrifice of love such as St. Francis of Assisi casting off all his possessions down to his very clothing in order to have God alone.

How about you? What do you think of when beauty is the subject?

St. Thomas Aquinas calls beauty the splendor of being. Every beautiful thing has integrity (absence of defect or brokenness); due proportion or harmony; and brilliance (glow).

The philosopher Dionysius says that creatures share in God's beauty by means of luminous rays of light. Beauty is a gift to us, that our eyes and ears can sense the Divine. The beauty around us is like a visible form of God's invisible love.

Pope Paul VI once wrote that "true beauty is the privilege of love, because love alone is able to detect beauty as gift freely given. Beauty contains meaning, amazement, joyful and grateful understanding.

John Paul II wrote a Letter to Artists. Among other thoughts he says that we have the power with grace to make our own lives works of art.

The English poet John Keats wrote "beauty if truth, that is all ye know on earth and all ye need to know." I think he means that beauty check-mates the skepticism, cynicism and despair that can flood our souls at worst moment of life.

Given these praises of beauty as a gift of God's love, what are we to make of the often heard sentence "Beauty is in the eye of the beholder?"

which seems to suggest that there is no real beauty out there. Is what we think of as objective beauty just a projection of our individual, subjective biases?

Well, of course, there is disagreement. You may think a certain piece of clothing is gorgeous and I think it is vulgar? You may think a certain style of music is terrific but I think it is trashy. Parents think their babies are the most beautiful in the world. The parents in the next delivery room vote instead for their progeny.

In spite of such disagreement, however, there is a lot of agreement. Why do some musical pieces withstand the test of time so that they are still loved many centuries after they were composed? Have you ever heard of anyone suing the Highway Department for putting up signs, "Scenic View – 2 miles on your right," because they found nothing beautiful in the designated water fall?

Lack of agreement about beauty has a lot to do with background and education. Examples? At first the Japanese hated Western symphonic music, now they understand and love it. At first Westerners didn't understand African carvings. Now we love them.

What about God? Is God beautiful? We are taught that one day if we make heaven we will see God face to face and the sight will make us ecstatically happy. Since God doesn't have physical parts, being pure Spirit, it is hard to picture this. We use analogies such as the beauty of radiant light.

SPIRITUAL EXERCISES:

1. Make a list of your favorite beauty spots; favorite music, art, dance, etc. Thank God for each one as you go along.

2. How would you define or describe beauty?

3. Do you thank God for everything beautiful you see or hear?

4. Pray to the Holy Spirit that your life may become more beautiful because more full of love.

FOR PERSONAL REFLECTION AND GROUP SHARING:

1. **Describe in detail moments of experiencing sublime beauty.**

2. **In what ways do you make your life more beautiful all the way from cleaning house, arranging food or flowers in a pleasing manner, to artistic creativity, to making your contacts with other people more loving?**

If you wish, write your own teaching about theories of ministry roles for a class for children, teens or adults, or a homily you might give in the future? You could include a song, a drawing, or dance? If you so choose, you can share what you create with the group at the beginning or end of some other session of the *Way of Life.*

SESSION

15

LIVING YOUR PERSONAL WAY OF LOVE IN THE FUTURE

Any ideas about beauty that surfaced since the last session?

You have gone through fourteen sessions of the *Way of Love*. Don't you need to catch your breath? But you have one last challenge: deciding what you want to take from your journey for the future?

Here are two ways you could do this. If you can think of a third way, check with Dr. Ronda if she thinks it will work.

1. Bring *The Way of Love,* Vol. 1, and all your responses to a quiet place. An adoration chapel? A beautiful place in nature? Read it all over and as you do this write a piece called "Living My Personal Way of Love in the Future" by _____your name. You might start with a favorite Scripture and end with a prayer. I suggest you then type this up and surround it with pleasant graphics and pin it up on a wall in your room or keep it in your pocket or purse to refer to often, especially when you are feeling the most unloving!

2. Less ambitious, but could work just as well, would be to just select the best lines from the *Way of Love* and from your journal notes and type them up for use whenever the Holy Spirit so directs.

If you are part of a group share with your comrades.

My closing prayer is this:

Dear Sacred Heart of Jesus, full of love for us, we thank you for this time to focus on the nature of love, and to embark afresh on the way of love. Heal our wounds, purify our hearts, and strengthen our feet for the way ahead.

VOLUME 2
OVERCOMING OBSTACLES
TO LOVE

SESSION

1

INTRODUCTION

"I have fought the good fight. I have run the race to the finish, I have kept the faith." (2 Titus 4:7)

Greetings reader/participant in the second book of the series *The Way of Love*: *Overcoming Obstacles to Love.* Some of you may not have read and studied the first volume: *What is Love?* If that is the case, here is a brief, brief, summary.

There are many definitions of love and many types of love. The definition that was used throughout the first booklet comes from the philosopher Dietrich Von Hildebrand: "love is a response to the unique preciousness of the other."

Types of love we studied were passionate love, affectionate (primarily family) love, friendship love, and caring/serving love for the needy.

We also had sessions about marriage, virtues, loving and unloving ethical decisions, masculine and feminine ways of loving and love of beauty.

The booklets are divided up into sessions. An individual person can work his/her way through, but *The Way of Love* is primarily oriented toward group sharing. Each session will include a scripture, a teaching, spiritual exercises, and questions for personal reflection (you could use these for journaling) and group sharing.

To turn now to this booklet, *Overcoming Obstacles to Love*. There are many obstacles to love, for example rejection, or separation from loved ones by wars or death. Many of these are beyond our control. Here we are concerned with obstacles coming from emotions: strong ones, such as anger; and weaker ones, such as moods. Other obstacles we will deal with are engrained traits of character such as addictions. Our perspective will be how God's love, called grace, can help us over time to overcome these.

We will begin with emotions. What is an emotion? According to Webster's dictionary, an emotion is a state of feeling; a conscious ... reaction (as anger or fear) subjectively experienced as strong feeling usually directed to a specific object and typically accompanied by physiological and behavioral changes in the body. The Encyclopedia Britannica web-site adds joy and sadness to anger and fear as examples.

According to Thomistic philosophy (based on the writings of St. Thomas Aquinas), an emotion is a mental awareness, a bodily response to that awareness, and an affective (feeling) response. For example, you sense danger to yourself or others. That is a mental awareness. Then you may experience trembling in the body, and also fear as an affective response. This leads to a decision between fight, flight, or standing your ground.

Emotions are studied by psychologists and moralists. Here we are more interested in what could be called *spirituality* of the emotions. The term spirituality can be widely defined as "the way to God," or more specifically, for Christians, as an individual's obedience to the Holy Spirit in the quest for union with God.

Since we have many negative as well as positive emotions, we have to be willing to change the bad ones. Dietrich Von Hildebrand, one of the greatest Christian philosophers and spiritual writers of the 20th century, considered that no one could become more holy without a readiness to change. As St. Paul told us, we need to beg the Holy Spirit for greater "love, joy, faithfulness, gentleness, self-control." (Galatians 5:22)

To be transformed, we need to struggle with negative emotions such as uncontrolled anger or trustless anxiety and despair. In His love for us and for those around us, God wants to give us the grace (supernatural love energy) to become more peaceful, and joyful. And this, as all the saints prove, can happen even while we endure the small and large crosses of life.

A key factor in our growth will be getting away from irrational passions into the emotional responses that are due to the specific realities we encounter. Examples: Going from fear of a disabled person to desire to help. Another one would be that instead of feeling annoyed about a glitch in preparing a perfect meal, we need to be more grateful that we have any food to cook at all. It is easy to see in the case of cooking that gratitude is better than petty annoyance about glitches. Harder, as you will see, will be rage at the faults of others to be replaced by gratitude for their virtues.

Spiritual Exercises:

1. Go through a typical day in your life tracking such emotions as anxiety vs. trust; indifference vs. friendliness; irritation vs. acceptance; anger vs. peace; boredom and annoyance vs. serving with love; despair vs. hope.

2. Ask yourself in prayer before God if you are really eager or ready for change?

3. Check with others who know you what is your worst fault. Start thinking about whether you are eager to pray for the grace to change in this area of weakness.

For Personal Reflection and Group Sharing:

1. How would you define the word emotion? How do you think emotions, in general, are regarded in society and/or in the Church?

2. Tell about emotions you struggle with present or past.

3. In battling with negative emotions what means have you found helpful such as talking to friends, seeking professional counsel, spiritual directors, prayer. Other?

4. Pray in the group with each member in a manner acceptable to the participant, such as silence, holding hands, formal prayers most members know, or in a charismatic mode.

If you wish, work on a presentation for the group reading this booklet or other groups you minister to. You can use power point, song, drama, art, dance to make the insights you found in this session available to others.

SESSION

2

MOODINESS AND ANXIETY VS. STEADINESS

"God indeed is my Savior. I am confident and unafraid. My strength and my courage is the Lord." (Isaiah 12:2)

(Is there anything you want to share about emotions in general or your personal experiences of emotions since the last session?)

Definition of moodiness: a tendency to fluctuate in states of mind and dispositions.

So, how is moodiness an obstacle to love? And how is steadiness a form of love? Think of this: Before approaching someone you ask, "What mood is he or she in?" The very question implies that you can't count on this person to be in a steady kindly disposition. With moody people you anticipate a possible unpleasant encounter.

Of course no one is always in one steady frame of mind. But we call someone moody if we surmise the moods fluctuate too quickly, usually on the bad side. If you are a moody type, an incentive to try to change your moodiness is to realize that people are a little afraid of you sensing you are unpredictable.

Good moods can sometimes be a special grace wafting us above feelings of drudgery. Bad feelings can sometimes come from the devil trying to sink our ship.

But bad moods can also be influenced by more by physical realities such as illness, weather, certain medications. As well, those of a melancholic temperament are usually more moody than the more happy-go-lucky type of person.

Many moods are related to good or bad expectations. Few of us get into a bad mood if we just won the lottery! Thinking something unpleasant or burdensome is in the offing can cause a mood swing.

Sometimes bad moods reflect self-centeredness. Since we were created for heaven, we cannot help wishing every day would be heavenly. Some of us have an attitude that the people around us are there primarily to serve our happiness. If they fail to do so we think they should be controlled and manipulated. If this also fails we easily fall into a bad mood. Since, however, we know that life after the Fall is full of crosses, we should have an abiding steady frame of mind accepting that there will be good and bad experiences in every day. The spiritual component of such experiences can be to unite the sufferings of disappointment with the pain Christ, who was God Himself, suffered when thwarted in building His kingdom.

When extreme, good moods such as manic-like elation, can be followed by a fall at the slightest negative that bursts the bubble. It is not good to have a frothy feeling that everything will go well for the rest of your life, etc. "Try not to get too high," I have been advised. One mentor of mine used to respond to such moods of mine with the humorous command, "Down, Fido!"

Bad moods can be like quicksand leading to unobjective ideas about reality in general, low self-esteem, or dire predictions about one's personal future. If only out of proper self-love we need to beware of sentences such as, "Life isn't worth living," or "I'll never amount to anything." If you are in a bad mood when reading this paragraph you might even think that these ideas are valid instead of effects of bad moods or suggestions of the devil. Consider: if a cup of coffee, a nice dessert, or a phone call from a loving friend is enough to dissipate a bad mood, then you probably don't really believe that life is not worth living and that you are a total failure!

Emotions should be a response to objective realities as in grief if someone died; joy at the birth of a new baby; compassion as a response to neediness of others or delight in their virtues or pleasant personality traits. However, with moods we tend to just ride a state of mind as if it were permanent. We largely forget what is objectively worthy of joy or hope such as the reality of the living God and His providential love for us, transcending even the worst earthly tragedies.

What about anxiety? Sometimes the word anxiety is used as a synonym for fear. But most students of the emotions distinguish anxiety from fear. Fear is a response to danger. If I see fire coming out of a window I ought to be fearful so that I will call 911. By contrast, anxiety is more subjective. Some of us experience what psychologists call "free floating anxiety." This happens when without any identifiable reason we feel tremulous and insecure. This sort of anxiety is a mood in that it isn't permanent, but fluctuating.

Three remedies often suggested for anxiety are these: first try to trace the anxiety back to a childhood experience. For example, a child of a severely alcoholic battering parent might feel anxious whenever alcohol is served even in benign social situations. Once a childhood source of anxiety is identified we can ask the Holy Spirit to give us counsel about whether to avoid such circumstances or, instead, go to them but offering the anxiety in prayer for the conversion of addicts.

Secondly, physical work or exercise is recommended for free-floating anxiety. Thirdly playing enjoyable or spiritual music can be mood altering for the best.

Such remedies contrast with a tendency many of us have to simply sink into negative moods. Wouldn't it be better to pray to God for a steady disposition, eager to approach every problem that arises with loving concern?

A Christian psychotherapist, Clare Ten Eyck, suggests that when a painful mood begins to flood our consciousness we need to focus on the feeling of the mood and bring it to Jesus. Don't tough it out, she advises, but cry to God out of the depths. Sitting in front of the Blessed Sacrament is another good choice. Sometimes when we attack bad moods through this kind of "spiritual warfare" God gives us the grace to realize what part our own choices cause negative patterns that lead down dead end roads. Sometimes we emerge from prayer so grateful for the good in life that we now feel in a very good mood.

Once Jesus told me in my heart "You need never worry another day in your whole life if you trusted in me."

Spiritual Exercises:

1. Between now and the next session track any negative moods on a little piece of paper. As you track these make a plan for

spiritual warfare against those moods such as calling out to God for help in your own words or saying traditional prayers or spending more time in Church.

2. Consider if you are one who tends toward anxiety. Try talking to friends or mentors about roots of your insecurity.

FOR PERSONAL REFLECTION AND GROUP SHARING:

1. Do you have other theories than mine about moods?

2. Do you think fear and anxiety are different or more degrees of the same emotion?

3. Try analyzing a mood you are prone to that you wish to overcome.

4. Describe people you have known who have the kind of steadiness that leads to persistent loving-kindness.

Loraine Cox   *HDL*
Fr. Louie ?   *Sr. Theresa & other sisters*

If you wish work on a presentation for the group reading this booklet or other groups you minister to. You can use power point, song, drama, art, dance to make the insights you found in this session available to others.

SESSION

3

INDIFFERENCE VS. FRIENDLY ZEALOUS SERVICE

"Whatever you do, work at it with your whole being. Do it for the Lord rather than for men, since you know full well you will receive an inheritance from Him as your reward." (Colossians 3: 17)

(Do you have any thoughts from the last session on moods and anxiety?)

The word lazy has become almost a politically incorrect word in our culture, like fat. Yet sloth is one of the seven deadly sins. If you don't like to even think about laziness as an obstacle to love, let's think of the milder word "indifferent," as contrasted to friendly zeal to serve.

Most of us are zealous about some things, such as work we enjoy or checking out e-mail, but lack-luster about other things, such as routine office work or household chores.

How can indifference be an obstacle to love? Consider the early part of the day. Even those of us who pride ourselves on being friendly may often allow ourselves to fall into an indifferent or even surly mood upon awakening. We may fail to greet those we see first in the morning. By contrast loving people are friendly and seem to be eager to help at any time. Their very smiles suggest openness to serve.

The contrast between the joyful first greetings of newlyweds and those of older married couples is proverbial. Delight vs. a grunt with, perhaps, absence of any greeting, or a reminder of a chore to be done – by the other, of course!

Of course, those who consider themselves "morning persons" are better at showing love or respect first thing than those who feel only half alive until after breakfast or at the first pause between classes at school or at the coffee break at work. Is this grumpy morning indifference just something everyone has to put up with or might we consider praying to do better?

We are called as Christians to love one another as Christ loved us. Can you imagine Jesus, Mary or Joseph greeting each other for the first time of the day with indifference? Can you imagine them avoiding serving each other in whatever way was needed?

We have many excuses for indifferent behavior. "I'm very busy," "I'm too tired to do anything now, ask me tomorrow." "If I do things for others they'll take it for granted and I'll be twice as burdened as I am now."

I believe that if we wish to grow in love as Christians we need to look carefully at such seemingly minor matters. In the Psalms it describes a country as terribly pagan because "The passersby say not 'God Bless You.'"

Once I noticed that a check-out woman never smiled or exchanged any comments with the long line of people going through her counter. I decided to try smiling at her and always saying hello. It took a month, but finally she did respond. A friend reported trying the same experiment with people she dealt with. She got the same result.

Maybe you feel it is artificial to pump up what seems like unreal friendliness to strangers or to relatives and friends you are on the outs with. An incentive might be considering how it makes you feel when every day you have to be in the company of an unfriendly, glum, or disgruntled person. For myself, I know that such people make me feel alternately used, unappreciated, unloved or even worthless.

Turning to zealous service, in our culture, there has developed an attitude that except during work hours everyone should be free to play games on their computers or I-phones. Wouldn't it be more loving to relax only after all necessary chores are finished? How often do we ask the Holy Spirit to show us what choices to make?

Of course, you may be muttering to yourself, "I would be friendlier and kinder more often if those around me weren't so self-centered. Why should I have to make all the effort? If so, go back to the Scripture at the beginning of this session: "Whatever you do, work at it with your whole being. Do it for the Lord rather than for men, since you know full well you will receive an inheritance from Him as your reward." (Colossians 3: 17) Introduced to Mother Teresa of Calcutta at her home for the dying destitute, someone remarked, "I wouldn't do that for a million dollars." She replied, "Neither would I. I do it for God."

SPIRITUAL EXERCISES:

1. Do you have a different theory about why some people are indifferent and others so friendly and helpful?

2. Go through a weekday and then a weekend day noticing occasions for expressing love for others by means of friendliness or zealous service?

3. Write a short prayer to Jesus that you could say whenever you are reluctant to be friendly and serving.

4. Think about planning a time for relaxation and recreation each weekday and for each weekend. Consider planning to use the rest of the time in helpful service.

FOR PERSONAL REFLECTION AND GROUP SHARING:

1. Describe people you have known or read about whom you consider to be exceptional in friendly loving service to others.

2. Tell of moments when friendliness of others has touched your heart. *J.a.P.   Joan C.   Fr. Ed   Fr. Louie*

3. Are there times when you made a breakthrough to overcome reluctance to help?

If you wish, work on a presentation for the group reading this booklet or other groups you minister to. You can use power point, song, drama, art, dance to make the insights you found in this session available to others.

SESSION

4

IRRITABILITY VS. ACCEPTANCE

"Learn from Me, because I am meek ad humble of heart and you will find rest for your souls." (Matthew 11:29)

(Do you wish to share any fresh insights you got about indifference vs. friendly zealous service?)

A large part of my book *Taming the Lion Within: Five Steps from Anger to Peace* is devoted to the problem of irritable anger at the frustrations of daily life.

In a world marred by original sin filled with broken and sinful people how could we expect things to run smoothly? Ignoring this truth, we wish instead that we could be the heroines or heroes of the drama of life. Everyone else should be secondary or walk-on characters who would do everything to bring about Hollywood endings for success in our personal goals.

With this expectation we become outraged at drivers who cut us off or slow us down, at machines that fail us when we are in a hurry, at spouses who seem to have an agenda opposite to ours frustrating our plans, etc., etc. ,etc.

Later in these sessions we will deal with anger just and unjust concerning major issues, but here we want to work on irritability about minor matters. Here are a few insights from psychologists and Christian teachers about irritability vs. acceptance.

In the 1940's, Dr. Abraham Low, psychiatrist and forerunner of cognitive therapy, developed a self-help group program called Recovery, Inc. for dealing with anger, anxiety, and depression. I learned about the groups when I was in my late 50's and have benefited greatly. Following are some of the most helpful ideas in this program about irritability and acceptance:

"Not a 911." Low claims that most irritable people blow up ordinary difficulties of daily life into big melodramas. The usual day can be rather boring, but, as some examples will show, the day can become more exciting if you yell curses through a closed window at the bad drivers on the road as if every discourteous driver is a villain deserving of hell! Or, to take another example, muttering about the short life span of modern kitchen devices changes a dull occurrence into a condemnation of all the manufacturing companies in the world! When a schoolmate, family member, or co-worker neglects a small chore, a sarcastic comment changes plain annoyance into a mini-victory of wit.

Recovery, Inc. members recommend that when daily annoyances occur we need to come up with an amusing phrase such as "It's not a 911," or "Expect frustrations every five minutes, you won't be disappointed."

A similar "tool" is "self-induced expectations lead to self-induced frustrations." In other words, if you nurture overly optimistic hopes for the smoothness of the day's agenda you are more likely to be upset by roadblocks.

Many of us are so used to being irritable that we don't even see how unloving such anger can become. Peaceless trigger responses to every difficulty of ordinary life are not just bad for us but display a lack of forgiving patient love.

Watch how loving acceptance is related to another key insight of Abraham Low. This brilliant psychiatrist recognized that we cannot be peaceful unless we accept what he calls averageness. We are urged to accept the fact that average people in an average family, school, work place, or Church, will be only so-so in meeting our wishes for perfection. And we will often fail in meeting the expectations of others, for example, their wish that we would make less of a big deal about trivial matters.

This does not mean that we should have no hopes for others or ourselves and wallow in mediocrity or worse. It is good and right to try to improve things when that is feasible. However, in many cases changing things would entail an entire renovation of society or personality. We might work slowly to achieve our goals but we cannot expect that just wanting things to be different, cursing others, or nasty remarks will change the world into paradise.

From a spiritual standpoint, we have to accept the fact once and for all that total happiness is only in heaven. On earth, no matter how hard we try to arrange things for smooth success, there will be frustrations. But these little crosses have great spiritual value if we bring them to Jesus and offer them to him. Here is the way many Christians often pray about annoyances:

Jesus, in heaven you had perfect happiness. You chose to come down to earth to suffer for our sins. You endured all the petty frustrations we do. I would like to complain and mutter, or make sarcastic remarks when daily life is so irksome, but I will "take up my little cross and follow you," to join in bringing down graces on the world for (names of people who need special favors.)

A meek person, following the teaching of Jesus, simply doesn't allow daily annoyances to disturb his or her peaceful pursuit of loving purposes. Such acceptance is compatible with trying to change unjust conditions when possible, but it isn't compatible with an attitude of perpetual annoyance.

SPIRITUAL EXERCISES:

1. Think of an average day in your life. What are the annoying people and circumstances likely to come up? Are they 911's?

   Are they worth becoming angry about?

2. Would you be willing to pray before each anticipated frustration not to be irritated but to patiently try to work on the problem?

3. Write a prayer for patient acceptance of the average behavior of those closest to you.

FOR PERSONAL REFLECTION AND GROUP SHARING:

1. What do you think about irritability in others and in yourself?

2. Do you know anyone who is patient and peaceful? How are those virtues related to a loving disposition?

3. Have you ever made a breakthrough in overcoming chronic irritation at the faults of anyone else?

4. Do you want to be prayed over for the virtue of acceptance?

If you wish, work on a presentation for the group reading this booklet or other groups you minister to. You can use power point, song, drama, art, dance to make the insights you found in this session available to others.

SESSION

5

BOREDOM VS. INTEREST

"Near restful waters He leads me, to revive my drooping spirit." (Psalm 23, 2-3)

(Did you get any fresh insights after the last session on irritability and acceptance?)

I suffer with what could be called the 1:30 PM syndrome. It usually follows my after lunch nap. As I lie half awake I get this feeling that everything I do with my life is absurd and meaningless. I think of my plans for work or for visits with others and it all seem worthless, distasteful. The tiniest glitches in washing up and preparing a snack I find intolerably

annoying. I feel too blah to even register irritation or anger about such frustrations.

Then, what do you know? Five minutes after guzzling down tea or coffee and a snack I feel fine, raring to go, and eager to pursue my goals.

However, about 4 P.M., I get tired again. Not as bad as at 1:30 PM but sort of blah, lack luster – and this persists until a surge of energy while eating dinner, unless....

Here's the point. If I happen to have scheduled in a late afternoon swim, I don't have that blah feeling. Instead I feel fresh, and even exhilarated and eager to see family or friends or get in a little more work before dinner.

I never bothered to analyze this syndrome much until working on a course called Spirituality of the Emotions. What strikes me most is that if a cup of coffee or a swim can change boredom, annoyance, or down blah feelings to good feelings, emotions have a lot more to do with the body than I imagine. Dr. Abraham Low insists that moving your muscles in any form is an antidote to low feelings as well as anxiety.

Low feelings can become what is called depression. It is important to distinguish clinical depression which is a steady state usually requiring medication, from the kind of milder depression that can be fought by spiritual warfare.

Since we are called to zealous loving service as Christians, we need to come against feelings of boredom, lethargy, and non-clinical depression so that we don't end up wasting time. Is it really God's will to do paid work in a sloppy manner, possibly faking work but really playing computer games? Is it good to doze off during afternoon classes at college? Or, is it okay to shirk necessary chores at home in favor of interactive web games? Is the excuse that "I feel so yucky, I need distraction," permissible as a typical reason for a Christian to be half-hearted in his or her work?

Let's see what one of many alternate Christian scenarios might be. I notice after lunch that I feel dull, dispirited, bored and cranky. I turn to the Lord and pray:

> "Dear God, you want me to serve you this afternoon in a productive or otherwise fruitful way. Please revive me by special grace or through the instrumentality of something that will pep me up, whether it be food, drink, exercise, prescribed medicine, or whatever would help me get out of this downer state."

or

> √ "I offer to You whatever is annoying or just uninteresting about my afternoon duties, in gratitude for the good goals my activities involve, or for the sake of special grace for someone I love, or as a penance for the sins of my past. I look forward to coming back to you in prayer as evening falls that I might know your approval for my sacrifices."

Of course, sometimes those down feelings are symptoms of a way of life that needs not acceptance but change. A university student might need to avoid afternoon classes if possible in favor of sports and night classes. A person whose work is always dull and unchallenging might need to look into alternate employment opportunities. A housewife might decide to accomplish chores as fast as possible in the early afternoon to have more time for recreation before making dinner.

Everyone dislikes boredom but is there a way that it is also unloving? I think so. I don't like to be around bored people. They bring me down. Their attitude seems like an indirect statement that I am not worth talking to or doing anything with.

Another aspect of down-feelings could be your temperament. Zealous service is much more appealing to choleric (raring to go) types than to phlegmatic (laid back) ones. But just as activist people desperately need to take time to relax and to pray quietly; so more relaxed people, even when they don't feel pushed by natural energies, need to pray for the grace to do whatever contributes to the common good in a quietly efficient manner.

Many times playing Christian music can lift one out of those dull, lethargic feelings. Recreation in the form of walking, sports, or playing games can also help unless these become overly time-consuming and addictive.

My prayer when I feel bored is often something like this: "Jesus: Every moment of your day on earth was given to prayer and working for the Kingdom of Love. You know how tired, discouraged and low we can sometimes become. Send the Holy Spirit to rouse us to spend more free time in prayer and to accomplish the goals You want us to achieve no matter what the setbacks."

Spiritual Exercises:

(Perhaps you are one of those who is almost never bored. In that case just pray for the rest of us.)

1. Think about circumstances or events or particular company when you tend to feel bored.

2. During the next week, whenever you feel bored consider the points made in this session. Try one of the strategies such as moving your muscles, prayer, or music.

For Personal Reflection and Group Sharing:

1. What is your theory about the boredom so prevalent in our society these days?

2. Do you think boredom is in the control of the will?

3. Tell others in the group about your experience of boredom. Let anyone who can share about ways he or she has overcome boredom.

If you wish, work on a presentation for the group reading this booklet or other groups you minister to. You can use power point, song, drama, art, dance to make the insights you found in this session available to others.

SESSION

6

ANGER VS. PEACE IN CONFLICTS

"Woe is me! For I am lost ... I dwell in the midst of a people of unclean lips." (Isaiah 6:5)

(Did you learn anything about boredom vs. interest that you could use during the time since the last session?)

Last session we talked about frustrations of daily life. In this one I want to begin to deal with more major conflicts, especially on-going ones. For most of us, no day passes by without some chronic conflict. Let's take a professor who reads old lecture notes in class but then gives huge assignments from a book he or she rarely goes over in class. Or, let's take dealing with a fellow employee who shirks, leaving more work for you.

In both examples, there is an injustice experienced often, not just by yourself, but by others as well. It is unhealthy to just suppress feelings of anger and fake that all is well. If there is any possibility of change to bring about justice you should try.

Often, however, you cannot bring about change because, say, the professor really thinks the reading is easy or the shirker is the friend or relative of the manager.

What, then? Our feelings of anger are not wrong in themselves. But they usually escalate to become toxic and sinful because they become disproportionate, harsh, unforgiving, or vengeful.

Here is the analysis of the psychiatrist, Dr. Abraham Low. When we are unable to get a real victory over a person who is thwarting our goals, we feel weak and angry. So we try to get a SYMBOLIC VICTORY over that person. For example, we make sarcastic remarks to our friends about the one who is so stubbornly recalcitrant. We save up instances of the unjust person's acts to gossip about with our friends. This is rightly called PUTTING SOMEONE DOWN. We like doing it because it makes us feel not weak and under the thumb of the unjust adversary, but instead above that person since we are judging him or her from the height of our own superiority. We may indulge fantasies about how one day that person will suffer for hurting us. Or we might take revenge by always coming late to class or losing necessary papers the shirker could need.

Why is this called trying to get a symbolic victory? Because there is no real victory. To use the previous illustrations, putting down the annoying professor over lunch with other students doesn't make him teach better. Trying to get back at the worker who slacks off so we have to do his or her work by messing up the things on his or her desk doesn't mean we still don't have to do the extra work. *Symbolic* here means that in our own minds we feel triumphant. It is as effective as trying to assuage hunger by eating a picture of a hamburger.

This principle of avoiding symbolic victory also covers cold anger. Some of us who are not prone to sarcasm or open revenge cherish anger in the form of withdrawal. "I will never forgive my brother for doing that to me. I will never talk to him again." This makes us feel powerful – we are in a position to shun another person who hurt us. Often we are the one most hurt because we escape the faults of the one we condemn but lose all the good things in the relationship. How much more powerful would we really be if through God's love we could bring about repentance and reconciliation?

Pride is usually behind over-reacting anger. We like to feel that we are smart, efficient, and successful in our endeavors. We hate being in a position of having to beg for what is only just. When others treat us badly, it stings our pride. They are in the power position and we have to accept unpleasant conditions.

Trying, in the midst of conflicts, to come to peace requires spiritual warfare. Over and over again, and sometimes only after many hours of struggle, we have to accept the fact that life is hard and only God knows how much we are suffering at the hands of others. We have to place before our imaginations the injustices Jesus suffered and remember how He forgave His enemies. In prayer we must ask Jesus to help us to be merciful to those who stand in our way. We need to set our sights on heaven instead of churning over our hurts.

But, but, but, we still like to think of ourselves as virtuous and others as being the sinners who deserve our anger. St. Augustine comments this way on Nathan the prophet upbraiding David for adultery with Bathsheba and the murder or her husband.

"Let us never assume that if we live good lives we will be without sin; our lives should be praised only when we continue to beg for pardon. But men are hopeless creatures, and the less they concentrate on their own sins, the more interested they become in the sins of others. They seek to criticize, not to correct. Unable to excuse themselves, they are ready to accuse others…Your heart must be crushed…For a clean heart to be created, the unclean one must be crushed" (Office of Readings, 14th Sunday in Ordinary Time)

In a novel by Gertrud Von Le Fort, *The Pope from the Ghetto*, the hero is incensed by the injustices going on in society and in the Church. A holy bishop gives him this advice: "If you are looking for justice you will find it in hell. In heaven is mercy, and on earth there is the cross."

SPIRITUAL EXERCISES:

1. Make a list of all the people you are angry at right now. If you aren't angry at anyone make a list of past reasons for your anger.

2. One by one ask Jesus to show you the crosses past and present in the person who frustrates or hurts you.

3. Pray for each one asking God to give you reasons to forgive.

FOR PERSONAL REFLECTION AND GROUP SHARING:

1. Take one example of chronic conflict. In silence, make an individual plan for spiritual warfare to come to peace in that area of anger, including personal prayers, traditional prayers and Christian services, and talking to friends or mentors. If you are in a group take down the names of the other people

and promise to pray for them by name throughout the next week.

2. **Repeat this practice whenever conflicts arise with the same people or with other ones.**

If you wish, work on a presentation for the group reading this booklet or other groups you minister to. You can use power point, song, drama, art, dance to make the insights you found in this session available to others.

SESSION

7

DISAPPOINTMENT, DESPAIR, AND FEAR VS. GRATITUDE, HOPE AND TRUST

"But rejoice in so far as you share in Christ's sufferings, that you may also rejoice and be glad when his glory is revealed." (1 Peter 4: 13)

(Any thoughts about anger you want to talk about with the group)

This may be one of the most difficult Scripture passages you will ever read!   Rejoice in suffering? Are you kidding? Well since it is St. Peter who wrote it there isn't much chance he was wrong, is there?

Let us repeat here the prayer in the opening of *The Way of Love: Overcoming Obstacles to Love*:

Dear Father God, You have created us with minds to know, wills to choose, and hearts to feel. You wish our hearts to be full of peace, trust, hope, joy and love in the midst of pain. Liberate us with Your saving grace from the uncontrolled anger, anxiety, despair, disappointment and bitterness that keeps us from being Your faithful disciples.

The most famous quotation from the writings of our great American philosophy Thoreau is "most men lead lives of quiet desperation." Bitter, indeed. For awhile, Thoreau sought liberation from the bitterness of life in solitude at Walden Pond.

In youth many of us take delight in fantasies of perfect cars, perfect friends, perfect careers, perfect spouses, perfect houses, or of myself, a perfect saint. Since there is no perfection except in heaven, such fantasies have to end is some degree of disappointment. When the daydream is replaced by the nightmare, normal disappointment can easily become full-blown despair.

Different but even more painful is the grief we feel for the losses in our lives. In spite of faith in eternal life, the death of loved ones leaves a hole in the heart that no one else can fill.

In the twilight of the evening and the darkness of midnight, with less to distract us, the choice can become more poignant: despair or hope. My godfather, a philosopher, Balduin Schwarz, used to say that if you add up all the reasons to despair and all the reasons to hope it is only Jesus, crucified and resurrected, who can tip the balance to hope.

St. Ambrose wrote "Let your door stand open to receive him, unlock your soul to him, offer him a welcome in your mind, and then you will see the riches of simplicity, the treasures of peace, the joy of grace. Throw wide the gate of your heart, stand before the sun of everlasting light that shines on every man. This true light shines on all, but if anyone closes his window he will deprive himself of eternal light. If you shut the door of your mind, you shut out Christ. Though he can enter, he does not want to force his way in rudely, or compel us to admit him against our will…His light is received by those who long for the splendor of perpetual light that night can never destroy. the sun of our daily experience is succeeded by the darkness of night, but the sun of holiness never sets." (*Office of Readings* p. 866-867)

On our way home from a day of school or work, as dinner time approaches, we can lift our minds to God in thanksgiving or all the gifts of the day. Then in the night before sleep or at times of waking if we feel dark despair overwhelming us, we need to cry out from the depths of our hearts to our Savior. Our hope cannot be in earthly good fortune for that comes and goes but must be anchored in faith in an eternity of love in the kingdom of God.

Surely, Jesus allows the very things in our life that seem to push us toward despair as a way to draw us into His Sacred Heart. Immersed in the love of God we let go of anger at not having gotten our way, we let go of our sadness that the bad seems to have won out in our lives and in the world and that good has not triumphed. Only God can make it come out right in the end.

Always helpful at times where despair is tempting is giving your heart just as it is to Jesus. An old prayer being revived at this time is to Our Lady of Knots – not Knock, the apparition site in Ireland, but Knots as in snarls. On the novena card is an image of Mary unraveling knotted skeins of wool. We ask her to unravel those knots that come in areas of our lives where we feel stuck. She helps us see the good and forgive the bad.

So, disappointment and despair, at first understandable, if dwelt on, can become rejections of God's love.

Since, very often, those in the throes of despair don't feel God's love, even if they do have faith that He is real even when hidden from view, a helpful antidote to despair is planning little deeds of love for others. Joining the stream of God's love for others puts us in touch with the God of love once more.

My husband, afflicted with disabling, frightening asthma most of our married life, used to play beautiful classical music, often sacred music every evening. It gave him hope.

I have included fear in this session because in some cases it can become as acutely painful as disappointment and despair and has many of the same supernatural remedies.

When we read accounts in the New Testament of disciples going to martyrdom, we marvel at their fearlessness. Surely awaiting being eaten by lions or crucified would total horror and despair. Yet the martyrs were full of trust that Jesus would help them in their torments and bring them to eternal happiness.

Many are our fears. They range from fear of being late for an appointment, fear of failing examinations, fear for our loved ones in trouble or danger, all the way to fear of terminal illness or fear of violence including, sometimes, that of members of our own households; finally, to fear of eternal punishment.

We are taught that "fear of the Lord is the beginning of wisdom."(Psalm 111:10) Since we are weak, sinful creatures subject to all kinds of evils and sufferings, we are called to work out our salvation "in fear and trembling." (Psalm 2:11) Even small threats to our security or welfare can trigger an immediate sense of fear. This fear can be positive when it causes us to be careful, plan well, and do whatever we can to avoid failure. Trusting in God in such situations helps, but may not remove a certain tremulous weakness.

Just the same, we need to avoid sinking into a quicksand of fear when challenged by situations we cannot control. We need to beg God to give us trust in His perfect love; in His provident care, even when results are disappointing or tragic. In the end, even if the worst things happen on earth, what matters most is our salvation and the salvation of those we love. We believe that God loves us and them even more than we do. When our fear becomes tortuous, we need to cast ourselves in prayer into His loving heart.

SPIRITUAL EXERCISES:

1. Bring to the Heart of Jesus, one by one, the greatest disappointments and sufferings of your life. In each case ask Him to comfort you in a personal way you can believe is real.

2. Even if it is painful, make a list of your worst fears. Then bring each one of them to Jesus and ask Him to quiet your soul.

3. Slowly meditate on these passages from Scripture:

    "Neither death, nor life… nor things present, nor things to come, nor anything else in all creation…Nothing can separate us from the love of God in Christ Jesus, Our Lord." (Romans 8:37-39)

   "Perfect love casts out fear" (1 John 4:18)

   "Come to Me, all you who labor and are heavy-laden, and I will give you rest." (Matthew 11:28)

   "Cast all your cares on Him because He cares for you." (1 Peter 5)

   √ "In the world you have tribulation; but be of good cheer, I have overcome the world." (John 16:33)

"I will wipe away all your tears. (Revelations 7:17)

Conclude your meditation with this passage from the Night Prayer of the Church on Mondays:

"Eyes will close, but you, unsleeping, watch by our side; death may come: in Love's safekeeping, still we abide. God of love, all evil quelling, sin forgiving, fear dispelling, stay with us, our hearts indwelling, this eventide."

FOR PERSONAL REFLECTION AND GROUP SHARING:

1. Read aloud these famous words of St. Teresa of Avila. "Let nothing disturb you, nothing affright you; [all things are passing,] God never changes; patient endurance attains to all things; who God possesses in nothing is wanting; alone God suffices." If you are working on *The Way of Love* alone, personalize this gem of spiritual wisdom by adding in brackets what each phrase means in your life. If you are in a group share your responses.

2. Read the following quotations and respond in your journal or talk about the with the group:

    "Charity means pardoning the unpardonable, or it is no virtue at all!" Chesterton

    "Dreams are only nightmares with lipstick." Toni Morrison

    "Thou shalt love thy crooked neighbor with thy crooked heart." the poet Auden

    "If the devil can't make you bad, he will try to make you sad." (Mother Mary Paula, see a Gentle Witness Canticle May/June 2007, p. 2)

Session

8

Humble Acceptance of Limitations vs. Perfectionism

"No one is good, but God alone." (Matthew 18)

(From the long session 8 about disappointment, despair, and fear, have you experienced any graces of hope and trust from God?)

"I'm a failure." How often do we hear these words from the mouths of people who are doing okay, but want to attain greater heights of success? An average passing student feels like a failure. A worker earning enough for basic needs can feel like a failure for not having desired luxuries. Parents sometimes feels like failures if their children aren't exceptional in worldly terms. A dinner party is deemed a failure because of one missing ingredient in the main dish.

Do you notice how this line of reasoning makes it seem as if the purpose of life is earthly success vs. growing day by day in love of God and neighbor? How many parents ask their children when they come home from school, "how many kids did you show love to today?" How many of us ask when we are to be introduced to someone not what does he or she do but is this person loving?

Perfectionism is a good word for the way some of us build up expectations for ourselves and others that are almost impossible to attain. Some counselors help their clients to lower their expectations so they can accept more realistic levels of success. After all, in baseball if a player got a base-hit even half of the time, he would have a 500 batting average. It is never achieved! So being an average student, worker, or parent should not lead to a sense of overwhelming failure, but a satisfying sense of accomplishment.

In Christian spirituality, there is an intriguing expression: humility of reality. What it means is not mediocrity, but acceptance of limitations. The goal of our lives should be growth in love, which is limitless, given God's grace. All other goals need to be subordinate to that one. It is part of trying to be loving to go to school to gain knowledge of useful subjects, but that does not require an "A" average. It is part of trying to be loving to earn money to support oneself and/or your family, but that does not require becoming rich. It is loving to bring up your children well, but that does not mean that they will become important in the world. It is loving to share specially cooked food with family and friends, but that doesn't require a perfect dinner.

A striking true story tells of a Hollywood TV crew doing a documentary about street people. They put a mike up to a mouth of an old man with rumpled, torn clothing, scraggly hair and missing teeth who was sitting on the pavement. In a kind of chanting cadence He spoke these words: "His blood never failed me." The TV people were stunned. They decided to take the tape of those 5 words and repeat it over and over again against the background of a melody. The disc became a best-seller!

A bad side of perfectionism is that when we know we can't do something perfectly or even very well, we fail to even try. Some couples live together in immoral sex for years for fear their marriage would not be ideal. G. K. Chesterton taught "if anything is worth doing it is worth doing badly." Another useful adage is "the perfect is the enemy of the good." It means that instead of doing good things fairly well, in some areas we do nothing, since we can't do it perfectly!

Here is my prayer concerning accepting limitations vs. perfectionism:

Creator God, You willed to bring beings into the world with lesser intelligence and ability than Yourself. You want us to prepare for an eternity of love by valuing service above fame and/or fortune. Help us to be able to laugh at the unrealistic standards of the world and rejoice, instead, in little deeds of love accomplished with Your help.

SPIRITUAL EXERCISES:

1. Go through the story of your life. In what areas do you think of yourself as having failed? Can you detect perfectionism in some of these estimated failures?

FOR PERSONAL REFLECTION AND GROUP SHARING:

1. **How would a greater emphasis on the Christian value of love above worldly success change your attitude toward yourself and others? How might it change the world we live in?**

If you wish, work on a presentation for the group reading this booklet or other groups you minister to. You can use power point, song, drama, art, dance to make the insights you found in this session available to others.

SESSION

9

BALANCED VS. ADDICTIVE

"But I will not be enslaved to anything." (1 Corinthians 6: 12)

What insights came to you after the session on perfectionism?

In times past the word "addict" was used exclusively for enslavement to illegal drugs. Nowadays the concept of addiction has been broadened to include a spectrum including alcoholism, nicotine addiction, workaholism, gambling, over-eating, sexaholism, shopping addiction, co-dependency, and computer game mania. The dictionary definition of addiction corresponds to this range: to devote or to surrender oneself to something habitually or obsessively. By contrast, a balanced person enjoys whatever pleasures life affords, within moral boundaries, but not to an extreme or in such as way as to hurt self or others.

The word "surrender" characterizes addictive enslavement from simply interest or enjoyment. We do not consider ourselves or others to be addicts because we enjoy a drink or 2 every day, smoke a few cigarettes, eat with greater gusto than others, work hard, play cards, enjoy sexual pleasure in a moral manner, or play games on the computer an hour a day.

Many psychologists point to one single factor underlying all addictions: pain in the heart so hard to bear that we flee, trying to find solace in the pleasurable or numbing effects of the addiction. How so? Drugs and drink are sought by many for a state of relative oblivion. Over-eating gives a physical sensation of abundant well-being, Nicotine and casual compulsive sex provide pleasure and also a momentary release from tension. The risks of gambling can be an escape into fantasies of wealth without the usual hum-drum work required to earn money. Besides the enjoyment of each purchase, acquiring many possessions gives an illusion of success. Games can distract the mind from dealing with the causes of suffering. Filling every waking moment with work leaves no time to go under because of the tragedies of life.

Can you see how this kind of slavery takes away energy and time that could be filled with love of God and love of family, friends, and neighbors?

When addicts try to achieve balance over obsessive habits through will-power, they can be surprisingly ineffective. Some Christian therapists try to bring addicts back to the original pain from which they are fleeing. They help us to find Jesus right in the midst of that wound. Twelve step programs help addicts to surrender to God in all the misery of enslavement. Through deep prayer we can then cling to the love of God precisely when the temptation of the addiction seems overwhelming. Even a few moments of postponement of the habitual addiction can be the first step in a growing ability to make balanced choices.

Father God, see me, your child, a slave to addiction. Hold me close. Pour Your love into my wounds. As I reach out to grasp the pseudo-salvation of my preferred addictions, pry open my fingers, and give me trust that you will fill my hands with what is truly good for me.

Spiritual Exercises:

1. Ask the Holy Spirit to show you how bad for you and those you love are those habits which have become for you addictions. If you think you don't have any addictions ask those close to you if they think you do.

2. Pray yourself and seek prayer to admit that you cannot control these addictions by will-power alone and to beg God to help you.

For Personal Reflection and Group Sharing:

1. Have you known anyone well who has an addiction? What has been the story of that enslavement? Can you share about someone conquering the worst part of any addiction through God's help? If you wish give your own personal witness on this.

2. What has been your experience or that of people you know of with 12 Step. In what ways are the 12 Steps similar to Catholic teachings? In what ways can Church teachings bring people even further?

If you wish, work on a presentation for the group reading this booklet or other groups you minister to. You can use power point, song, drama, art, dance to make the insights you found in this session available to others.

SESSION

10

CARING VS. SELF-CENTERED

"Greater love has no man than this, that a man lay down his life for his friends." (John 15:13)

(Any new thoughts about balance and addiction since the last session?)

A caring person is one whose love of God shines forth in concern for all those who need him or her. Sometimes such caring flows naturally without effort when our talents or inclinations make us apt instruments of His love. At other time we show our love by being willing to make heavy sacrifices.

It is part of our fallen nature to be self-centered. In a way we have to be. Unless we are totally disabled, we, ourselves, are responsible for taking care of many of our daily survival needs. We don't blame a person for eating or sleeping. We are not to blame for wanting the good things in life whenever we can have these without harm to others or to our own souls.

We think of people as self-centered whose desire to satisfy their own needs makes them care little for those of others. The worst is to victimize others because of sinful needs. Some examples would be carelessly victimizing others through drunk driving. Others enjoy the torture of prisoners. There are those who avoid the sacrifice of bearing a child in the womb and giving the child up for adoption by choosing abortion instead. If you have done any of these things do not despair. Jesus wants to forgive you. Sexually abusing others is clearly selfish as is venting anger at the frustrations in life by beating family members. Forgive us and heal us if we have ever committed such sins.

Less extreme examples of self-centeredness would be trying to get the biggest piece of cake at a dinner party, or pushing ahead of a line in a store, or ignoring the need of someone for advice because one prefers surfing TV channels or playing computer games.

Psychologists point to fear as a key underlying motive for self-centeredness. Not having experienced sufficient love as a child, an individual may feel that pursuing one's own goals is the only thing that counts. Christian moralists would point also to a tendency in our nature simply to be drawn to self-centered enjoyment of pleasure and to pride and passion.

Caring can grow for different reasons. Some become more caring when they fall in love; some when becoming parents. Often greater caring comes with a conversion (turning) toward God's love. Deeply believing that one day, God can give us perfect happiness in heaven, enables us to loosen our grip on earthly satisfactions.

One aspect of caring is giving money or time to help needy people not in our own families or circle of close friends. We all know from the global TV and Net that there are in the world many dying of starvation or lack of medical care. We know there are local, national and international groups who can alleviate these needs and who need our money and/or helping hands.

Of course, a really poor person with many family obligations may have no money or time to give to strangers. But what of those of us who simply pile up unneeded possessions and, beyond normal needed recreation, waste time on trivial amusements?

Some will use the excuse that the so-called needy are really dishonest manipulators or that money given to charities winds up in the pockets of the CEO's organizing them. But can anyone claim that the victims of floods, earthquakes and wars are all thieves? Or that heads of pro-life groups, mostly staffed by volunteers, who reach out to those with options for women with tragic pregnancies, are all keeping most of the donations for themselves? Would anyone think that Sisters and Brothers of the Missionaries of Charity founded by Saint-Mother Teresa of Calcutta whose rule forbids them, in solidarity with the poorest of the poor, to have anything better than newspaper for toilet use, are squandering the money that comes in?

If we actually saw a mother holding a starving baby in her arms in front of the store we were entering to buy a sixth sweater or our 50th CD would we easily step over her to buy our luxuries instead of helping that mother get food for herself and her child?

Jesus, you want us to have the joy of one day meeting in heaven all those strangers we have helped with money and/or time. You want to thank us for seeing You in "the distressing disguise" of the poor. Take away the blindness of indifference and may the Holy Spirit help us to find legitimate charities we can help whenever we have time or money.

Spiritual Exercises:

1. In what areas do you need to overcome self-centeredness to show more loving care?

For Personal Reflection and Group Sharing:

1. What is your theory about causes of self-centeredness?

2. What is your strategy for drawing out caring impulses in yourself? In others?

3. What new leap might Jesus want you to make in this area?

If you wish, work on a presentation for the group reading this booklet or other groups you minister to. You can use power point, song, drama, art, dance to make the insights you found in this session available to others.

SESSION

11

ENJOYING AND AFFIRMING VS. CRITICALNESS AND COMPLAINT

"But who are you that you judge your neighbor?" (James 4:12)

(Did pondering the need to become more caring lead you to any new resolutions?)

I have linked together the four words in the title because they usually go together. A person who knows how to enjoy is usually willing to lovingly affirm others. A person who is critical is also usually the first to complain.

The word "critical" is often used in the positive to mean the ability to discriminate between truth and error, excellent and poor literary style, or to detect phoniness and deception. All of us hope to be considered critical in those ways. We hope that by means of our critical abilities we will be able to improve things.

In the negative, though, a person deemed critical is judged as always finding fault; nit-picking, using the mind as a knife to cut the words or actions of others to pieces. Very unloving, indeed!

Such criticalness is associated with coldness, harshness, and arrogance. 'But, but, but,'...a reader might bridle, 'there is so much in the world that is shoddy, careless, stupid, and evil. How could I not be critical? Wouldn't it be phony to go around smiling and nodding as if everything were wonderful? And isn't lots of praise manipulative flattery?'

Granted there is much we cannot praise and that some affirmers are flatterers, but is that a reason to practically ignore all the good and speak only in carping criticism of others?

By contrast, affirming others is rightly considered to be a positive trait. How good others feel to be praised for virtues, work well done, and their loving deeds. How good we, ourselves, feel when we affirm others! In praising we dwell in the good. We might be said to be joining in God's delight in that good.

Besides critical *words* or affirmations, there are also disparaging *thoughts* and affirming thoughts. These can fill our minds with discouragement or with gratitude. And, of course, the one we may be most critical of is ourselves, leading to such low feelings we feel sapped of energy for doing good.

If you tend to be critical in this bad way, you might find this prayer of use:

> Dear God, when I become aware of all that is deficient and evil in the world, I want to criticize those responsible. Help

me to use the critical faculties You have given me in tandem with plans for bettering things. Never let me concentrate so much on the bad that I cannot joyfully praise everything worthy, thereby encouraging others to persevere in their good works.

Let us now turn to complaining as an unloving emotional pattern. Everyone agrees that life is difficult. In Recovery, Inc., anger management participants urge themselves to "expect frustrations every five minutes, you won't be disappointed." It is only natural to feel annoyed and to express it, at least sometimes. I think it is a particular way of expressing annoyance that makes others call us complainers.

There is a Yiddish word for a complainer that sounds just like what it feels like: kvetch – it has a growling muttering tone. "Kvetch" is a name for someone who acts as if his or her burdens are worse than anyone else's. When I "kvetch" there is an implication that others are to blame for not fixing things so I would be less miserable. Rarely do I think that I need to work harder to fix things myself instead of blaming everyone else.

For example, if I constantly complain about computer glitches maybe I should take the trouble to take courses in computers to better my skills!

Some psychologists would say that complaining about relative trifles is a symptom of feeling lonely or unhappy about bigger things. Instead of taking out these feelings on little situations, we may need counseling and prayer so that the Holy Spirit can help us find ways to change our lives.

The best opposite to complaining is gratitude. Contrast the beaming faces of those who enjoy life with the tight, well, kvetchy look of the complainer. I am overwhelmed when I read of political prisoners unjustly confined for years, actually making up jokes to amuse themselves. Trying to eat a burned chicken breast, one person complains about the cook while another sets aside the skin and relishes the juicy meat underneath. Most people complain about a dreary drizzly day; others exult in the unusual and needed rain. Even more importantly, some of us complain bitterly about the faults of those around us, while others enjoy those same individuals, laughing at their flaws as quirks.

I often tell God that He knows how difficult our life on earth is. I say, "You don't blame us for disliking all that is unpleasant. You want us to pray for those who make life hard for us. You also want so much for us to offset annoyances with grateful enjoyment of Your many gifts. Help us to savor all that is pleasant in our days."

SPIRITUAL EXERCISES:

1. Try going through a day and making a tally of your praise vs. criticism in words and thoughts.

2. Try for just one day to enjoy everything positive to the max, smiling or laughing at everything negative.

FOR PERSONAL REFLECTION AND GROUP SHARING:

1. Tell each other about how you feel when others praise and affirm you.

2. By contrast, how do you feel when others criticize you or complain about every deficiency in what you do for them?

3. How do you think you could help a critical complainer to take a more positive attitude toward life?

4. Try for just one day to enjoy everything positive to the max, smiling or laughing at everything negative unless it is truly tragic. Do you think that if Jesus, Mary, and Joseph came back to earth they would enjoy the gifts of God? Would they be affirming or critical or both?

If you wish, work on a presentation for the group reading this booklet or other groups you minister to. You can use power point, song, drama, art, dance to make the insights you found in this session available to others.

SESSION

12

SELF-CONFIDENT VS. ENVIOUS

"Let us have no...envy of one another." (Galatians 5: 26)

(Thoughts about criticalness and complaint to share?)

Envy is one of the seven deadly sins. Why? Think, for a minute, about the feeling of envy. It is a kind of leaden weight of self-pity mingled, usually, with animosity toward the envied one. Another person has qualities I wish I had: beauty, brilliance, physical strength and agility, fame, fortune, or power. By contrast I may feel ugly, stupid, physically weak, ordinary, poor, or powerless in the game of life.

Even more deeply, an envious person feels unlovable because she or he can't match up to those glittering qualities. A person we wish loved us more, seems to prefer another with a surplus of those attractive features. Naturally, the envious person feels inferior. There may also be anger at God. Why couldn't You have given me more of those gifts? It's not fair!

You might think that those who have many gifts feel self-confident. This is rarely the case. The one who comes in second in the beauty contest can feel envious. The smart kid with IQ ten points lower than his brother can feel inferior. One who doesn't quite make the team in spite of ability and practice can feel finished. A famous person can notice his or her ratings dwindling. A person who made millions on the stock market can worry about a depression. The all powerful manager can be envious of a younger associate climbing up the ladder right behind.

Many times envy comes from insecurity. The picture of security is a sleeping baby in the arms of a parent. No fear. Just peaceful content. Soon enough bliss changes to anxious cries as some needs must wait or some may never be met on this earth! The feeling that even when things are going well they could change for the worse even about survival has to make us insecure. Add on childhoods where there was abandonment or rejection it is easy to see why many of us suffer from a kind of chronic insecurity. Probably if you got to know an envious person well you would find that insecurity was a big part of his or her childhood.

On the other hand there are situations of relative security such as having loving parents, consistent teachers, a steady job, a good church. I try to remember to thank God for all the sources of security He has given me in my life, even if they are only for a time. "Thank you most, Father God, for your everlasting love. Teach me to hold onto You when I feel insecure so that when I pray I may have the security of a babe in arms."

Even when we become aware of some of these roots of envy we might wonder if envy is the wrong, and very unloving, response, what might be the right Christian way to think about oneself? The way I think of it is this: pride in one's gifts and accomplishments as if we should take the whole credit for them, is not Christian. We should realize that life itself and every talent, and even the energy for working hard for goals, is a gift from God. True, the popularity and success that can come from our talents and efforts can be good if used to build the kingdom of love. We can be grateful for them. But those qualities others envy are often negative if used for vanity, luxurious living, or the enjoyment of power. Most of the saints were not beautiful, brilliant, strong, famous, rich or powerful in their life-times. Compare Hitler, at the zenith of his power, to Jesus on the cross! Or the attractiveness of Marilyn Monroe to that of Mother Teresa of Calcutta!

The right kind of self-confidence could be expressed in this prayer: "Father, God, You created me to use my gifts in loving service. I am content with the way I look even if I am not beautiful by media standards. You can use my average looks to make me approachable. I am content with the mind you gave me since knowing You is the summit of all wisdom. I am thankful for everything my body can do even if it is much less than that of an athlete. Even if You allowed me to suffer with disabilities, my heart is not disabled, but able to love as much as any more agile person can. If I am not famous, I am known to You, whose "eye is on the sparrow." If I am not rich or powerful, if I follow You, I will one day have all of heaven and the power of immortality in eternal life. With confidence in Your personal love for me, and Your promises, I can admire the gifts others have in profusion. I can pray that those beneficiaries of natural gifts don't lose the greater supernatural gifts of faith, hope and love."

SPIRITUAL EXERCISES:

1. Who have you been most envious of among those in your family, school, work, or public figures? Have you ever experienced grace overcoming this envy?

2. What made you insecure as a child? What were reasons for relative security? Can you open yourself to God so that He can make you feel more secure?

FOR PERSONAL REFLECTION AND GROUP SHARING:

1. Why do you think God made us to be equal in being all sons and daughters of Him but so unequal in our attributes such as intelligence, beauty, physical skillfulness?

2. How could meditation on what heaven will be like assuage envy and insecurity?

3. "Let nothing disturb you....God alone suffices" wrote St. Teresa of Avila. Can you accept this advice as valid for you right now in your own heart?

If you wish, work on a presentation for the group reading this booklet or other groups you minister to. You can use power point, song, drama, art, dance to make the insights you found in this session available to others.

SESSION

13

WARM VS. COLD

"Love one another, even as I have loved you." (John 13:34)

(Do you want to share anything on envy and insecurity?)

Can you imagine anyone in Nazareth finding Jesus, or Mary, or Joseph cold? Why people pushed their way through crowds to touch Jesus; judging from her apparitions Mary, refuge of sinners, must have been encircled by townsfolk looking for love and guidance. And are the artists not right in picturing St. Joseph so often holding the boy Jesus on his shoulders?

Very outward-going people sometimes think of anyone who is quiet as cold. That is not fair. A smile, affection when needed, and little deeds of love prove the warmth of many an inward person. Background also has to be taken into consideration when making judgments about warm vs. cold. In some cultures warmth is shown by ready hugging; in others that would be taboo.

Yet, some of us whether extrovert or introvert are sometimes accused of being cold, at least to some people, at some times, and even to spouses, family members, or other parishioners. Reasons for being cold to others could vary from having legitimate grievances because of their behavior, all the way down to just being indifferent.

Analyzing coldness, psychologists think first of role-modeling in the family of our birth: a cold father or mother or both. Selfish reasons might be as simple as trying to be inapproachable to avoid getting involved in the knotty problems of others or being asked to perform annoying chores.

Feeling courageous? How about asking the people who have to be with you a lot whether you ever seem cold to them and in what way. You might be surprised. A dedicated very sacrificial priest once read in an evaluation: "you seem cold to us because the door to your office is always closed." Once aware, he changed that quickly. A grown daughter charged her mother with being a little cold because her Mom's hugs were so quick. That changed fast!

Prayer: Dear Jesus, Mary, and Joseph, we want to be like you. Please grace us with the warmth of your hearts; heal us of any coldness from others in the past that closed us up; let us be a warm haven for all who need our love.

Spiritual Exercises:

1. Ask family and friends if they ever find you to be cold? If so, pray to be warmer in the areas they have pin-pointed. Try expressing more warmth to people you encounter.

2. Meditate on the warmth of heart of Jesus, Mary, and Joseph. Ask them to inundate you with their love so that you may transmit it to those who need it most.

For Personal Reflection and Group Sharing:

1. Talk about examples of warmth from the lives of the saints.

2. What cultural differences concerning warmth have you observed in people from various national backgrounds?

3. What about women and men? Do you think women are warmer or only warm in a different manner from men?

If you wish, work on a presentation for the group reading this booklet or other groups you minister to. You can use power point, song, drama, art, dance to make the insights you found in this session available to others.

SESSION

14

FORGIVING VS. UNFORGIVING

"Forgive us our trespasses as we forgive those who trespass against us." (Matthew 6:12)

(Between this and the last session were you able to come to any new conclusions about warmth and coldness?)

All Christians know that Jesus has obliged us with those words to forgive everyone who has hurt us, no matter how badly. Many a time we think we have forgiven others but when we have to come into contact with them again we realize our hearts are closed in bitterness or hate. Perhaps you have noticed that your own sins can seem relatively minor to you and forgivable compared to the sins of others. Easy to understand, really. When you are the victim of someone else's sins, it stings. When you hurt someone else they feel the sting, but you don't!

If your list of sins committed against you is truly greater than the list of your own sins you are in good company in your forgiveness. Jesus, Mary, Joseph didn't sin at all and the other saints through the ages certainly sinned less and were certainly sinned against more. Would they have been saints if they "couldn't" forgive?

Meditate on these lines of Pope Benedict XVI (*Jesus of Nazareth* p. 158-159) "Forgiveness exacts a price – first of all from the person who forgives. He must overcome within himself the evil done to him; he must, as it were, burn it interiorly, and in so doing renew himself…in communion with the One who bore the burdens of us all."

Other images that could help would be letting go or dropping the anger into the ocean. My favorite is the one quoted before in *The Way of Love* from the poet W.H. Auden: "Thou shalt love thy crooked neighbor with thy crooked heart!" I start out thinking, yes, yes, yes, as a Christian I have to love my crooked neighbor and he or she sure is mighty crooked. But then I have to read the rest of the line: with *my* crooked heart! Even if my sins may not be as visible as the ones I want to reject, given all the graces I have been given, they are still serious and awful.

If you wish, work on a presentation for the group reading this booklet or other groups you minister to. You can use power point, song, drama, art, dance to make the insights you found in this session available to others.

Spiritual Exercises:

1. If you have the courage, make a list in writing of all those you have hurt from childhood to the present whether purposely, such as harshly judging others, or by omission, such as not obeying parents when they had a right to ask you to help in the house, or not giving all you could to the needy. In sacramental confession ask for pardon for any of these not previously confessed.

2. Now make a list of wrongs of others that have hurt you. (If you are like me, the lists are about equal!) Now forgive these sins against you slowly and from the heart.

For Personal Reflection and Group Sharing:

1. Why do you think Jesus makes our forgiveness of others the condition for forgiving our sins?

2. What are instances of asking for forgiveness in Scripture that stand out for you?

3. If you are in a group share with the others times in your life when you have forgiven others or received forgiveness of your sins from them.

Oh my Jesus, forgive me my sins. I try to forgive but often I fail. I need a big infusion of love from Your heart if I am to be free of the anger of non-forgiveness. Make my heart like unto Yours. May my forgiveness release my victimizers. May the forgiveness my victims offer to me release me that all of us may be more loving in the future.

SESSION

15

A MORE LOVING FUTURE?

"Stay sober and alert. Your opponent the devil is prowling like a roaring lion looking for someone to devour. Resist him, solid in your faith." (1 Peter 5: 8-9)

These pages have suggestions for you to consider when planning your program for the future. Before pondering the suggestions on these sheets print out the section at the end of this session entitled:

MY PLAN

FOR OVERCOMING OBSTACLES TO LOVE

WITH THE HELP OF THE LORD

As you read the suggestions below, fill in your sheet during this session and then gradually in the coming days.

When negative emotions arise what do I need to try? Ponder these suggestions. Check ones you think could improve your emotional life.

Prayer:

X **Talk to Jesus, offer things up**

Our Father

X **Rosary**

In depth praying for divine help

✓ **Mass more often when possible**

Sacrament of Reconciliation – more frequent than in the past?

✓ **Adoration**

✓ **Liturgy of the Hours**

✓ **Scripture Reading, personalized such as adding in your name to each passage as in "Jane, be of good cheer….."**

X **Repeated word or phrase such as Jesus; or Jesus, Mary, and Joseph; peace, praise prayer (in tongues?)**

X **A Scripture that helps you, repeated all through the day.**

X **Spiritual Reading**

Physical Helps:

Food – better or more or less

✓ **Longer sleep, naps?**

✗ **Sports or Exercise – move your muscles!**

Dance

✓ **Vitamins**

Medicine

Emotional Helps from Family, Friends, or Mentors:

Talking to someone about your problem

Using Recovery, Inc. Tools:

Not a 911

Expect frustrations every 5 minutes, you won't be disappointed

✗ **Expect the average**

Peace over power, don't try for symbolic victory

✓ **Will to bear discomfort to meet your goals**

✓ **Move muscles vs. brooding**

✗ **Humor is your best friend**

✗ **Cultivate positive emotions especially love, gratitude, and forgiveness, humor.**

Beauty:

✗ **Place yourself where you can enjoy the beauty of nature, music, art, literature.**

Examination of Conscience:

Throughout the day check out whether negative emotions prevail, moods dominate, first encounters are loving, frustrations are accepted if they cannot be avoided, conflicts are struggled with so that peace is the last word in your own heart if not in that of others; was my service in my work zealous and loving? Did I end the day with disappointment and despair or with gratitude and hope?

MY PLAN

FOR OVERCOMING OBSTACLES TO LOVE

WITH THE HELP OF THE LORD

Prayer on Arising:

Helps I will seek daily when possible and especially when negative emotions are taking over.

Prayers:

Physical Helps:

Emotional Helps:

Beauty:

Examination of Conscience – enter here areas of specific importance to you as an individual.

Night prayer:

VOLUME 3
MAKING LOVING MORAL
DECISIONS

SESSION

1

DECIDING TO MAKE LOVING CHOICES

Many people with loving qualities of character such as kindness, generosity, helpfulness, and compassion, have trouble with choosing between alternatives. Some of these choices are between 2 loving possibilities such as: should I respond to what I think is a call to the religious life as a priest or brother, sister, consecrated virgin or widow, or should I marry? Such decisions are certainly important, but they do not fall under the category of choices considered in this booklet. Why? Either choice, marriage or a specific consecrated vocation *is* are good. Moral choices, by contrast, generally involve choices between what is good and what is bad; right or wrong; obligatory or optional.

Examples would be choosing between stealing a computer from the office or waiting to have the funds to buy one; driving dangerously or following the law.

Now, you might be thinking that since you are a person who tries to be loving you would never make a choice for the bad. Maybe, not. But, consider that there are people who have questioned choices you have made, thinking they are not authentically loving. And you have questioned choices of others even if you would affirm their character in general as being good-hearted.

Toward the end of these sessions we will be considering how choices in the realm of morality are influenced by religious beliefs. Most of the session, however, will show how people make good or bad choices just on the basis of reason.

Throughout my study of moral decision-making I will be using an example concerning abortion. Perhaps you have been involved with an abortion yourself or with helping someone procure one. If so, the purpose of the *Way of Love* is not to scold and shame you, but to help readers to sort through the factors in such a choice. Fortunately there are wonderful groups for healing of women who regret abortion and the sacrament of reconciliation (confession) for those in Churches where this rite is performed.

Here is a description of the choice that will be carried through the sessions in the booklet:

Lisa has been going out with Mark ever since they started at St. Mary's college. They are very close. Both of them want to become doctors. They decided that they didn't want to have to make a choice between marriage and their careers, but instead would wait for marriage until they both finished medical school. Their parents are helping to pay their bills for room and board, but they are both on scholarship for the tuition.

In their junior year, Mark and Lisa decided it was old fashioned to wait for marriage in order to express their love for each other physically in the most complete way. Lisa, a biology major familiar with her own bodily rhythms, had a pretty good idea as to when the fertile time of her cycle was, so they just avoided intercourse on those days. But one night when they had been to a party, both of them were very high and went ahead, even though it was a borderline day in the cycle.

Now Lisa is pregnant. She is trying to decide what to do. Should she drop out of school, arrange a quick marriage, have the baby, and postpone her own plans for a career for many years while she brings up their child? Or wouldn't it be so much easier to call it a mistake, have a fast abortion, and be more careful in the future?

For the first sessions of this course, I am going to have Lisa decide for an abortion. In her deliberations, she will use such concepts as these:

"It's really for the greatest good of all concerned."

"The fetus is too small to suffer."

"Nowadays people realize that a woman's career counts too; she's not just a baby machine."

"Everybody's doing it."

At this point I will presuppose that Lisa and Mark agree that a fetus is human. Later I will explain why this is true. Farther on, I will have Lisa and Mark decide that abortion is an unloving act and that they will keep their baby.

As you study the decision-making steps, you will think about a decision you have to make now or can imagine yourself making in the future. It should be a moral decision: that is, not about 2 good choices but about a choice you think is good and an alternative you think is bad.

In a notebook write a brief description of the matter you will consider. If you are reading this as part of a course, check out your example with the professor. Later in the booklet I will refer to this example as "your own ethical decision." This way you will be able to use the steps in making moral decisions to help you with something in your own life.

Most of us, when we have to make a moral choice, go back and forth between pros and cons. Such analysis can be helpful, but if our decisions are to be truly loving it is best to begin with a recommitment to a personal philosophy of love.

I can tell myself: Ronda, your greatest desire is to become a loving person. Regardless of the cost to yourself in terms of money, fame, power, or convenience, you want to do what is right.

Such recommitment does not always mean choosing what will hurt us most. Often what is good for us is also good for others. It does mean not clinging to our own will regardless of the harm to those affected.

In the case of Lisa and Mark, the pre-med college students, I am supposing that their first reaction to the knowledge of the unwanted pregnancy was panic. Lisa started thinking of women she had known, including her own mother, who had married early in similar circumstances. "I don't want to wind up like her." Mark pictured dropping out of school, living in a trailer and working at the supermarket.

They did not stop to consider their deeper mutual wish to be a force for good in the world, starting with each other and their own family.

In the case of your own ethical decision—the one you have selected to reflect upon—before considering consequences, first of all commit yourself to love, in terms of your own personal way of viewing love in life.

In each of these sessions we will close with a prayer and then questions for personal reflection and group sharing should you be reading *The Way of Love* in a class or other group setting.

FOR PERSONAL REFLECTION AND GROUP SHARING:

1. Do you tend to approach ethical decisions by recommitment to love or more in terms of pros and cons?

2. Think of moral decisions you have made in the past. What was loving or unloving about some of them?

A Prayer: Lord, you taught us that growing in love was the meaning of our lives. Help me to want the loving choice even if it would be more difficult for me.

SESSION

2

AVOIDING SELF-CENTERED EXCUSES A

In Lisa's panic certain phrases came immediately into her mind: "I've gotta survive; nobody's going to be hurt if I have an early abortion." Mark thought, "We'll feel guilty the day of the abortion but later we'll be glad. Our consciences won't bother us because what we're doing is for the greatest good of all concerned. Unwanted babies are unhappy. We can have as many as we want later on. Think of the good Lisa and I will do in our medical work!" Just before the abortion Lisa began to feel guilty. It seemed terribly wrong to snuff out the life of a tiny human being. Then she thought, "It is wrong, but nobody's perfect. I'm not a saint. God will forgive me."

Some of you might think the reasoning used by Lisa and Mark is justified. I think that even though they were trying to be good, they were using self-centered excuses. Here are some ways that the phrases Lisa and Mark used can be shown to spring often from selfishness rather than love.

"I Gotta Survive."

It was on a university campus during the '70's that I first started to hear the phrase, "I've got to survive," used as a self-evident maxim. It puzzled me. Naturally I had read of cases in wartime or in totalitarian countries or in the history of the martyrs where people were given an immediate choice: "Do what we say or die." And there were also sudden emergencies when trying to save someone else might mean risking one's own life. Even though we laud heroes and heroines for choosing death over survival, we could understand if someone would refuse, saying: "My survival counts too." In such situations the concept of survival seems like one of many good motivations—not a phony excuse. But in the contemporary use of the concept of survival, there is usually no question whatsoever of so radical a choice. To have a right to survive seems to mean simply that nothing should be allowed to stand in the way of what I conceive to be my own fulfillment.

At the foundation of survival as an excuse, we can find the very old philosophy of egocentric hedonism. In Runes' Dictionary of Philosophy hedonism is defined:

'A doctrine as to what entities possess intrinsic value. According to it, pleasure and this alone has positive value, is intrinsically good...the contrary hedonic feeling tone is displeasure...and this alone has negative ultimate value...the total value of an action is the net intrinsic value of all its hedonic consequences."

In simpler language, when a hedonist is egocentric, he or she will maintain that it is perfectly all right to seek the greatest possible pleasure for oneself, wherever that may lie, no matter how many victims. There are different kinds of pleasures. The most obvious are the sensory delights associated with eating, sleeping, sexuality, sun-bathing, etc. But some people are ready to give up many of these sensual pleasures for more complicated ones such as the excitement of power, or pride in climbing one rung after another of the ladder of success.

For some of us the word hedonist sounds ugly. We would not apply it to ourselves with gleeful bravado. However, if we have the courage to check on ourselves, we may detect such a philosophy behind the most ordinary perceptions. For example, when we say, "I had a good day," we usually mean that many pleasurable things happened—i.e., I had a nice lunch, someone praised me or I won out over my chief enemy at work. By a "good day" we rarely mean a day devoted to the welfare of others amidst many frustrations. Such a day we more aptly describe with the negative: "My whole day was shot!" A "lousy day" is often one without pleasure because we were forced to be helpful to others!

Many factors go into making a decision, but for the sake of philosophical clarity, let's isolate the hedonistic elements in the decision of Lisa and Mark. Aborting their baby has lots of pluses for this couple. It means they can enjoy the freedom to pursue their careers without obstacles. It means they don't have to contemplate the ills of living poorly at the start of their marriage. They don't have to worry about getting into a "forced marriage" they may later regret. Of course there is the pain of guilt and a fear of possible bad physical consequences of abortion.

They may have to cope with disapproval if their parents find out. But balancing things out, the pleasures seem to far outweigh the pains. This is not the only reason Lisa and Mark decided for the abortion but it is probably a large factor, for it is only human nature to want to choose what seems most desirable in terms of our own individual needs.

Now consider the ethical issue you are debating in your own life. Could the pleasures and displeasures over-weigh in your mind the question as to which decision would he most loving? Write your tentative answer in your notebook.

But, you may ask, why is hedonism unloving or wrong? Isn't it loving to want to maximize pleasure and minimize displeasure? Here are some problems concerning hedonism for you to consider.

First of all, our decisions often have unwanted consequences. We simply do not know the future well enough to predict what is for the greater good. In later life Lisa may discover (and this would not be unusual) that because of the first abortion she will have a real difficulty in carrying a baby to term. After many miscarriages she may deeply regret her college decision. Also, her boyfriend may have pretended to go along with that decision but might not respect her as highly as before. Lisa may not find her medical career as thrilling as she imagined and may wish she had not sacrificed her baby for it. Plunging into their studies, Mark and Lisa may have less and less time for each other. Their ideal match may never work out. The drive to succeed, which led them to decide to sacrifice their baby, may also lead them to lose their love for the value of life, so that their humanitarian motives for being doctors may fade, leaving them with a sense of emptiness. The sense of guilt may grow rather than diminish. Some women who once opted for abortion can't look at a baby on the street without feeling a wrench of pain. Some have nightmares all their lives.

In the case of your own ethical decision, can you think of any unwanted consequences that could occur if you make a selfish choice?

For Personal Reflection and Group Sharing:

1. When have you used the excuse "I gotta survive" for something you later regretted?

2. Are you sometimes taken in by a hedonistic (pleasure above all) way of thinking?

A Prayer: Holy Spirit, please give me good counsel when I am tempted to exaggerate the feeling that I have to survive no matter what the consequences or moral wrongness of a decision I am making.

SESSION

3

AVOIDING SELF-CENTERED EXCUSES B

Here is an analysis of some of the other excuses Lisa and Mark make.

"My Conscience Doesn't Bother Me."

"I feel good about it. My conscience doesn't bother me!" This is probably one of the most frequently heard excuses for moral evil. Of course, as we shall see later on, there can be a legitimate conscience claim in a choice that runs counter to the usual pattern of a society. We can all think of heroes who after long introspection made brave decisions that shocked persons who were blind to some particular moral value. Socrates was tried for impiety. Jesus, for blasphemy. Gandhi and Martin Luther King were subjected to ridicule for their non-violence. In these cases great sacrifices, even to death, were necessary in the following of conscience.

Recently, however, it seems that the word conscience has been most often used not for making hard decisions that demand sacrifice but for rationalizing refusal to accept the sacrifices demanded by morality. "Conscience" always seems to instruct us that we don't have to overcome temptations or endure hardships. Notice that Lisa and Mark tried to make a decision in conscience, but that the decision also turned out to be what each favored for his or her own reasons.

One problem which enables persons to make unloving decisions "in good conscience" is value-blindness. In his book *Ethics,* Von Hildebrand develops the penetrating concept of value-blindness in order to explain why there can be so much divergence among people's ideas of right and wrong. (Dietrich Von Hildebrand, *Ethics* (Chicago: Franciscan Herald Press,1953), pp. 46ff.

Just as some people may be blind to certain colors, human beings can also be blind with regard to particular objective moral values. Examples that readers would certainly agree with would include the blindness of the Nazis to the worth of the Jewish people or the blindness of some Americans of the past and even of our own times to the dignity of Black people.

A fascinating commentary on value-blindness can be found in this comparison chart that recently appeared in a newspaper:

Another "Civil War" that <u>Must</u> Be Won -If the U.S. Is to Survive!

1857 'DRED SCOTT' DECISION 1973

IN THE INFAMOUS "DRED SCOTT" SUPREME COURT DECISION OF 1857, THE "BLACK SLAVE" WAS LABLED AS JUST "A PIECE OF PROPERTY" OF <u>THE WHITE MAN</u>

IN THE EQUALLY NOTORIOUS RULING BY OUR PRESENT SUPREME COURT, THE "INNOCENT CHILD" IS NOW DISMISSED AS JUST ANOTHER DEPENDENT "SLAVE" BELONGING TO A <u>WOMAN</u>...TO DISPOSE OF AS SHE SEES FIT!

THUS:

Slavery-1857	Abortion-1973
Although he may have heart and a brain, and he may be a human life biologically, a slave is not a legal person. The dred scott decision by the United States Supreme Court has that clear.	Although he may have heart and a brain, and he may be a human life biologically, an unborn baby is not a legal person. Our Court has that clear.
A Black man only becomes a legal person when is set free. Before that time, we should not concern ourselves with him because he has no legal rights.	A baby only becomes a legal person when he is born. Before that time, we should not concern ourselves about him because he has no legal rights.
If you think that slavery is wrong, than nobody is forcing you to be a slave-owner. But don't impose your morality on somebody else!	If you think that abortion is wrong, than nobody is forcing you to have one. But don't impose your morality on somebody else!
A man has a right to do what he wants with his own proper- ty.	A woman has a right to do what she wants with her own body.
Isn't slavery really some- thing merciful? after all, every Black man has a right to be protected. Isn't it better never to be not free than to be sent unprepared, and ill-equipped, into a crual world. (Spoken by some- body free)	Isn't abortion really some- thing merciful? after all, every baby has a right to be wanted. Isn't it better never to never be born than to be sent alone, and unloved into a crual world. (Spoken by somebody already born)

Some value-blindness comes to us as a cultural heritage. In certain countries polygamy has been practiced for so long that almost everyone is blind to the higher value of monogamy. Such value-blindness, according to Von Hildebrand, is relatively blameless, although in the case of many participants the custom is adhered to partly because it satisfies a vice common to people of all countries, such as lust.

But other types of value-blindness come because we allow our desires to overcome our original moral feelings, principles or religious convictions. For example, Lisa's frantic fear of seeing her career dreams go down the drain may temporarily blind her to the great objective value of the life within her womb.

If you can, describe value-blindness as it might function with regard to your own moral issue. Write the description in your notebook.

One-sided sympathies can be another cause of blindness. Persons close to someone who has to make an ethical decision may be accused of a special sort of blindness, due to one-sided sympathies which lead to a sincere but erroneous conscience.

Let us think of Lisa's example. Suppose she turns to her father for advice. The father is probably very sympathetic to his daughter's plight. He may resent the boyfriend and rage against the stupidity of the young man in being so careless. The question of the baby's right to life may scarcely cross his mind. After all, his daughter who cries hysterically in her bedroom looks like the main victim, whereas the baby has no voice. Since Lisa's father has a good motive in wanting to protect his daughter, he may have a clear conscience about recommending abortion.

False liberation is another reason why peoples' consciences may not bother them even if their decision is unloving. Many people feel positively liberated when they plunge into what they previously knew to be evil. Why is that? For one thing, after the long, hard struggle of a difficult decision, it is a relief to decide either way. Then again, most of us hate to feel constrained from doing what seems most pleasurable or advantageous to ourselves. As a passionate desire overwhelms us, the principles we live by begin to seem very cold and remote—not really powerful enough to win the battle. It is a good feeling to be done with them and to swing totally into the rhythm of our desires. We feel triumphant when we can overcome all scruples and do what we want to do. Only later may we come to see that evil did not really liberate us. Meanwhile, we may feel very happy and readily convince ourselves that our decision cannot be so wrong.

Lisa has a very strong desire to keep up with the timetable she set for her advancement from college to medical school. She doesn't want to have a baby right now. In the face of her thwarted ambitions, the ethical principle that life is sacred seems a distant ideal rather than a burning reality. Compared to the nightmare of years of being stuck with diapers and housework while her husband flies along ahead of her at medical school, the idea of abortion provides a false sense of liberation.

Even though conscience can be used as an excuse for unloving behavior, many consider it our best source for making decisions. Situation Ethics is the name of the theory which states that we should try to discover what is right to do by examining each unique situation and listening to our consciences instead of following a set of ethical rules. In defense of conscience, the situation ethicist will claim that it is impossible to just walk through life with a rule book. That would be tunnel vision. We must make our own judgments, for it is the glory of being free human beings that we can decide for ourselves.

If we have good motives, wanting to do the most loving thing in every situation, why should we doubt that we will accomplish more good than evil by relying on the judgment of conscience? The situation ethicist declares that even should one's conscience be erroneous at times, it is still better to decide for oneself than to let others make the decision.

In response, I would agree that in many situations the consciences of good persons will warn them away from objective evil and show them the good. However, I would disagree with the situation ethicist on the whole, because I think that more often than not, especially in situations involving crisis and sacrifice, conscience does not function as a register of the objective good but instead conforms with principles which are questionable.

The situation ethicist pictures conscience as a light shining in the darkness, whereas I picture conscience as a very complex product of early training, fear of punishment, need for approval, false principles—not always a pure response to what is objectively good and evil. Because of the ambiguity in the way conscience functions, I cannot regard it as a self-evident proof of ethical goodness if I feel good about something and my conscience doesn't bother me.

We must draw our moral convictions from a source other than our own subjective judgments in each situation.

Having established a set of objective values, as we will attempt to do in a later session of *The Way of Love*, we will be able to form our conscience by these, so that it can warn us of violations in the disturbing, tempting situations in which we find ourselves.

FOR PERSONAL REFLECTION AND GROUP SHARING:

1. Can you think of instances of value blindness in history or in the present not already covered in this session?

2. How about instances of false liberation?

A prayer: Oh God, how I regret sins in my past where I ignored Your moral commandments out of value blindness or a desire for false liberation. Help me to bring such sins to sacramental confession if that is available to me or to personal prayer if not. Guide my conscience in the future.

SESSION

4

AVOIDING SELF-CENTERED EXCUSES C

"It's for the Greater Good. Nobody Will Be Hurt."

Lisa and Mark may object that they are not hedonists but humanitarians. They really think the abortion is for the greater good because nobody will be hurt.

Many people base the lovingness or unlovingness of a choice on whether anyone is being hurt. For example, in a secret adultery the unfaithful husband or wife often

claims that since the spouse doesn't know, it's okay; it may even hold the marriage together if the unhappy partner has some joy elsewhere.

One of the problems with this excuse is that not all victims scream. The rejected spouse may know all along and feel very hurt but be afraid to complain for fear of losing the adulterous spouse altogether.

Lisa may try to picture the fetus as a clump of cells rather than a tiny baby able to suffer pain. With regard to the sentiments of her boyfriend, who may have secretly wished she had kept the baby, she will erase the memory of his hurt and shock from her mind by thinking of his eventual relief at a decision involving less sacrifice for him. If her parents are very upset about the decision, she will decide that they have no right to feel bad since it is none of their business. In this way she will build up her defenses against any hurt she has caused, until she may really think that her act has been without victims. The fetus didn't scream aloud so it doesn't seem to have been maltreated, although evidence now shows the baby in the womb does try to scream as its limbs are dismembered.

Besides quiet victims there can be long-term victims. Lisa's decision may influence other friends to take the same course of action, increasing the number of victims in the world. Her boyfriend, Mark, may find himself adopting a previously unwelcome pro-abortion position as a way of defending himself against guilt feelings. This pro-abortion stance may influence his friends and his own practice of medicine in years to come.

Can you think of any possible quiet or long-term victims in the case of the ethical choice you yourself must confront?

Even when one sincerely wants to find out what is for the greatest good, it is very difficult to know. This has been one of the chief criticisms of the theory of utilitarianism. Utilitarianism is defined in Runes' Dictionary of Philosophy as "the view that the right act is the act which, of all those open to the agent, will actually or probably produce the greatest amount of pleasure or happiness in the world at large."

The greatest advocate of this theory was John Stuart Mill (1806-1873), a prominent liberal reformer of his day. Oppressed by the visible suffering of the poor and the violation of the natural rights of women, he sought to replace moral ideas based on tradition with a more open ethical system based on evidence and concern for consequences.

By means of the utilitarian formula—act to produce the greatest good for the greatest number—Mill sought to overcome that selfishness which tends to count the self alone as important and others as zero. Since you, yourself, would only count for one in any utilitarian survey, you would be bound to see the necessity of sacrificing your own claims in the face of the needs of so many others. Mill believed that through education mankind would gradually learn to realize that one's personal greatest good is whatever is the greatest good for the whole

Although Mill himself never drew from his theory the consequence that the end would justify the means, according to many critics this seems to follow without fail, both philosophically and historically. Given grave enough concern for particular goods for a large number of people, will not any means seem justified?

Historically, have not totalitarian regimes insisted that the progress of all humanity in ages to come justified the death here and now of a few thousand or even of millions?

As mentioned earlier in connection with other excuses, it is not easy to predict accurately how many victims will result from a particular action. Mill was himself inclined to think that there were certain rules which would always bring about the greatest good for the greatest number. Murder, for example, would always be judged to lead to further bad consequences for mankind at large in terms of creating a general climate of fear and defensiveness, even if in the short run it might seem justifiable.

However, utilitarian philosophy led to other worldwide consequences that Mill did not predict. Freed from the idea that some deeds such as murder were always wrong (and therefore, of course, unloving), many leaders in such movements as Nazism and Communism justified mass genocide. Later, some such leaders repented of their false calculation, for the result of their acts was not heaven but hell.

In regard to abortion, Bernard Nathanson, a doctor who spearheaded liberal abortion laws and ran a huge abortion clinic, finally saw that the fetus is human.

Dr. Nathanson now exhausts himself trying to undo the laws he initiated. Many observers see lack of accountability of fathers, infanticide of the disabled, acceptance of euthanasia, and forced sterilization all as a domino effect from abortion.

"Everybody's Doing It!"

To many, otherwise loving people, it seems impossible that anything can be too unloving if "everybody's" doing it."

This excuse takes many forms. I see it hidden behind such statements as these:

"That opinion went out with the Middle Ages. Boy, are you old-fashioned!"

"Even person X thinks it's okay, so how could it be wrong?"

"Statistics show...."

"The laws of the land allow it."

Of course, it could sometimes happen that the majority view, or the latest view, or the one held by an admired person or the one just voted in, would really be the right view. But, as I will try to show later, it seems to me that a view is not made true because many people hold it, or because the best people believe it, or even because it is the newest view. An opinion is true if it corresponds to what is really right. More of this in a later chapter; for now, let us examine "majority wins" exclusively as it functions in rationalizing a wrong act.

Lisa certainly feels less guilty about her abortion when she hears of lots of other college girls doing it. When the act was illegal she would have hesitated much more, not only because of risks to her health, but because of reluctance to move out of the stream of what decent citizens thought was right. The idea that the Supreme Court of the land, so respected by most Americans, has left it up to her and her doctor is reassuring. The connection of the word "liberal" with abortion adds a sheen of progress to the idea, for it links "anti-abortion" with forces of regression.

How does this excuse apply to one side or another of your own ethical dilemma?

Sociologists have popularized the very apt term "peer pressure," showing the impact of this force on the individual. We all greatly need to be accepted by the people around us. Thinking, speaking or acting contrary to the majority view of our group is experienced as very painful and disconcerting, and only the brave few can withstand such a force toward conformity.

But we also know from history that every era has its particular blind spots. The marvelously intellectual and artistic Greeks were blind to the evil of slavery. There were times in gentlemanly England when it was thought harmless to base the economy on the labor of young children. Some societies tolerated infant sacrifice in religious rites. Millions of Germans considered Hitler a tremendous force for progress. This shows that even the most admired leaders can be insane tyrants, hardly to be followed with blind trust.

History also shows that there are cycles of decay within whole societies where what once would have been considered repugnant and criminal becomes an accepted lifestyle.

For the same reasons, the fact that many consider abortion as a viable option is a weak argument. The legalizing of abortion could be a sign that our society is decaying. The abolitionists certainly thought that the legalization of slavery was a terrible infringement on the original spirit of the Declaration of Independence. The fact that most people accepted it as a necessary evil in no way convinced them that this practice could be tolerated.

How would this critique apply to the moral problem you are working on?

"Nobody's Perfect; I'm Not a Saint."

What about the final excuse Lisa gives: "I know it's wrong, but I'm not a saint"?

Here again we find ourselves with a statement that sounds almost self-evident and yet can be used in very phony ways as an excuse.

Everyone knows that human beings are not perfect and that very few are saints. It can seem harsh to demand so much authenticity of Lisa and Mark. But even so, it hardly seems right that a person who is victimizing you should demand that you exonerate him or her on that basis. Suppose a thief were in the act of stealing your car, and you yelled at him to stop and he said, "I'm not perfect and neither are you—what do you expect?" Not only would you refuse to buy this excuse, but you would consider him to be adding insult to injury!

If you were Lisa's baby and could speak, wouldn't you want a chance to live even if Lisa and Mark were not perfect? After all, our own real-life parents were not perfect, yet we are glad they were good enough to have given us life.

I find the phrase "nobody's perfect" interesting to analyze. In the mouth of someone consoling a guilt-stricken person who is unable to forgive himself or herself for some past deed, the words "nobody's perfect; you're not a saint" are meaningful and helpful. And yet, in the mouth of someone excusing himself from a moral obligation, the words are full of unjustifiable anger, pride and insulting bravado.

When used as an excuse, "Nobody's perfect" seems to throw the blame on the ideal in question instead of on the guilty party. It is as if God, society, parents or friends, in holding up an ideal of motherly protectiveness of the young, had proposed something impossible for the sole purpose of making others feel guilty.

But surely any system of ethics, whether religious or humanistic, must be based on some ideal which overreaches man's natural tendencies to selfishness, especially as these gain ascendance in moments of crisis! There could be no society at all if everyone simply felt free to trample on everyone else, totally giving in to the lowest instincts of one's nature without a struggle. We should forgive and yet also inspire others to be better.

Referring to the ethical situation you are studying, what effect would you predict if all ideals were taken out of the picture?

FOR PERSONAL REFLECTION AND GROUP SHARING:

1. Do you ever find politicians arguing that something is for the greater good that you think is bad?

2. When have you used the excuse that everybody's doing it?

3. When do you accept "I'm not a saint," and when do you find it phony?

A Prayer: Jesus, when I think of these excuses I have also made such as it's for the greater good, everybody's doing it, or I'm not a saint, I shudder. On that basis you should have fled from the cross instead of suffering to redeem us! Help me set my standards by true morality instead of excuses.

SESSION

5

ETHICAL INTUITION

In the next 3 session you will read about authentic ways of finding out what is are loving moral choices.

In this section, I will try to show how Lisa and Mark become more loving by deciding to keep their baby. I will suppose that, after the shock of finding out that Lisa is pregnant, all the excuses described in Sessions 3-5 pass through their heads—but that finally they agree that these could be just selfish excuses.

They spend some time deliberating about what would really be the right—i.e., the most loving—course of action. It happens that Lisa and Mark are both taking ethics at this time. The professor brings in a film about abortion. When it shows how abortion works by methods which dismember the fetus, vacuum it out, burn it to death with saline solution, or kill it by other methods equally horrifying, Lisa and Mark "just know" that such an act could not be an act of love for a baby.

A more formal name for "just knowing that something is right or wrong" is ethical intuition. The use of the word "intuition" here is a precise philosophical one. It does not mean an irrational hunch but rather an immediate intellectual apprehension. An ethical intuitionist is one who believes that we know the goodness of the good and the worth of various values by an immediate apprehension rather than by deduction of consequences.

For example, once you have experienced a genuinely reverent person, you can easily see that, in terms of goodness, reverence is preferable to manipulation. By reverent I mean a person who approaches others with sincere respect rather than seeing others as contacts to be used. As long as you compare manipulation to the pseudo-virtue of passivity, you may think that manipulation is not so bad, but when you have an intuitive intellectual grasp of the essence of reverence as a moral quality, you cannot help but perceive its goodness.

Exponents of ethical intuitionism are such philosophers as G. E. Moore, Max Scheler, John Paul II, and Dietrich Von Hildebrand. The key objects of ethical intuitionism are the good, quality, in the sense in which Pirsig uses it in his popular Zen and the Art of Motorcycle Maintenance, and value.

Of the good, the contemporary British intuitionist Iris Murdoch states that no realist can deny that goodness really matters. We can pretend that egoism is justified, but we all know that ruthless stampeding over the rights of others is wrong.

In the philosophy of the Catholic moral philosopher Dietrich Von Hildebrand, value is viewed as a type of importance. Good is the property of a being which enables it to motivate our will or to engender an affective response in us (a feeling or a desire) because of its positive importance. A value is something intrinsically important. We recognize that whether we get a lollipop or not is of no intrinsic importance, but whether we act justly or unjustly does matter very much.

Discussion of value theory is rather confusing to most modern people, because the word "value" is used in at least two very different ways, not only in ordinary language but also in philosophy and education. Value theory springing out of the pragmatic school of thought makes it seem as if there is no intrinsic value in an object—instead, we decide to give something value in accordance with our own personal taste. For example, in a book called *Values and Teaching* by Raths, Harmin and Simon, we find references which describe values as individual, created by us, changing, and never to be indoctrinated. The function of man is not to watch over ancient values, but to enjoy the excitement of forming his or her own lifestyle. As we will see, ~~this way of~~ this way of describing values is very different from that of the philosophers I mentioned as ethical intuitionists.

In a market economy it is natural for us to think of economic values as the paradigm—and such values go up and down with the stock exchange. Such a meaning of value, in which nothing is fixed and we create values ourselves, is exactly opposite to the notion of values in the European phenomenological school, in which we discover rather than create values. Values are seen as eternally valid, as transcending relativism. (In a later session of this book you will see why relativism, the theory that what are considered to be absolute values are just programmed into us by our culture, is a false theory).

The noble deed of a Roman senator has a value which can be perceived by a reader in the 20th century. Risking one's life to save someone else is always the embodiment of high value. To be kind rather than cruel must be understood as good in itself. If in a particular culture cruelty is exalted, this is described by thinkers such as Von Hildebrand as a form of value-blindness.

Of course, some object: How can you know if anything is really absolutely good or evil—since philosophers disagree, and so do whole societies? This difficulty will be met later on. For now, suppose that there are some intrinsic values, and let's see how these values can be divided to help us to understand the intuitive knowledge that Lisa and Mark reached regarding their decision.

Von Hildebrand has provided us with some very helpful categories for the analysis of conflict and value-blindness. In his book, *Ethics* (Franciscan Herald Press), he distinguishes between what he calls the subjectively satisfying (what gives us personal pleasure regardless of its objective goodness, such as smoking, a particular flavor of ice cream, etc.); the objective good for the person (what is truly of benefit to the human being, though changing, such as education, dishwashers, cars); and unchanging intrinsic values (what is precious in itself in time and eternity, such as beauty, truth, peace, the unique selfhood of a human person, God).

In many cases of moral choice we find a conflict between these three categories—the subjectively satisfying, the objective good for the person and the intrinsic value.

For example, we find Macbeth contemplating the murder of the king, perfectly aware that loyalty to his king, a man of high moral character, is an intrinsic value, and that hospitality is an objective good which he owes to the king. Yet, on the other side, there is Macbeth's passionate ambition for the subjective satisfaction of his pride: he wants to be king himself. As the witches prophesy his ascent to the throne, and his wife urges him to the terrible deed of murder, the longing for the subjective satisfaction of being king overwhelms him, temporarily blinding him to the intrinsic evil of the deed.

In the case of Kitty Genovese—a woman raped and murdered in front of an apartment development while thirty-eight people watched from their windows and did nothing, in order to avoid getting involved—we have an example of temporary blindness to the intrinsic evil of failing to help save a neighbor from death. This blindness stemmed from fear of the subjectively dissatisfying annoyances connected with calling the police and being interrogated.

In the case of the decision of Lisa and Mark, here is a list of elements in conflict:

Subjective pleasures or displeasures:

> anticipated joy of fondling the baby
>
> or disgust with drooling, diaper-using babies
>
> fun of being free
>
> fun of being unencumbered
>
> displeasure from morning sickness, fatigue, labor pains
>
> displeasure of males at one's pregnant image
>
> displeasure from ridicule for being unwed mother
>
> pleasure of parental approval
>
> or displeasure of parental anger

Objective goods at stake:

> baby—the good this child can experience and bring to others
>
> health of mother—damaged by pregnancy or abortion
>
> psychological health of mother and father—threatened by pregnancy and abortion

smooth continuation of career without interruption

not being forced into early marriage which might not work

finance—strained by having a baby

quality of life of baby

Eternal values:

unique personhood of baby

unending bond of love between mother, father and child (in potency)

A pro-life proponent would insist that those who approve of abortions have simply become blind to the eternal values at stake because of concern for a category of lesser importance—objective goods or subjective pleasures. To the pro-lifer, the unique personality of the baby is the highest value on the human level, and no other consideration can be higher.

A defender of the abortion option would claim that there is no eternal value at stake. This person's highest value would be one of the items listed under "objective goods" or rarely, but conceivably, one of those listed under "subjective pleasures." With eyes fixed on some objective good, such as the psychological health of the mother or the anticipated quality of life of the infant, a pro-abortionist would think that he or she was doing something good in helping a young woman to decide for an abortion.

It should be noted that the option of giving the child over for adoption preserves the unique value of the baby while avoiding many of the subjective displeasures and objective sacrifices.

Now turn to the ethical issue that you are working on and list the subjectively satisfying pleasures, objective goods and eternal values involved.

Although ethical intuitionism can trace its roots as far back as Plato and Augustine, it has only become prominent as an explicit theory of ethical knowledge in the 20th century.

FOR PERSONAL REFLECTION AND GROUP SHARING:

1. When have you, yourself, neglected an eternal value in favor of a subjective pleasure or an objective good?

2. When have you observed others around you, known personally or only heard of, making wrong choices because of blindness to an eternal value?

A Prayer: In spite of all the subjective displeasures my own parents might have faced and the objective problems, they chose for me to live. Thank you for that choice. May my choices reflect your hierarchy of values, God, creator of heaven and earth.

SESSION

6

NATURAL LAW ETHICS

A more traditional Christian ethical philosophy which shows that some acts are objectively evil, and therefore clearly also unloving, is the philosophy of natural law. Germain Grisez gives a very clear explanation of this theory. According to Grisez, moral goodness and badness can be discerned by comparing the essential patterns of possible human actions with the intelligible structure of human nature considered both in its inner complexity and in its intrinsic relationships. (Germain Grisez, Contraception and Natural Law (Milwaukee: Bruce, 1964).

When we examine human nature we discover, as did Thomas Aquinas, that all men seek: life and its preservation, sex, care of offspring, etc. By virtue of our rational faculties, we seek truth, life in society, etc.

For example according to Thomas Aquinas lying is evil in itself'. Since words are naturally the signs of what is understood, it is unnatural for a person to signify by word what he does not have in his mind. A lie has the character of a sin not only because of the damage that is done to a neighbor, but in its own disorder.

By means of practical reason we apply the natural law to the ordering of our lives, seeking principles about objectives. The first principle of natural law according to St. Thomas Aquinas is: "The good is that which all things seek after. Good is to be done and promoted and evil is to be avoided."

Relating the needs of human nature and the overall principles enunciated above, you can come up with such clear concepts as: Life is a good and actions which preserve it are good, whereas actions opposed to life should be avoided. Good food preserves life and is to be preferred to poison.

Since the basic needs of mankind are deemed by natural-law theorists to be self-evident, it is wrong to take action against any one of them in order to maximize another, for example, to improve society by getting rid of half its members. It is the work of ethical philosophers and social and political theorists to work out the basic principles of natural law to be applied to the issues which arise in our changing historical situations. The meaning of a universal rule is very carefully defined through reasoning.

For example, most natural-law theorists would not make a blanket statement such as "do not kill" without first defining the difference between murder, self defense, etc. Natural-law theory, while aiming at universality so that an individual does not selfishly exclude himself, is not simplistic in its pronouncements, because the rules include the necessary specifications, such as self-defense.

In order to relate natural-law theory to a topic such abortion, it is first necessary to define terms in view of the best available estimate of the facts. Taking it as self evident that it is morally wrong to destroy the life of a human being except in self-defense, it is necessary to determine whether in fact the organism within the mother's womb is a human being.

Being pre-med students, Lisa and Mark are especially interested in the following facts when trying to decide about their own problem. Here is a summary of the biological traits of the unborn baby at different points in time.

Conception: the fertilized ovum has its own unique genetic code with human cells;

4 weeks: eyes, spinal cord, brain, thyroid gland, lungs, stomach, liver, kidneys, intestines. The heart begins beating between the 18th and 25th days. The head is taking definite shape; arms and legs forming. The fetus is 1/3" tall.

4 weeks: The eyes have retina and lens; ear clefts; arms and legs are developing with fingers and toes. The fetus floats in amniotic sack. Facial features are visible.

5 weeks: mouth and tongue formed; baby teeth forming in gums; major muscle system developed, eyes complete; mouth has lips; fingers and toes complete.

6 weeks: swims in surrounding fluid.

8 weeks: Brain is complete; brain waves measurable on EEC Baby is capable of feeling pain. MOST DECISIONS FOR ABORTION MADE AT THIS TIME.

12 weeks: 3-1/2" tall. Swallows regularly; vocal chords
complete; cries silently; fingernails appear; may start
sucking thumb.

16 weeks: 5-1/2" tall; weight 6 oz. Eyebrows and lashes appear;
grasps with hands; swims; kicks; somersaults.

20 weeks: has a chance of survival as premature infant outside
the womb.

The facts clearly indicate that the unborn entity in the mother's
womb is certainly not a mere blob of cells. A mother who decides
for abortion on the basis of such a conception is basing her
choice on false data.

On the other hand, the question which many raise is whether the
human life in the womb is to be considered a human person in
the full sense of the word.

Most pro-lifers reason that any designation except personhood at
conception makes no sense. It is at conception that the genes of a
human, rather than those of a cat, join together. It is the very
nature of human selfhood to begin small and develop. No one
stage of development can be decisive—only the beginning. As the
philosopher James Hanink expresses it: "Every identifiable and
existing adult human being has once been a fetus—though never
just a sperm or an ovum. But unless some adult human beings
have a history of past membership in other species, or in none,
no existing adult has ever not been a member of homosapiens. So
fetuses are humanbeings." (James Hanink, "Persons, Rights and
the Problem of Abortion," Ph.D. Thesis, Michigan State
University, 1975. See also Stephen Schwarz, *The Moral Question
of Abortion* (Chicago: Loyola Press, 1990) for a complete study of
the ethics of abortion based on facts and reason, not on religious
truths.)

It is further argued by such natural-law theorists asFr. Robert Taylor, S.J., of Loyola Marymount University, that properties of humanity such as consciousness, intelligence free will, etc. are manifestations of the more fundamental reality of being a subject. The unconditional value of the human being is grounded in being an individual subject. This value does not disappear when the subject fails to manifest a certain potentiality, as in the case of a fetus, a person in a coma, etc.

If we think of natural law in terms of theology as well as philosophy, we can see that each individual is infinitely precious as one loved into being by God, the Father of all being. (Dietrich Bonhoeffer, Ethics, (New York: The Macmillan Co.,1955, pp. 149ff.)

Do you think there are any natural rights pertaining to the very nature of the human person in society which are at stake in your own ethical issue? List them in your notebook.

For Personal Reflection and Group Sharing:

1. Has your concept of human nature ever differed from the one described under natural law ethics?

2. Do you think of the baby in the womb as a person or a clump of cells? If you now or previously thought of the baby as a clump of cells of no value, did the fact sheet alter your opinion?

A Prayer: Creator God, thank you for creating me as a human person. I regret if I sometimes take this for granted and act just out of my immediate needs instead of considering what is right for me as a member of the human family.

SESSION

7

UNIVERSALIZING YOUR CHOICE

Lisa and Mark decide to discuss their decision with their ethics professor. Later, when the excuses will begin to seem attractive, they will be helped in overcoming temptation by remembering a one-line injunction that their teacher told them had first been enunciated by the philosopher Immanuel Kant (1724-1804):

"There is but one categorical imperative: act only on that maxim whereby thou canst at the same time will that it should become a universal law."

Let us try to explain it in simple terms. You are about to do something—say, tell a lie. Before making the decision to go ahead, ask yourself this question: "What would happen if everyone told lies?" You will discover that you could never will the universal maxim, "Everyone should tell lies." Why? Not just because lying is evil, but because as a pure intellectual judgment it is self-contradictory. If everyone told lies there would be no truth-telling and no one would ever believe any statements at all. In that case lying wouldn't work!

For Kant, the word "categorical" meant the opposite of hypothetical. In a hypothetical proposition you are asked to choose: "If you want to be happy, then you must be good."

But Kant wanted ethics to be based on a non-hypothetical obligation of reason, to which the will ought to conform irrespective of individual passions. Whether you are inclined to be honest or not, it is clear that dishonesty is contrary to reason.

Some say that Kant's very philosophically-worded formula can be summarized much more simply in the well-known Biblical injunction: "Do to no one what you would not want done to you" (Tobit 4:15).

Since we have already shown how Kant would deal with lying, let us now turn to the abortion issue which Lisa and Mark are facing. Here are some of the considerations which might occur to them:

1. Could I will a universal law that all mothers who do not want their babies should abort them?

   How could I? Am I sure that 1 was wanted at the moment of my mother's first knowledge of pregnancy? In case she did not positively want me would I prefer never to have existed?

   (How would you, the reader, answer that question?

2. Could 1 will the universal law that anyone has a right to kill anyone whom he or she doesn't want—even if that person is

psychologically harmful? Even in the case of rape, since I condemn the rapist for venting his own torments on an innocent person, should I not condemn myself if I vent on the innocent baby my torment at being pregnant?

3. If I say that all handicapped fetuses should be killed, would I universalize that to say that all less-than perfect adults should be killed? Would I think I should be killed if I lost an arm in an auto accident? Should any woman who had a syphilitic husband and had given birth to a stillborn child, a deaf and dumb child, and one with tuberculosis, risk another pregnancy? Beethoven's mother did. Should any woman who is pregnant out of wedlock, has no housing, has no money, and lives in an over-populated area, abort the child? Mary didn't!

4. Would I have wanted my own birth to depend on what year of college my mother was in, or how far along she was in her career?

5. Would I have wanted my own birth to depend on what year of college my mother was in, or how far along she was in her career?

6. Which proposition would I rather universalize — all unwanted babies should be killed, or all unwanted babies should be put up for adoption by couples who want a baby?

7. Could I universalize the proposition that all laws that are steadily violated should be taken off the books? If anti-abortion laws, why not anti-speeding laws?

Now turn to your own ethical dilemma and try to work out questions which could be asked in terms of the categorical imperative.

Just as Lisa and Mark are about to commit themselves to keeping their baby, a new doubt comes in the form of a question raised in class by a philosophy major.

After learning about ethical intuition, natural law, and the categorical imperative, this young woman argues: "I still can't see how anyone could be absolutely sure something was intrinsically loving or unloving in a universal way.

I'm sure that slave owners thought they were being loving in taking care of their slaves and bringing them the Christian faith. Now we all think they were terribly unloving in their blindness to freedom. Perhaps what we see as good we will later see as evil.

Here are some of the ways this student's professor tries to refute her skeptical and relativistic ideas.

Arguments such as this flow from skepticism and relativism. There are various forms:

1. No human being is God, so you should not claim to know anything with absolute certainty, especially not concerning morality. (Ethical Skepticism)

2. There are different ideas of right and wrong in other cultures. One should not set up the norms of one's own society as an absolute. Since 500 miles away the people might accept as natural the same act morally frowned upon in our country, we should realize that moral rules are arbitrary. George Bernard Shaw argued that morals are mostly only social habits and circumstantial necessities. A. J. Ayer claims that the causes of moral phenomena are psychological rather than ethical. Saying 'thou shalt' is but another way of registering your own desire that the other perform in a certain manner, it has nothing to do with moral absolutes. (Cultural Relativism]

(Paragraph 3 is about Marxist Relativism. It is very long but read it carefully since it represents the thinking of the leaders of a large part of contemporary humanity.)

3. We are all conditioned by economic and historical forces to set up certain values as absolutes, but there is no eternal sanction for any of them. This concept is especially important in Marxist philosophy, as indicated in the complicated but highly interesting quotation from Engels:

    "The conceptions of good and bad have varied so much from nation to nation and from age to age that they have often been in direct contradiction to each other. But all the same, someone may object, good is not bad and bad is not good: if good is confused with bad there is an end to all morality, and everyone can do and leave undone whatever he cares...."

If it was such an easy business there would certainly be no dispute at all over good and bad; everyone would know what was good and what was bad. But how do things stand today? What morality is preached to us today?

There is first Christian-feudal morality, inherited from past centuries of faith; and this again has two main subdivisions, Catholic and Protestant moralities, each of which in turn has no lack of further subdivisions from the Jesuit-Catholic and Orthodox-Protestant to loose, 'advanced' moralities. Alongside of these we find the modern bourgeois morality and with it, too, the proletarian morality of the future, so that in the most advanced European countries alone the past, present and future provide three groups or moral theories which are in force simultaneously and alongside of each other. Which is then the true one? Not one of them, in the sense of having absolute validity...

"But when we see that the three classes of modern society, the feudal aristocracy, the bourgeoisie and the proletariat, each have their special morality, we can only draw the one conclusion, that men, consciously or unconsciously, derive their moral ideas in the last resort from the practical relations on which they carry on production and exchange.

"But nevertheless there is much that is common to the three moral theories mentioned above—is this not at least a portion of a morality which is externally fixed? These moral theories represent three different stages of the same historical development, and have therefore a common historical background, and for that reason alone they necessarily have much in common. Even more. In similar or approximately similar stages of economic development moral theories must of necessity be more or less in agreement. From the moment when private property in movable objects developed, in all societies in which this private property existed there must be this moral law in common: Thou shalt not steal. Does this law thereby become an eternal moral law? By no means. In a society in which the motive for stealing has been done away with, in which therefore at the very most only lunatics would ever steal, how the teacher of morals would be laughed at who tried solemnly to proclaim the eternal truth: Thou shalt not steal!

"We therefore reject every attempt to impose on us any moral dogma whatsoever as an eternal, ultimate and forever immutable moral law on the pretext that the moral world has its permanent principles which transcend history and the differences between nations. We maintain on the contrary that all former moral theories are the product, in the last analysis, of the economic stage which society had hitherto moved in class antagonisms, morality was always a class morality: it has either justified the domination and the interests of the ruling class, or, as soon as the oppressed class has become powerful enough, it has represented the revolt against this domination and the future interests of the oppressed. (Friedrich Engels, "The Communist Manifesto," from The Marx-Engels Reader, ed. Robert C.

Tucker (New York: Wm. C. Norton & Co., Inc., 1978), p. 489.
(Marxist Relativism)

Having presented in outline the three main standpoints favoring
the idea that there are no absolutes — ethical skepticism,
cultural relativism, and Marxist relativism— let us now turn to
some refutations:

Ethical Skepticism: the theory that we cannot know anything
for certain. I hold that even though we cannot know all truth
because we are only finite human beings, it is still possible to
have some valid insights. Look at this list of acts. Put an 'X' next
to those you think are certainly wrong and put a '?' next to those
you think could be right:

a) torture an innocent human being

b) murder an innocent human being

c) maim a child

d) cause an innocent friend to go to jail for life

e) be a spy for an evil group of people who are

   enslaving one hundred innocent people

f) rape someone

g) earn your living by setting up a slave system.

Do you think that you would have to be God in order to be sure
about the wrongness of those acts (a-g)?

Here is another relevant question: why is it that when we are the
victim of a blatant injustice we are perfectly sure that the act
was wrong, whereas when we are strongly tempted to do
something usually considered wrong, we are quick to invoke as
an excuse the idea that there are no moral absolutes? For
example, if a teacher gives an unfair grade you don't react by

saying—'Maybe her (or she) is right. There are no moral absolutes.' But if you want to cheat you'll most likely deny that cheating is totally wrong.

Cultural Relativism: based on the fact that people in different cultures have varying moral rules. I argue that plurality of rules does not prove that no one rule is better than another. Few really think Nazi Germany's ethics as good as those of post-Nazi Germany.

Also, it can be argued that even if people of different cultures differ in the application of basic moral ideas to specific cases, most agree on the essence.

Here are some passages by moral philosophers trying to refute relativism in these terms. Underline what strikes you as true and put a question mark next to anything you disagree with:

"Everyone has heard people quarreling. Sometimes it sounds funny and sometimes it sounds merely unpleasant; but however it sounds, I believe we can learn something very important from listening to the kinds of things they say. They say things like this: 'How'd you like it if anyone did the same thing to you?"

'That's my seat; I was there first.' — 'Come on, you promised....' Now what interests me about all these remarks is that the man who makes them is not merely saying that the other man's behavior does not happen to please him. He is appealing to some kind of standard of behavior...some kind of Law or Rule of fair play and decent behavior or morality or whatever you like to call it, about which they really agreed.

"Now, this Law or Rule about Right and Wrong used to be called the Law of Nature of Human Nature. The idea was that, just as all bodies are governed by the law of gravitation and organisms by biological laws, so the creature called man also had his law— with the great difference that a body could not choose whether it obeyed the law of gravitation, but man could choose to obey the

Law of Human Nature or to disobey it.... Taking the race as a whole, they thought that the human idea of decent behavior was obvious to everyone. And I believe they were right. If they were not, then all the things we said about the war were nonsense. What was the sense in saying the enemy were in the wrong unless Right is a real thing which the Nazis at bottom knew as well as we did and ought to have practiced....

"I know that some people say the idea of a Law of Nature...is unsound, because different civilizations and different ages have had quite different moralities.

But this is not true. There have been differences between their moralities, but these have never amounted to anything like a total difference. I need only ask the reader to think what a totally different morality would mean. Think of a country where people were admired for running away in battle, or where a man felt proud of double-crossing all the people who had been kindest to him. You might just as well try to imagine a country where two and two made five...selfishness has never been admired.

"But the most remarkable thing is this. Wherever you find a man who says he does not believe in a real Right and Wrong, you will find the same man going back on this a moment later...if you try breaking [a promise] he will be complaining, 'It's not fair....'"

"It seems, then, we are forced to believe in a real Right and Wrong. People may be sometimes mistaken about them, just as people sometimes get their sums wrong; but they are not a matter of mere tastes and opinions any more than the multiplication table." (C. S. Lewis, *Mere Christianity* (New York: The Macmillan Co., 1943), pp. 17-18.

"From the diversity of many moral judgments; ...the fact that certain people hold a thing to be morally evil while other people believe the same thing to be morally correct...in no way proves that the object to which the opinion refers does not exist.

The fact that the Ptolemaic system was for centuries considered correct but is now superseded by our present scientific opinion is no justification for denying that the stars exist or even that our present opinion has only a relative value....The truth of a proposition does not depend upon how many people agree to it, but solely upon whether or not it is in conformity with reality.... Even if all men shared a certain opinion, it could still be wrong, and the fact that very few grasp a truth does not therefore alter or lessen its objective validity....

"Sometimes we find that those who are in a rage against the notion of any objective norm and any objective value nevertheless strive against them in the name of 'freedom' or 'democracy'; and thereby they fully admit the character of the value of freedom or democracy. They do not speak of freedom as if it were something merely agreeable or as if they wanted it for personal reasons, but they speak of it as an 'ideal'....(Dietrich Von Hildebrand, *Ethics* (Chicago: Franciscan Herald Press, 1953), pp. 108ff.

Marxist Relativism: based on the theory that morality reflects the economic conditions of a people rather than an absolute ethical stance.

Although theoreticians such as Engels claim that morality is no more than an effect of economic conditions, it is impossible for them to actually hold this concept consistently.Why? Because Communist ideology involves inspiring people in non-Communist countries to revolt in indignation against the moral evils of capitalism. We are supposed to detest the injustice of exploitation of the poor.

But how could we truly believe exploitation to be unjust if there is no such thing as justice, if justice is merely a bourgeois concept caused by economic necessity?

What is more, we are supposed to be motivated by our moral indignation to actually sacrifice our lives and those of others for the victory of the Party. But to sacrifice for the future of the human race presupposes that it is good to altruistically set aside our own legitimate personal desires for the good of others.

How can altruism be a virtue if there are no virtues, only economic conditions favoring a false belief that virtues are ethically good?

Having heard these refutations, Lisa and Mark feel strengthened against doubt. They realize that at all times it must be wrong to kill an innocent baby. They see that it is value-blindness that makes so many in our culture go along with abortion.

Do any of these ideas about skepticism and relativism fit in with arguments regarding your ethical issue?

FOR PERSONAL REFLECTION AND GROUP SHARING:

1. Have you ever been skeptical about a moral truth others thought was absolute? Did you ever experience surprising enlightenment?

2. Did the refutations of skepticism and relativism seem cogent to you? If not, compare notes with others in the group.

A Prayer: When I was an atheist, before my conversion in 1959 (for more about this see www.rondachervin.com – click on books – e-leaflets – Saved!) I was a total sceptic and relativist. Forgive me God, for ignoring everything that might have reached me to show me the wrongness of my actions. May all who are now skeptics and/or relativists see more of the absoluteness of moral truths.

SESSION

8

SOCIAL JUSTICE

Here begins an analysis of specific controversial issues.

As you read, underline any ideas new to you.

Central problem: minimalism—the idea that Christians can pursue their own individual needs with a minimum of concern for others.

Scripture and Church Teaching:

"Is not this the fast that I choose: to loose the bonds of wickedness, to undo the thongs of the yoke, to let the oppressed go free, and to break every yoke? Is it not to share your bread with the hungry...?" (Isaiah 58:6-7)

In the biblical concordance there are more than 200 listings under just and justice and thousands of others explaining how important it is to care deeply about the needs of the suffering.

In his excellent catechism the American theologian Fr. John A. Hardon, S.J. gave a very balanced view of how these injunctions can be brought into harmony with the right to private property:

"Pressed on the one side by the evils of unbridled ownership and on the other by the theory that private property leads to abuses and therefore all ownership belongs to the State, the Church in our day has had to steer a clear course between two extremes. It has defended ownership and denounced theft as sinful; but it has also insisted on the rights of society and decried selfish greed as morally wrong.... [The Christian] must respect private ownership as divinely ordained, a right inherent in the human person which means that the seventh and tenth commandments are still as valid as they were when first revealed on Sinai. And he must realize that ownership is not an absolute, but that society too has rights for which the author of man's social nature equally demands recognition...." (John A. Hardon, *The Catholic Catechism* (Garden City: Doubleday, 1975), pp. 386-389.

The bishops of the Second Vatican Council stated: "God intended the earth and all it contains for the use of all men and peoples, so created goods should flow fairly to all, regulated by justice and accompanied by charity" (*Church in the Modern World,* n. 69.)

I would like to add to this, personally, that it is estimated that the garbage of the United States alone could feed the entire world!

In his Encyclical, *The Development of Peoples*, Pope Paul VI summarized and applied the constant teaching of the Church in this regard: '"If someone who has the riches of this world sees his brother in need and closes his heart to him, how does the love of God abide in him?' (1 John 3:17) It is well known how strong were the words used by the Fathers of the Church to describe the proper attitude of persons who possess anything toward persons in need. To quote St. Ambrose: 'You are not making a gift of your possessions to the poor person. You are handing over to him what is his. For what has been given in common for the use of all, you have arrogated to yourself. The world is given to all, and not only to the rich.' That is, private property does not constitute for anyone an absolute, unconditioned right. No one is justified in keeping for his exclusive use what he does not need, when others lack necessities. In a word, according to the traditional doctrine as found in the Fathers of the Church and the great theologians, the right to property must never be exercised to the detriment of the common good. If there should arise a conflict between acquired private rights and primary community needs, it is the responsibility of public authorities to look for a solution, with the active participation of individuals and social groups." (10. Paul VI, The Development of Peoples (Boston: St. Paul Editions, 1967), n. 23.)

The common good may require expropriation. The rich should not divert wealth from their own countries for their own personal advantage.

In the Pastoral Letter of the U.S. Bishops *To Live in Christ Jesus* it is stated that "Law and public policy do not substitute for the personal acts by which we express love for neighbor; but love of neighbor impels us to work for laws, policies and social structures which foster human goods in the lives of all persons."(U.S. Bishops' Pastoral Letter, *To Live in Christ Jesus* (Washington: United States Catholic Conference, 1976), p. 23.)

The same letter spells out some of the injustices flowing from discrimination against women, minorities and the elderly. [Since the time I wrote *Living in Love* it is necessary to stress the injustice of sexual abuse, emotional abuse, and physically violent abuse as extreme cases of injustice not only in the actions of the victimizers but also the injustice of various forms of toleration of such situations.]

In every way possible we must seeks to overcome the type of minimalism that sees simply the omission of certain grave sins as proof of moral rectitude, leaving out the clear importance for the Christian of positive acts of justice and charity.

The Pastoral of the U.S. Bishops on the economy further clarifies ways these general principles can be related to problems of our day.

FOR PERSONAL REFLECTION AND GROUP SHARING:

1. In your opinion is social justice adequately addressed in your circle of friends, in the workplace, or in the Church? If so, you might want to write about or share about efforts you endorse.

2. Did this reading challenge you in any way?

A Prayer: Dear God, how often we excuse ourselves from involvement in social justice or in personal charity on the basis that there is dishonesty and fraud in the processes of distribution of wealth. Send your Holy Spirit to guide us to work for causes and charities that are legitimate and truly helpful.

SESSION

9

WAR AND PEACE

Main Problem: Because of nationalism and other causes many Christians fail to see that most wars are unjust and therefore anti-Christian. On the other hand, some Christians insist that total pacifism is the only genuine course.

Scripture and Tradition:

The passages relating to being peaceful are countless. Jesus continually greets others with the words: "Peace be to you." He proclaims that the peacemakers

shall be blessed (Matthew 5:9), and he is called the prince of peace (Isaiah 9:6).

On the other hand, in the New Testament the role of being a soldier was not looked down upon as evil in itself. Luke reports: "And the multitudes asked him [John the Baptist] 'What then shall we do?' And he answered them, 'He who has two coats, let him share with him who has none; and he who has food, let him do likewise.' Tax collectors also came to be baptized, and said to him,'Teacher, what shall we do?' and he said to them, 'Collect no more than is appointed you.' Soldiers also asked him, 'And we, what shall we do?' And he said to them, 'Rob no one by violence or by false accusation, and be content with your wages'" (Luke 3:10-14).

Tradition emphasizes both the intrinsic evil of deliberately killing an innocent person, and the importance of seeking all possible methods to eliminate causes of violence and seeking peace; but it also makes it clear that self-defense can be justified, even to the extent of going to war.

Here are some of the main points of the tradition as summarized by Fr. John A. Hardon, S.J. :

"In a world wholly governed by Christian principles, war would be ruled out as at variance with the moral teachings of Christ.... But since Christians are also citizens of secular order in which the exercise of force is sometimes necessary to maintain the authority of the law, the Catholic Church has held that the method of war and the active participation of Christians in it are on occasion morally defensible and may even be praiseworthy." (*The Catholic Catechism*, pp. 346-351.)

The doctrine of the "just war" was developed to try to distinguish on which occasions Christians could be morally justified in supporting a war. Such criteria include the following:

a) based on the authority of the lawful government (vs. personal or family vendetta)

b) for a just cause (i.e., defense against an unjust aggressor)

c) using proper means (not causing terrible suffering with no hope of victory, or directly killing the innocent).

"All warfare which tends indiscriminately to the destruction of entire cities or wide areas with their inhabitants is a crime against God and man, to be firmly and unhesitatingly condemned." (Vatican II, *Church in the Modern World*, n. 80.)

A document entitled "The Holy See and Disarmament" further emphasizes that it is criminal to stockpile nuclear weapons designed to wipe out whole populations, even as a threat, [some time after this document it was clarified that using them as a threat could be tolerated if diplomatic means were being employed to get rid of them) especially because the funding of such ventures diverts resources from helping the needy.(See The Pope Speaks, Vol. 22, n. 3 (1977), pp. 243-244.)

It is also part of the tradition to object on the basis of conscience to a given war or to all wars, and no nations may demand blind obedience of its citizens to participate against their consciences. (See Pastoral of U.S. Bishops, *To Live in Christ Jesus*, p. 34.)

What is more, we are constantly being enjoined to play the role of peacemakers as Jesus preached, doing our best to defuse the causes of war rather than easily conforming to nationalistic propaganda.

The United States Bishops' Pastoral on peace and war adds concepts to this summary helpful for the formation of conscience of Americans.

FOR PERSONAL REFLECTION AND GROUP SHARING:

1. Making use of the criteria listed in the teaching in this session, which of the many wars you have studied or participated in do you think were just?

2. Given the controversies about the facts that rage during any war, how would you help a person trying to decide whether to enlist in a war to determine whether the war was just or unjust?

A prayer: Jesus, even as we pray and work for peace, let us always laud the bravery and sacrifice of those in the armed forces who participate in just wars in loving service to us. May the Holy Spirit enlighten leaders everywhere in the world in the avoidance of unjust wars and in actions within just wars that are cruel and exploitative such as torture and rape.

SESSION

10

EUTHANASIA

Main Problem: Many people wonder whether it is required to sustain life by extraordinary means in cases which involve great suffering or expense. In the case of someone in excruciating pain or born with extreme defects, could not a positive act of ending the life of such a person be more charitable than letting him or her live on?

Scripture and Tradition:

"Thou shalt not kill!" The biblical injunction against killing is supported by the Greek Hippocratic oath taken by all doctors:

"I will neither give a deadly drug to anybody who asks for it, nor will I make a suggestion to this effect."

Direct killing of innocent persons for any reason has always been ruled out in Judeo-Christian morality. (In the case of capital punishment or war it is usually maintained that a person who unjustly kills others forfeits his or her own right to life.)

Killing an innocent person, including oneself, is a way of usurping God's power over creation and death. This doctrine was reiterated by Pope Pius XII during Nazi times in response to questions regarding eugenics and genocide. This doctrine also reflects the religious conviction that every human being is infinitely precious regardless of any consideration of development, race, creed, etc.

"Not only does man have intrinsic dignity, but God has inalienable rights. The divine lordship over human life is an article of...faith, namely, To believe in God the Father Almighty, Creator of heaven and earth.' As a creature of God, to whom man owes every element of his being, man is entrusted only with the stewardship of his earthly existence. He is bound to accept the life that God gave him, with its limitations and powers; to preserve this life as the first condition of his dependence on the Creator, and not deliberately curtail his time...on earth.... Ours is not mastery but only ministry of our own lives as of the lives of others." (16. John A. Hardon, The Catholic Catechism, op. cit., pp. 331-332.)

On the other hand the Church teaches that we do not have to use extraordinary means to keep a person alive who is in great pain with no hope of cure, or that is causing tremendous burdens. What extraordinary and ordinary means consist of often requires a committee of ethical and medical experts to determine. This makes it impossible to apply some neat, exact measure to every situation. However, moral theologians normally say that ordinary means are those commonly accepted, readily available, without extreme difficulty in terms of pain and expense. Recently it has been clarified that nutrition through feeding tubes is not an extraordinary means.

An issue that has surfaced recently is that of living will documents which authorize procedures considered by the Church to be euthanasia but by others to be licit. It is wise to bring any living will document to a priest for review.

This teaching is short because it is about an area the author is the least expert about, but I am including it anyhow since it is so important.

FOR PERSONAL REFLECTION AND GROUP SHARING:

1. How do you view the ethics of euthanasia with regard to yourself or others?

2. Can you give examples of extraordinary means extending life in a good way or in a way that was not necessary?

A prayer: Jesus, you died an excruciating death on the cross and experience terrible mental sufferings throughout your life as well. Help us to overcome by human effort any sufferings we can, but not to employ immoral means as if we would challenge your sovereignty and disbelieve in your love for us and in the hope of heaven.

SESSION

11

SEXUAL MORALITY

Main Problem: Given the tremendous emphasis on pleasure in contemporary society, it is very difficult for people to impose restraints on themselves. Also since many think that marriages should not be entered into before the age of twenty-one or even later, it is thought to be too difficult to restrain sexual impulses until that time. Although all Christians reject free-love, some think that in the case of engaged couples who have to wait a long time for marriage, pre-marital intercourse could be all right. Others think that in the case of marriages involving great difficulties, extra-marital sex might be licit.

Scripture and Tradition:

The scriptural word for pre-marital sex is fornication, and for extra-marital sex—adultery. Some people claim that these matters are not emphasized in Scripture, because they do not realize to what these terms refer.

Scripture contains many references which forbid any form of fornication or adultery—see especially the commandment "You shall not covet your neighbor's wife"(Exodus 20:17); the book of Hosea; Matthew 5:27-30; Hebrews 13:1-4; 1 Corinthians 6:9, 18.

Tradition has been very strong on these two temptations. Contrary to some opinions, these doctrines have in no way been changed in recent years. They have been reaffirmed in authoritative documents to the present. (See Sacred Congregation for the Doctrine of the Faith, *Declaration on Certain Questions Concerning Sexual Ethics* (Boston: St. Paul Editions, 1976), n. 7ff., and U.S. Bishops' Pastoral, To Live in Christ Jesus, pp. 17-19.)

In view of the great difficulty for many in accepting these doctrines, I am hoping that these reflections of mine may help. Underlying Catholic sexual morality is to be found a philosophy of sexuality as a physical means of expressing a deep, intimate union of two people in love, open to the creation of a new human being—the child. This love must reach the point of a real giving of the self in the emotional, volitional, and spiritual dimension before its physical expression is justified.

The spectrum of possible situations and attitudes of two people engaging in sexual activity has an enormous range. The possibilities described below are necessarily sketchy and incomplete but still may serve to clear up certain difficulties in understanding the morality of sex.

1. Isolated sex. This term is used by Von Hildebrand in his books *In Defense of Purity* and *Man and Woman*. It refers to

the type of relationship in which sexuality is isolated from love and is experienced merely as a means for getting pleasure. It is a typical I-it relationship in which the other partner is viewed as dispensable and as an object, rather than as a unique person lovable and worthy of care and consideration. In such a relationship, it is very clear that the physical giving is completely separate from any emotional and spiritual giving and there is obviously no commitment of the will.

Such a sexual act is immoral, because the sexual sphere is an expression of the intimate depth of the personality rather than a surface dimension which is morally neutral, as eating and sleeping usually are. Because of this, it is wrong to use sex to buy love, enjoy pleasure, or for popularity, status, etc.

The despair that results from pursuing a life given to isolated sexuality is well described by Rollo May in his book *Love and Will*. The reason for this despair is that such a person sees his or her selfhood as something used. He or she throws it away instead of seeing it as something cherished which will engender lasting love.

Whereas in the relationship of married love the sexual relationship is part of the I-Thou love directed to the irreplaceable unique being of the other, in isolated sex what is given can be replaced by any other woman or man with the same sexual parts.

2. Sex in the love affair. In such a situation sexuality is given a romantic aura which raises it above the level of isolated sex. Two people feel attracted to each other and hope for a relationship lasting longer than one evening. They relate to each other as individuals rather than as sexual organs and measurements, but their interest in each other has little self-giving on an emotional, spiritual or volitional level.

All they give to each other is their passing emotional states—they do not unite their hearts and souls or vow to stay together longer than they happen to give each other pleasure. Such relationships are generally filled with self-deceit, for the persons involved will tell one another that they love each other without believing it, flirt with others at the same time, often try to avoid facing the possibility that one or the other might meanwhile have become serious about the relationship and therefore be hurt by it. To be convinced that such sexuality is immoral, however, it is necessary to believe that a real I-Thou love is possible and that a person ought to preserve so deep an experience as sex for such a relationship. Most often people engaged in love affairs lack this hope. Sometimes one believes that such an affair reflects real love while the other party is sure that it does not, and in these cases such affairs may leave lifelong scars of disillusionment and despair.

3. The engaged couple and sex. Many hold that isolated sex and sex in a love affair are wrong, but that sexual intercourse for the engaged couple is fine because in this case there is a real I-Thou love which is being expressed in the physical sphere. Usually marriage is postponed only for exterior reasons involving finances, family difficulties, decisions about finishing school first, military service, etc.

   But does the engaged couple really feel joined in a total I-Thou commitment? The couple will argue that they really are married and certainly don't need a piece of paper to prove it; but is it really true that they have made an interior binding vow and that the certificate or religious ceremony is but a conventional trimming of no deeper significance?

   That an engagement is not an interior marriage lacking only exterior forms can be seen by asking one simple question: is it a sin to break an engagement? The fact that breaking an engagement is always considered possible and not seen as a divorce proves that no one thinks that an engagement represents the same degree of unity as a marriage. Each person is still free to change his or her mind because of the recognition that this love was not as deep as was originally supposed. Hence the engagement expresses the hope that this love is so great that the couple wishes to spend life together, but this hope is not expressed through a full, irrevocable vow of marriage. In case the young people do not marry they may be thankful for all those exterior obstacles which made them postpone marriage.

4. Marital love and sex. The moment of marriage is one of the most dramatic times in life, because it unites all the aspects of the person in the joining of oneself to another. It is the "hyphen" which joins I-Thou. It makes the couple two in one, as Christ proclaims. Here there is no disparity between the body, the heart, the mind, the will, and the spirit. They wish for this union and do not hold themselves back by placing conditions on their love. This overflow of love into the joining of life on every level is gloriously expressed in the possibility that sexuality may bring about a new person, the fruit of the couple's love.

   It is an indication of a couple's lack of readiness for sex in pre-marital sexuality if the fruit of the couple's love is viewed as negative and to be prevented or destroyed or at best is viewed as some kind of disaster. In the case of an unmarried couple, that a human person born of the flesh of the person one most loves could be considered something negative reveals the lack of love hidden within the relationship. If, instead, the couple rejoices in this baby and decides to marry, this reveals that their sexual love was an expression of an I-Thou love.

   The essence of the sacrament of marriage is the mutual vow of permanent union. However, the making of the vow in the Church before the witness of the priest is a beautiful symbol of the fact that Catholics who marry receive each other in Christ, in the midst of their spiritual I-Thou relationship to Christ. It also symbolizes a rather subtle metaphysical reality: fundamentally a person does not belong so much to himself or to the people surrounding him as to God, and it is God who gives him or her into the hands of the spouse.

In this sense it is also true to say that pre-marital sex is immoral because one's body belongs to one's future husband or wife—it has been destined by God to belong to the one person who will love it and cherish it in a whole, total love. Because it belongs to the future husband or wife, it is not mine to throw away or trade for some advantage or use as a plaything.

To use another analogy, one could say that a person's sexuality is like a secret closed garden to which only the ultimate lover is to be given the key. It ought not to be received by the spouse as a garden trampled upon and wasted, full of the weeds of random visitors who did not cherish its flowers but picked them and strolled away.

5. Difficulties. But, you may well ask, if this is God's plan why should it be so difficult to live by such ideals? Why should we have to fight against the lure of isolated sexuality? How can we be asked to wait for the perfect love when we don't know if we will ever find it and meanwhile have overpowering sexual needs and desires and pressures?

Much struggle and despair underlies such questions. It is very difficult to live up to Catholic moral ideals unless one's religious life is deep and concrete. It is then, within the context of a living I-Thou relationship to Christ, that we have the faith in God's providential love which will enable us to postpone immediate longings for the sake of the deeper experience of marital sexual love.

Unless we love Christ as intensely as we love those who attract us physically and emotionally, we will not have the strength to live in hope that he will give us the gift of a true love. This is the question: do we want to seek the good things as gifts of his love as he has planned, or do we want to listen to the voices of the majority, which always say that we must grasp the tangible, desired things with both hands before it is too late? Do we "seek first the kingdom of heaven and its justice and all things will be added unto you" (see Matthew 6:33), or do we "look out for number one and let the future take care of itself"?

I think that every time of life calls for the making of a particular decision which is always very difficult but which is the most important thing one can do in order to transcend egoistic norms and become more loving in following Christ. For a child the hardest thing might be to avoid joining gangs or cliques and to be friendly with everyone, even the kid the others make fun of. For the teenager and young adult it might be to believe in the ideal of marital sex when all his friends boast of conquests, or to pass up that Saturday night date if she knows where it would lead to. Later it might be to choose a career which is more worthwhile but pays less; and later on to overcome the discouragement that comes from not having achieved what one had dreamed of in order to value the love of the family and friends more than external success. For others it might be to become part of a difficult good cause or to become a priest, or to remain honest in the midst of corruption.

When we see how easily we fall, should we lower the ideal so that we can be comfortable, or should we ask for forgiveness and start again? It is in the midst of temptations to forsake the ideal that we discover the deepest meaning of Christian truths. We discover our weakness — our desire to clutch onto what promises so much and to turn away from Christ's path, and the reality of his forgiveness, and the miracle of the gifts he sends us, which we find to be so different from what we imagined, so much better!

FOR PERSONAL REFLECTION AND GROUP SHARING:

1. Do you think that reserving sex for marriage is impossible even with grace?

2. Have you known any people who have remained chaste in spite of temptations and been happy to have done so?

3. Did any of the reflections in this session help you to understand the Christian view of love concerning sex?

A prayer: Jesus, you told us that with God nothing is impossible. If we failed and still fail in living up to your ideal of married sex, please forgive us as abundantly as you forgave Mary Magdalene!

SESSION

12

CONTRACEPTION

Main Problem: Due to the great difficulty of raising families in cities, the problem of poverty, and many other obstacles, many couples think it unwise to have large families. Of these many are unacquainted with the natural rhythms of the woman's fertile cycle, which when properly understood require only a minimum of abstinence from sexual intercourse to avoid an untimely pregnancy. This state of affairs has made the alternative of artificial contraception more and more attractive to many Christian couples.

Scripture and Tradition:

In *The Catholic Catechism*, Fr. John A. Hardon, S.J. shows that throughout history many different methods of preventing birth have been used. Such practices were describedas "using magic" and "using drugs." (See, for example, Galatians 5:20; Revelation 21:8; 22:15.) Throughout history the Church has condemned such practices over and over again (see Hardon, pp. 368-381), culminating in the Encyclical Humanae Vitae in 1968.

Again, as in the case of sexual ethics, since this issue is so controversial, I would like to explain it in my own way:

A Married Woman's Reflections on Humanae Vitae (This article was first published by Faith and Reason,The Journal of Christendom College, 1978.)

"You're the first person I've ever heard defend Humanae Vitae," a seminarian told me recently. Discussions of the famous encyclical still focus very much on the question of who is raising points pro or con. When a priest defends Humanae Vitae, his arguments are often dismissed as irrelevant for lack of experience—although if a priest dissents, he is listened to with great respect because of his superior theological training.When a father defends Humanae Vitae, his views are often dismissed as based on a sentimental, idealized portrait of motherhood. However, if a father dissents, he is usually listened to with respect as representing the infallible voice of the laity. As for mothers, it is taken for granted that most accept contraception: less-educated women on the basis of intuition, and college-trained women as part of a philosophy of self-fulfillment, both seeking freedom from the exhausting burden of one baby after the other. Awoman who avoids contraceptive means is often thought of as suffering from "slavish fear" of authority.

In view of the above, could any witness be considered credible in defense of the encyclical?

Yes, I believe so. As wife, mother and philosopher, I feel that I can draw upon my own experience in the home, the classroom and the Church, to formulate a new objective argument which can appeal to all Catholics, irrespective of their roles in the Church.

The first experiences, fundamental to all the rest, are the traditional ones you would expect to find at peak moments for any woman: the day of my wedding; and the birth of each of my children. It was overwhelming to see the baby who had been nurtured for nine months in my own womb appear before my eyes for the first time.

But even before birth, there is another moment, less often discussed, which is very precious to parents. This is the time of sexual union with a difference! The couple knows that it is the fertile time, so that added to the joy of the love union there is the mystical sense of participation in an event which goes beyond the subjective toward the incarnational mystery...a unique new person may be conceived at this moment!

This experience is crucial to a deeper insight into Humanae Vitae's description of sex as a divine gift and human life as sacred. (21. See Paul VI, Humanae Vitae (Boston: St. Paul Editions, 1968), n. 13.) The sense of awe before the experience of conception and childbearing has to be at the center of any feminism worthy of the name—how much more a Catholic feminism!

To dwell on the words of Sigrid Undset, the Nobel Prize winning woman writer:

"No other belief can give the people of our day courage to live according to nature and accept the children that God gives them, except this—the belief that every child has a soul which is worth more than...the stars in the heavens, though at times she is near fainting under the shower of the stars." (Sigrid Undset, Stages on the Road (Ayer Co., Publishers).

With the subjective experience of the miracle of fertility in mind, we are encouraged to penetrate the mystery even further through a bold set of comparisons:

As our Lady was prepared by the Immaculate Conception to be ready at the sacred time for the Incarnation of Jesus, making a sacred space of her womb... so, too, at the sacred time of the Mass, through the words of the priest, Christ becomes really present on the sacred place of the altar... so, too, at the sacred time of fertility, through the sexual union of the parents, the life of a new creature begins, making the mother's womb into a sacred space.

It is in the light of such religious insights that we must understand Humanae Vitae's insistence that sexual union is sacred and not to be violated. Not that the sacredness of fertility cannot be understood without religious belief. Any human being can marvel at it, and humanists of all types do express their awe of creative sexuality. Nonetheless, it must be admitted that in our times the sense of sacredness is being lost as other values are given greater weight; so that a return to the Source of the sacred is necessary to renew our appreciation of its natural forms.

Returning to the analogy of the Mass as the peak experience of the priest, and conception as the highest metaphysical fulfillment of the married couple, and carrying it still further — A priest incarcerated in a Communist prison is subjected to unbelievable physical and psychological torture. On Christmas Day he begs to be allowed to say Mass. Permission is given. With awe and bliss he intones the words of the liturgy—but, horror of horrors, at the moment of the Consecration when he is about to say the holy words, the torturers gag him and shout, "This is not my body; this is not my blood!" What a diabolic desecration!

Now, here is the comparison:

It is the fertile time. There is the couple joined in sexual union: a new life can enter the world! But no! Instead, the life-giving sperm is contained in a little rubber bag, later to be discarded. Or, perhaps even more grotesque, the woman has taken a pill which prevents conception by causing a simulated pregnant state —mocking, betraying the natural state and making real conception and child-bearing impossible. What a desecration!

I believe that the argument I have just advanced based on the sacredness of the fertile period is sufficient to show why its violation is intrinsically evil as Humanae

Vitae states (n. 14) in language less vivid but just as insistent.

Other related and important arguments against contraceptives were also advanced before or shortly after the promulgation of the encyclical; they certainly deserve greater consideration than they received at that troubled time. (See the excellently phrased discussion in the collective pastoral letter of the U.S. Bishops, Human Life in Our Day (Boston: St. Paul Editions, 1968). For a fine phenomenological defense based on the importance of love, see Dietrich Von Hildebrand, The Encyclical Humanae Vitae: A Sign of Contradiction (Chicago: Franciscan Herald Press, 1969). For an ingenious discussion in terms of natural law, see Germain Grisez, Contraception and the Natural Law (Milwaukee: Bruce, 1964). An analysis in terms of the historical situation at the time of Humanae Vitae which also gives very concrete arguments can be found in the book by Christopher Derrick, Honest Love and Human Life (New York: Coward McCann, 1969), p. 145.23)

[Another analogy about the goodness of the fertile time occurred to me after the publication of this article and of the book *Living in Love.* I was delighted when black Americans stopped trying to look like white people by flattening out their hair and sometimes wearing lightening make-up. I thought it grand when black people started wearing African hair-dos and beautiful African clothing, with the slogan: Black is Beautiful. Here's the comparison. Instead of a woman thinking of her fertile time as the "bad time," and wishing that, like a man, she could have sex without conceiving a baby in her own body, wouldn't it be wonderful if she boasted of her "miracle, glow, fertile time"?

Of course, some problems remain. Does this mean every couple should have up to 24 children! That is not the teaching of the Church. For serious reasons, determined by the couple, they may postpone childbirth using the very successful natural family planning method. (If you are doubtful there is more about this method later in this teaching.) But, then, what about the normal physical expression of marital love during the fertile days which are to be skipped?

As the Encyclical explains:

Unitive sexual love without intent to procreate – corresponds to the non-fertile time unitive sexual love with intent to procreate - corresponds to the fertile time.

Both experiences of love are God-given and blessed. The conformity of one's sexual life to such a natural rhythm is no more a desecration than the conformity of a farmer's planting times to the seasons of the year.

In the past, special problems arose because some couples had difficulty determining the fertile period. They thought that the rhythm method did not work and that the practical choice might be between total abstinence or yearly child-bearing. (Incidentally, it is important to realize that it is not part of the order of nature to conceive every year. The mother's body is designed for breast-feeding, which in former times lasted several years, in most cases rendering her less fertile, with a resulting natural favorable spacing of births.)

Looking back at the time just before the encyclical, the 1950's and '60's, and reviewing my own experiences, I must say that there were no lack of ambiguities connected with blaming rhythm for unwanted pregnancies. Many couples used guesswork, when more precise methods were available and known to them. How can we explain such inefficiency about a matter so important?

I am convinced that it came about because the strong physical, emotional and spiritual motives behind the joys of participation and experience of the whole creative cycle often outweighed any prior considerations. Except in certain cases, the impulsive leap of faith involved in love-making at a time when fertility is possible though not probable, seems to me to be part of the family vocation.

The acceptance of the extremely heavy burden of child-raising for the reward of another beloved little one is a sign of holiness. Those who regard couples having many children as objects of scorn are in my view as misguided as those who regard saintly priests, sisters and brothers as lacking in moderation when they exhaust themselves in their ministries.

Nonetheless, there certainly were instances involving heroic sacrifice, for example, if a new pregnancy would imperil the mother's health gravely and she had an irregular cycle which was hard to predict, so that almost total abstinence was required.

The plight of such couples was the motive behind the hope for a change in the Church's ban on contraception. Possibly the "pill" would provide the loophole, since its use did not directly mutilate the sexual act. (Now, of course, the pill is considered to be very dangerous to health and hopefully is no longer being recommended as a solution.)

Pope Paul was aware of the sufferings of couples who could not work successfully with the rhythm method. When his final decision was made, it was with absolute conviction of reflecting the will of God, but with a heavy heart and with prayer that new methods would be discovered which would eliminate trial and error and thus insure to couples who had serious reasons for avoiding procreation more time to experience unitive sexual love. (See Humanae Vitae, nn. 24, 25.)

Thanks be to God, there was an answer—an accurate system discovered by two doctors (an Australian married couple), whose research began with women for whom previous methods did not work. It is called the Natural Ovulation or Billings Method. (There are booklets available on it at most Catholic bookstores and short courses for couples at hospitals.)

The discovery of this natural method is a great breakthrough. The method should be studied by every young couple. It is even being adopted purely on health grounds by people with no interest in Catholic moral teachings.

From my own personal experience with three children and five miscarriages, after each one of which doctors advised me to allow a period of one year without pregnancy, I can witness to the fact that the new method is easy. It takes only minutes per month to calculate and usually demands no more than seven days of abstinence per month—often fewer.

If with God's grace celibacy is possible, who can doubt that married couples can make such a small sacrifice? At first it may seem hard, because many women are more desirous of sexual union at the fertile time, but with practice many married people find that periodic abstinence heightens sexual enjoyment, turning the non-fertile days into little honeymoons.

Moreover, this kind of abstinence is really participation through sacrifice in the mystery of fertility—I experience it as a sort of reverent bowing before the plans that God has written into nature.

(Here again, another analogy came to me after my ethics book was published to explain why contraception is wrong but natural family planning for serious reasons is good. Suppose a child gets a beautiful bicycle for Christmas. Alas, it is snowing out. He or she can't ride the bike. One response would be to postpone riding the bike and storing it in the cellar. This shows gratitude for the gift. Another would be to wreck the bike. This would show disdain for the gift. Postponement of the use of fertility is different from desecrating it.)

(At the time I first wrote the article I wished that married couples with sound theological, spiritual and psychological training would take up the idea of forming a ministry to other families in the parish, as suggested by Pope Paul in the encyclical. In the meantime this has been founded. Search for Couple to Couple League on the web.)

For Personal Reflection and Group Sharing:

1. If your parents had the same ideas about birth control that you do now, would you have been born?

2. If it is not too personal what have you experienced in the area of birth control and natural family planning?

3. Did any of the ideas in this session strike you as true?

A prayer: Holy Spirit, break through the tremendous confusion in this intimate area so important for marital happiness.

Session

13

Homosexuality

Main Problem: In recent years due to causes psychological, sociological and moral, there has been an enormous increase in open homosexuality. There is agitation among homosexuals who consider themselves to be Christians that their lifestyle be accepted as an alternate one rather than condemned as intrinsically disordered.

Scripture and Tradition: Scripture refers to homosexual activity, masturbation, fornication with animals, etc., as unnatural, unclean acts. Passages condemning these acts include: Genesis 19:5 ("know" = to have intercourse); Leviticus

18:6-23; 20:13; Judges 19:22; Wisdom 14:22-29; Ephesians 4:19; and the most often quoted Romans 1:24-27, 32:

"For this reason God gave them up to dishonorable passions. Their women exchanged natural relations for unnatural, and the men likewise gave up natural relations with women and were consumed with passion for one another, men committing shameless acts with men and receiving in their own persons the due penalty for their error....Though they know God's decree that those who do such things deserve to die, they not only do them but approve those who practice them" (Romans 1:24-27, 32).

Note that in Scripture "to know" in a sexual context means to have intercourse.

The wrongness of homosexual practices has been reaffirmed over and over again through the present day. (See Hardon, *The Catholic Catechism*, p. 355, and footnote 43, p. 585.

On the other hand, having a homosexual orientation as opposed to practice is not in itself blameworthy, since many times it is rooted in psychological disorders. Growth in Christian maturity makes it possible to control such desires, and intense counseling may lead to the healing of psychological problems, and growth in heterosexual orientation to the point of making marriage to a woman a good option, but only if the person involved wants to change.

As Pope Paul VI states:

"The Master, who speaks with great severity in this matter [of chastity] does not propose an impossible thing (Matthew 5:28). We Christians, regenerated in baptism, though we are not freed from this kind of weakness, are given the grace to overcome it." (Paul VI, "To Live the Paschal Mystery," address, May, 1971.)

Essentially the reasoning behind seeing homosexual acts as intrinsically disordered is that God created the sexual organs primarily for reproduction. To cast aside the gift of fertility in sexual acts with same sex partners is a rejection of the way God created us as male and female. Love between any persons can be expressed in innumerable ways that don't contradict the nature of the human person.

Since writing *Living in Love*, I have become acquainted with the wonderful work of Courage – a support group for chaste homosexuals. Their work is reported by the founder, Fr. John Harvey, in his books such as *The Homosexual Person*. This book gives an illuminating account of theories by different psychologists about the origin of homosexual orientation and means of healing. Harvey favors the theory that a distance in childhood with the same sex parent either because of abandonment or simply coldness leads to a desire to bond with people of the same sex for compensation, which then can lead into a sexual form of bonding. I also recommend the writings of Joseph Nicolosi, a Catholic psychotherapist specializing in work with homosexuals.

FOR PERSONAL REFLECTION AND GROUP SHARING:

1. If it is not too personal, what has been your experience with homosexual orientation or activity? Have you known anyone who has been able to struggle with homosexual urges so that even if there are set-backs, he or she is able to live in joyful acceptance of God's will?

2. Can you add to the reasonings given above?

A Prayer: God, only you know the story of each ~~individual~~ oriented and/or active homosexual's innermost problems and agonies. Help each one to be healed and able to follow your moral teachings so as to manifest the greatest love for others and for You.

SESSION

14

IS THERE A GOD OF LOVE?

In the last two sessions of *The Way of Love: Making Loving Moral Decisions*, I want to reflect with greater emphasis on the way God enters into the making of loving moral decisions.

A person might have a vague belief that there is a first cause of the universe without being religious. The word "religio" in Latin means bond. Such a vague belief would not necessarily involve a bond with the intelligent designer of the universe.

By contrast, the God of most religions is seen not only as a cause or force, but also as a person – not a human person with a body, but nonetheless a consciousness, and especially a love for His creatures.

This type of God clearly has importance for decisions about love. In most world religions, though not all, it is believed that God loves us and wants us to grow by doing His will.

But how do we know if there is a God of Love? Many of us would say, by faith in the Bible. ~~Here is the way philosopher, Stephen Schwarz, explains why even those who don't have such faith can find there way to the God of Love:~~

Here is the reasoning of Dr. Stephen Schwarz, a Catholic philosopher and professor teaching at the University of Rhode Island, a secular campus:

1. "What can I do if the existence and nonexistence of a God of Love are both uncertain? "

2. Consider the possibilities:

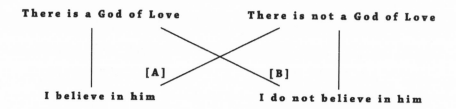

"In this diagram, the top part represents two possibilities regarding the objective situation, how it really is. The bottom represents two corresponding positions that can be taken by each person. The four lines represent four possible combinations among the four elements of the diagram.

Thus:

3. If there is a God of Love, I should believe in him. If there is not, I should not believe. So much for the vertical lines, which are clear.

4. But, I may be in error: diagonal lines. Both are tragic in that I am mistaken. I have been deluded. I have made the wrong commitment. But from this point of view (truth) they are equal.

5. Leaving aside the viewpoint of truth, where they are equal, how do A and B compare otherwise?

6. Line A is tragic because I am fooled—I wasted my time believing in a God who doesn't exist.

7. Line B? Isn't this an infinitely greater tragedy? There was, after all, Infinite Love waiting for me, with consolation for all my sufferings, with salvation from the evils and absurdities of life. There was Love and I ignored him. Truly my life was wasted. How much worse to be wrong in this way!

8. And perhaps the God of Infinite Love has prepared an eternity of happiness for those who respond to him. Can I afford to risk such a loss?

9. The stakes are great if there is a God of Love: the loss or gain of an infinity, an eternity of happiness.

10. But really the deepest and greatest tragedy of B is not my loss, here and afterwards, but that I have failed to give the response due to Infinite Love. How tragic when human love is rejected, how much more when Infinite Love is rejected."

Now that I realize how much is at stake, I ought to seek to find out if there is a God of Love. This can be done through reasoning, through questioning others who believe, through making contact with God in prayer.

Schwarz argues that if we seek God then we have to decide whether to trust experiences which seem to show that there is a God of Love. Failure to seek or trust is tragic for us. Not only does it shut the door on such infinite love, but also we will be unable to give the due response.

Here are some ways in which belief in the existence of a God of Love affects a person's ethical behavior:

-If the ultimate foundation for the universe is its creation out of love by a God of love, then our life goals should be related to love.

-If God thinks love is most important, being a loving person takes precedence over amassing possessions, achieving status or fame, or just "doing your own thing.

-If God loves love and hates indifference, one's eternal destiny might be a result of how much one followed the way of love in time.

-A God of love may have given us commandments on how to live in love which we must follow.

-If there is a God of love, our efforts to procure good for those whom we love do not end in failure because of death. We can live with a horizon of victory over death which prevents ultimate pessimism and the tendency to give up.

In the case of large personal sacrifices entailed by love for others, we know that God wants these and will recompense us.

Returning to our original example of the couple making the decision about abortion, let's say that Lisa and Mark study the traditional arguments for the existence of God and also Schwarz's argument and begin to pray more frequently and fervently.

Lisa and Mark start to read the New Testament. Certain main truths become clearer with implications for ethics:

We Belong to God

In the religious vision of the meaning of life, we are not seen as merely material entities thrown by chance into the world, but rather as sons and daughters of a loving Father who, therefore, deserves our obedience. St. Paul writes in his letter to the Ephesians: "He chose us in him before the foundation of the world, that we should be holy and blameless before him" (Ephesians 1:4). And in the letter to the Romans it is written: "None of us lives to himself, and none of us dies to himself. If we live, we live to the Lord, and if we die, we die to the Lord; so then, whether we live or whether we die, we are the Lord's" (Romans 14:7-8).

The Catholic theologian, Hans Urs Von Balthasar, writes: "God and God alone, has the right to demand all from man because His word is salvation and demands only in order better to give."(A Theological Anthropology (New York: Sheed & Ward: 1967).

The Protestant theologian, Dietrich Bonhoeffer, explains in his book *Ethics*: "The question in ethics for the believers is not how can I be good or do good but what is God's will. If it is the first two questions, then I and the world would be the center, not God. But God is the ultimate reality.,... What is central in Christian ethics is that God became Christ. The question is not the relationship between is and ought, motive and act, but rather participation in Christ. Since only God is good, it is only by sharing in Him that we become good."(Op. cit, pp. 188ff.)

God Blesses Goodness

God loves and cares for us. He has prepared for us an eternal kingdom of bliss. Therefore we ought to be willing to sacrifice earthly fulfillment if it conflicts with the needs of others—that man may not be the victim of man. Very often when we are asked to make very difficult sacrifices we are tempted to imagine that the Church is heartless in demanding so much. And it would be terribly harsh of God to insist that we give up all hope for human happiness for the sake of the good of others.

The invitation to lay down our lives for others (see John 15:13) contains the promise of our own personal fulfillment through divine love. How else could Jesus admonish us with the words: "What good is it for a man to gain the whole world, yet forfeit his soul?" (Mark 8:36-NIV) It is through an ever-deepening appreciation of God's love that we are able to accept the seeming impossibility of the Christian doctrine that it is better to suffer than to sin. We are willing to take up the cross because we are following him through the cross to the resurrection.

The Struggle Between Good and Evil

Because of the nature of our fallen humanity, the choice between egoism (the worldly spirit) and sacrificial love involves a terrible struggle. Being seduced by worldly values means being sensual, acquisitive, complacent, defensive, proud, contemptuous, fawning, possessive, irritable and vengeful, whereas: "The fruit of the Spirit is love, joy, peace, patience, kindness, goodness, faithfulness, gentleness, self-control" (Galatians 5:22-23). "Do not be conformed to this world but be transformed by the renewal of your mind, that you may prove what is the will of God, what is good and acceptable and perfect" (Romans 12:2).

We are not allowed, as Christians, to settle into a compromise position. God does not say, "Be a nice guy, be a nice gal," but he calls to us with a voice thundering yet thrilling: "You shall love the Lord your God with all your heart, and with all your soul, and with all your mind.... You shall love your neighbor as yourself" (Matthew 22:37, 39).

The reader should now read the New Testament, especially the Gospels and Letters, and make notes regarding:

1. Which instances and words show how loving Jesus was? Which show his knowledge of the lovingness of God the Father?

2. Which virtues are lauded and which vices condemned?

3.   Which attitudes and deeds are considered loving and which unloving?

To follow Christ, however, depends on strongly believing that he is a supreme authority. Several people in the theology class Lisa and Mark are attending doubted whether it could be shown that Christ was divine.

The professor brought in the classical argument of C.S. Lewis in The Case for Christianity. The argument Lewis presents is extremely simple.

There are three possibilities if a man claims to be divine:

a)   he is a liar

b)   he is a psychotic

c)   he really is divine

Christ appears in the Gospels as an extremely good and truthful person. Far from being judged insane, he is held by many as the best man who ever lived, so there is

good reason to take his claim very seriously. Otherwise we would be in the absurd position of saying that the most admirable man who ever lived made the most absurd claims ever!

Doubters have found two main arguments for avoiding these alternatives:

1.   Christ did not claim to be divine; disciples and commentators made this assertion later

2.   Christ's claim to be divine was only a way of saying that every man is divine

To the first statement it can be replied that, in the context of Hebrew thought, to call oneself the Son of God is to claim divinity, and that the Jewish leaders condemned Christ precisely for this assertion, which they thought to be blasphemy.

Regarding the second contention—that Christ was only telling us that we are all divine—it must be noted that Jesus continually emphasized forgiveness of sin. It is incoherent to claim that Christ came to forgive the sins of men if he was actually trying to tell these same men that they were divine. Furthermore, instead of teaching them to follow him—to believe that he is the way, life, and truth—he would have taught them to seek the divine within themselves if he had believed that all men were equally divine.

FOR PERSONAL REFLECTION AND GROUP SHARING:

1. What did you make of the arguments for believing in or seeking a God of Love? Those for the Divinity of Christ?

2. What insights into the way belief in a God of Love helps us to be ethical did you agree with? Can you give examples from your life or that of others you know or have read about?

A Prayer: Thank you, God of Love, for finding me when I was not consciously looking for You. Thank you Jesus, for revealing Your Divinity to me when I hardly understood you. Thank you for giving me the strength after my conversion to make some loving moral decisions. Forgive me for wrong decisions I made in spite of knowing You.

SESSION

15

THE HOLY SPIRIT AS GUIDE TO MAKING LOVING MORAL DECISIONS

Many Christians who accept the teachings of Jesus in a general way are reluctant to see the teachings of the Church as definitive. These teachings purport to be based on Scripture, doctrine and tradition, but there are difficulties everywhere.

Some think it is childish to agree with blind faith to Christian moral injunctions. Instead, they hold, we should think everything out personally. Some find seeming contradictions within Scripture or between particular passages and traditional Church doctrines.

There is a great tension between fundamentalist interpretations of Scripture on the one hand and extremely "liberal" symbolic interpretations on the other, sometimes within the same Church, community or family.

Many moderate people conclude that the safe middle course is to use their own judgment, following the spirit rather than the letter. Many moral pronouncements in Scripture or from the pulpit, the Pope or Councils, seem so hard to apply to modern life that some "believers" assume that these ethical demands are exaggerations or ideals for the already holy. Shouldn't future changes be anticipated by adopting modern views that are more sensible and livable than the harsh pronouncements of Scripture and tradition?

In spite of such apparently plausible and very widespread reasons why many tend to rely solely on personal judgment in moral decision-making without submitting to any higher scriptural or doctrinal authority, it is very hard to square such an individualistic stance with the basic truths about human nature and Christian truth.

 Can a person be said to belong to God who ignores God's views except when these happen to coincide with his or her own? Given our weak nature, don't we need an objective admonishment from the Lord? In the book of Proverbs (28:26] we find the terrifying line: "He who trusts in his own mind is a fool; but he who walks in wisdom will be delivered."

The Protestant theologian, Bonhoeffer, quoted earlier, points out that, whereas for the natural man conscience is the call to unity with self, for the Christian, unity is to be found only in surrender of the ego to God. (*Ethics,* pp. 243-245.)

It is interesting to find in a novel written by an agnostic (Iris Murdoch's The Bell) a pithy contemporary admonishment containing the basic truth about man's need to submit humbly to doctrine:

"We should think of our actions and look to God and his Law. We should consider not what delights us or what disgusts us, morally speaking, but what is enjoined and what is forbidden. And this we know, more than we are often ready to admit. We know it from God's Word and from his Church with a certainty as great as our belief. Truthfulness is enjoined, the relief of suffering is enjoined, adultery is forbidden, sodomy is forbidden. And I feel that we ought to think quite simply of these matters, thus: truth is not glorious, it is just enjoined; sodomy is not disgusting, it is just forbidden. These are rules by which we should freely judge ourselves and others too. All else is vanity and self-deception and flattering of passion.... The good man does what seems right, what the rule enjoins, without considering the consequences, without calculation or prevarication, knowing that God will make all for the best. He does not amend the rules by the standards of this world." (Iris Murdoch, The Bell (New York: Penguin Books, 1987).

In view of the gravity of the crisis among many believers regarding whether to accept doctrine and tradition as a check on one's own ethical reasoning, I will try to present the issue in still another light for your consideration. In order to understand the controversial topic of moral authority in the Church, especially as it pertains to Catholic moral authority, I would like to begin with a reflection on the famous Myth of the Cave devised by Plato in his dialogue, The Republic, centuries before the birth of the Catholic Church.

Here is Plato's mythical image: There is a dark cave in which prisoners have been chained to the floor, able to face only one wall. Behind them there is a fire blazing at a distance, which casts onto the wall their own shadows and those of people passing by on a walkway behind them. Never having seen their own bodies or the forms of the citizens of the outside world, these prisoners imagine that only shadows are real.

Next Plato asks us to imagine that one of these prisoners breaks free and sees the other people in the cave and finally emerges from the cave and sees free people, the stars and the sun. This is Plato's image of the wise man—the philosopher. Whereas most men on earth see only physical things, the enlightened philosopher sees the intangible element of the world, the souls of men and the truths about being. Ordinary men count shadows and pride themselves at their skill in this (Gallup Poll?) but the wise man looks for more essential truths.

To continue the image of the cave, Plato remarks that if the free man comes back into the cave, his fellow prisoners will by no means automatically believe his visions of the outside world and of their own true natures, especially because the man of light will find it hard to see in the dark anymore and will lack skill in counting the shadows. The analogy is to the attitude the ordinary man takes toward the philosopher. He regards this "wise man" as having his head in the clouds and not understanding the real facts of survival—to lapse into contemporary language. Thus the philosopher will probably be able to enlighten only a few, since the rest will not listen and will not even want to dwell in the light, preferring to rest, secure in their chains.

What would you have done if you were a character in Plato's myth? Would you have been the one who left the cave? On his return, would you have followed him out or would you have remained with the shadow-counters?

I would like to note in regard to similar situations three interesting conclusions that can be drawn from Plato's myth:

1. The freed prisoner who left the cave could be right about the world outside, even if he were one against a hundred in the ideas he held to be true.

2. The freed prisoner could be an idiot in shadow-counting or even a "bad guy" and still be right about the essential truths of the outside world as against the opinions of brighter shadow-counters and better people.

3. The people in the cave could be convinced that they were right, but they might not be right.

Now, let us leave Plato's fascinating myth for a while and turn to an image as strange as his. Do you recognize this:

"Before the world was created, the Word already existed; he was with God, and he was the same as God....Through him God made all things; not one thing in all creation was made without him. The Word was the source of life, and this life brought light to men. The light shines in the darkness, and the darkness has never put it out....The Word was in the world...yet the world did not recognize him. He came to his own country, but his own people did not receive him. Some, however, did receive him and believed in him; so he gave them the right to become God's children....Grace and truth came through Jesus Christ. No one has seen God. The only Son, who is the same as God and is at the Father's side, he has made him known" (John 1:1-5, 10-12, 17-18-TEV).

It is striking to note the similarity and differences between the imagery of the Prologue to the Gospel of St. John given here and the Myth of the Cave.

Christianity is the fulfillment of Plato's vision. Whereas in Plato's philosophy man must make a tortuous ascent up the mountain of wisdom in order to find truth, in Christianity God descends downward with his message of love and promise of eternal happiness.

When Christ was departing from the apostles just after the Resurrection he said: "I am telling you the truth: it is better for you that I go away, because if I do not go, the Helper [the Holy Spirit] will not come to you. But if I do go away, then I will send him to you. And when he comes, he will prove to the people of the world that they are wrong about sin, and about what is right....I have much more to tell you, but now it would be too much for you to bear. When, however, the Spirit comes... he will lead you into all the truth..." (John 16:7-8, 12-13-TEV).

In fact, many people who discover a deeper relationship to the Holy Spirit in their lives, find that in a closer bond to the Spirit many things that they took for granted as being all right are really un-Christian. Furthermore, Christ tells the apostles that they are to remain in the world but not be of the world, and that he will guide them. He singles out Peter to be the head, and enjoins them to seek unity through truth. (How different Christ's emphasis is than those of individualism and scepticism!) We realize the importance of leadership in the Spirit very soon in the description of matters in the early Church. Disputes arise about rituals concerning food and circumcision. These are solved by direct visions given to Peter and by a Council during which Peter is convinced by Paul, but Peter gives the final assent.

To return for a moment to the Myth of the Cave, we could say that God himself enters the cave with a new message about the transcendent world and also about how to transform conditions in the cave. Some follow him—the disciples. These are like torchbearers. Many refuse to follow. As with the cave, it is easy to see that truth cannot be a "numbers game." Peter is right in following Christ even though public opinion is totally against him. It is right to follow Peter, even though Peter is not a genius. Peter doesn't even appear at first to be any sort of great hero, and yet he is still the true torchbearer, as against some very worthy man who might not follow Christ at all. As in the case of the cave, many who did not follow Christ or Peter were convinced that they were right, but the sincerity of their conviction did not make them right.

The significance of the comparison that has been drawn between Plato's cave and Christ's Church will become still clearer as we now proceed to leap into the 20th century and describe four typical stances taken by Catholics in the sphere of authority and morality. I am sure you will recognize these positions. As you read them you might check the one that comes closest to your own initial viewpoint and then see if you have reason to question this position as you read on.

1. Unquestioned fidelity: "If the Pope says so it must be so, even if I can't understand it."

2. Faith seeking understanding: "Through reading, thinking and prayer, I have come to see that what the Church teaches really is the truth."

3. Sincere dissent on the basis of conscience: "With regard to one particular doctrine or several doctrines I am convinced that the Church's teaching is wrong, at least for men in our times and in our circumstances, or at least for me in my situation."

4. Rebellious dissent on the basis of selfishness: "I don't care what the Church teaches—nobody can tell me what to do! I'll make my own mistakes, if they are mistakes. I have to go my own way."

Let us examine each of these positions a little more closely, taking the issue of abortion as an example.

Unquestioning fidelity to the Church's teachings:

At first sight it may seem that a person who holds such a position is just an uneducated, mindless idiot. But when we look a little closer, this attitude is not so absurd. Such a person might feel this way: "People can argue forever and not get anywhere.... You can find arguments on any side in any dispute. It's a good thing that Christ established a Church to bring light into the confusion of our minds. Throughout my life of prayer and experience I have come to see over and over again how right the Church is, and so I conclude that it makes sense to trust her voice even if it involves sacrifices." A very good case can be made for the fact that Christ wanted his followers to go out and love their neighbors, not to sit and debate issues. He gives different individuals different ministries to his people, and unity can only be achieved by having one supreme leader to enunciate his will in the midst of dispute.

To use an analogy: Suppose you are going on a mountain-climbing trip. You know very little about the mountain, but you have a leader who has been to the top very often. You trust him. You may even have blind confidence in him if you know he is the best guide in the world. Now you come to a certain point in the climb where it seems obvious to you that one path would be best but the guide chooses another path—will you follow him, or your own ideas?

One should note that probably a person would follow this expert guide up the mountain even if the guide had ridiculous political views and six mistresses and got drunk after each excursion.

Now, to apply the analogy. According to Catholic faith, the Holy Spirit is the absolute expert guide in the moral and doctrinal aspect of faith. The Holy Spirit guides all believers, but in the case of dispute, the Spirit speaks through the consecrated leader of the Church, the Pope. Even if some Pope is an immoral man in certain respects, as has happened in the past (the recent Popes have been very holy), or has very questionable political views, when he speaks solemnly to the whole Church he is the torchbearer of the Spirit and should be followed. A believer with unquestioning fidelity to the Church's teachings on abortion would take as absolutes the scriptural and doctrinal statements on the general subject of destroying the innocent and their application to the unborn child. (For references to statements throughout Church history condemning abortion at every stage of growth, see John A. Hardon, *The Catholic Catechism* (Garden City: Doubleday, 1975), pp. 338-341.

Here are some of the relevant statements:

"Cain said to Abel his brother, 'Let us go out to the field.' And when they were in the field, Cain rose up against his brother Abel, and killed him. Then the Lord said to Cain, 'Where is Abel your brother?' He said, 'I do not know; am I my brother's keeper?' And the Lord said, 'What have you done? The voice of your brother's blood is crying to me from the ground'" (Genesis 4:8-10)."Whoever sheds the blood of man, by man shall his blood be shed; for God made man in his own image" (Genesis 9:6).

"Do not slay the innocent and righteous" (Exodus 23:7).

"Cursed be he who slays his neighbor in secret" (Deuteronomy 27:24).

"Children are a gift from the Lord; they are a real blessing" (Psalm 127:3-TEV).

"You created my inmost being; you knit me together in my mother's womb....

My frame was not hidden from you when I was made in the secret place. When I was woven together in the depths of the earth, your eyes saw my unformed body.

All the days ordained for me were written in your book before one of them came to be." (Psalm 139:13-16-NIV)

"The Lord called me from the womb; from the body of my mother he named my name.... And now the Lord says, who formed me from the womb to be his servant..." (Isaiah 49:1,5).

"Before I formed you in the womb I knew you, and before you were born I consecrated you..." (Jeremiah 1:5).

'And when Elizabeth heard the greeting of Mary, the babe leaped in her womb; and Elizabeth was filled with the Holy Spirit and she exclaimed.... 'When the voice of your greeting came to my ears, the babe in my womb leaped for joy'" (Luke 1:41-42, 44).

"Do you not know that your body is a temple of the Holy Spirit within you, which you have from God? You are not your own; you were bought with a price. So glorify God in your body" (1 Corinthians 6:19, 20).

"Yet woman will be saved through bearing children if she continues in faith and love and holiness, with modesty" (1 Timothy 2:15).

"Whatever is opposed to life itself, such as any type of murder, genocide, abortion, euthanasia or willful self destruction, whatever violates the integrity of the human person...all these things and others of their like are infamies indeed. They poison human society but they do more harm to those who practice them than those who suffer from the injury. Moreover, they are a supreme dishonor to the Creator." (Second Vatican Council, *Pastoral Constitution on the Church-in the Modern World* (Boston: St. Paul Editions, 1966), n. 27.)

"Faith seeking understanding"

I have placed this phrase in quotation marks because it was the main way in which medieval man described the quest of Catholic philosophers. Some Catholics can rest perfectly content with simple fidelity. Most educated Catholics, however, seek to really appreciate why a given doctrine is held to be true. Even an uneducated person will try to ponder why the Church holds certain positions, especially if he or she finds the position obscure.

For example, in the case of a moral principle such as the condemnation of abortion, a relatively uneducated woman might question it before she became a mother, but then when she, herself, experiences the miracle of childbirth, she will understand in a deeply personal way that from the very start the new being in her is a little person, an almost invisible but real little one living within her womb. From the moment of conception the possibility of the child may fill her with awe. She will then shrink from abortion, not only because the Church teaches that it is wrong, but also because she understands that it is wrong.

The more educated woman will be able to describe the way in which all the elements of life exist as seed in the newly conceived fetus, etc. She will be able to speak about the spiritual dimension of the new creature which cannot be measured in terms of its physical development. She might regard those who allow abortion—depending on the months of development of the fetus—as being like the shadow-counters in Plato's cave who are simply blind to the true meaning of a new human person.

Dissent for sincere reasons of conscience

The Second Vatican Council reaffirmed the traditional teaching of the Catholic Church that even in the case of an erroneous conscience, a person must act in accordance with his or her own judgment. (See Church in the Modern World, n. 16.) This doctrine can be viewed as especially relevant to matters concerning religious and political liberty—for example, the civil rights of persons of other religions living in Catholic countries.

The passage has been quoted extensively, however, not so much in connection with tensions between Church and State as with regard to dissent on such controversial issues as birth-control, the subject of the famous encyclical, Humanae Vitae. In the explanation of dissent from the teaching of the Church on artificial contraception, the concept of the sincere conscience of the many Catholics using such methods as the "pill" was brought into prominence.

Here the good conscience of the sincere dissenter would consist in his or her summation of moral intuitions and arguments, usually accompanied by prayerful opening to God's will. (For a thorough and penetrating analysis of situation ethics and Catholic teaching, see Dietrich Von Hildebrand, Morality and Situation Ethics (Chicago: Franciscan Herald Press, 1982).

"Surely the Holy Spirit also speaks to the faithful Catholic seeking moral guidance as well as to the Pope?" the dissenter reasons. What is much more obvious now than when dissent on the birth-control issue began, is that the same reasoning would be used with many other issues, often to the horror of the original proponents of "sincere dissent."

What is certainly true in the emphasis on conscience in contemporary Catholic thought is that guilt is greatly mitigated when there is a sincere, if erroneous, conscience. An unwed teenager who decides that an abortion is the only route to take, because she is frightened to death of potential parental actions administered to a boyfriend who has fled from the scene, is certainly less guilty than a doctor who is running an abortion mill solely for the sake of greater profit than his previous medical activities provided him.

Knowing how much suffering can go into making difficult moral decisions, and horrified at the harshness of judgment sometimes leveled against the sinful by so called "decent" people who have never faced such a crisis, many religious educators have tended to focus on the authenticity of conscience of the moral agent as if the pain could make a wrongdoing become right.

Instead of following Augustine's maxim of "Hate the sin; love the sinner," they "accept the sin, out of love for the sinner." While showing the utmost understanding and compassion for those caught in moral dilemmas, I believe that it is part of being loving to communicate the wisdom of objective Christian doctrine. Christ and the Holy Spirit, teaching through the Church, would not forbid an act unless it was truly harmful. Knowing how blinded someone may be to the outcome of a decision, the priestly, pastoral, or educational minister must be the one to shed light on the wisdom of the doctrine in question, rather than yield to the erroneous conscience of the person seeking advice.

Another passage from the Documents of Vatican II helps balance the picture of how conscience and doctrine work together. "Conscience is the most secret core and sanctuary of a man. There he is alone with God, whose voice echoes in his depths. In a wonderful manner conscience reveals the law which is fulfilled by love of God and neighbor.... Hence the more that a correct conscience holds sway, the more persons and groups turn aside from blind choice and strive to be guided by objective norms of morality...recognizing the imperatives of the divine law through the mediation of conscience." (Church in the Modern World, n. 16.)

What distinguishes a Catholic conscience from that of a person whose ethics are formed by philosophical considerations alone is the conviction that the Holy Spirit is guiding the teaching authorities of the Church infallibly in matters of faith and morals. Unity of truth is a great gift of the Spirit to the Church, so that making a subjective idea of one's own into an absolute would have to be a denial of Catholic truth.

In our times, when there is a great problem of dissent in the Catholic Church, a Catholic cannot simply trust the views of a teacher or a priest but should consult Scripture, books such as The Documents of Vatican II, ed. by Austin Flannery, O.P. (Boston: St. Paul Editions);The Code of Canon Law (Washington, D.C.,

Canon Law Society of America, 1983); The Church Teaches (St. Louis: Herder, 1955) which summarize Council Documents from the beginning of Church history; the Catholic Encyclopedia; and approved catechisms such as *The Catholic Catechism* by Rev. John A. Hardon, SJ. (New York: Doubleday, 1975) or, of course, *The Catholic Catechism* published by the Vatican.

Dissent on the basis of selfishness

This is the case when someone has basically decided to "do his or her thing," as against "doing the will of God," but still wants to be part of the Church for reasons of sentimentality, habit, desire for the approval of others or, in the best cases, because in the heart of hearts one knows that he or she is in the wrong and hopes to return to the truth someday.

For Personal Reflection and Group Sharing:

1. How do you understand moral authority? If it is different from the options given in this session, explain your stance. Did anything in the chapter make you think in a different way than before reading it?

2. With regard to the moral issue you dealt with earlier in these sessions, how do you find that people on either side who are Catholic try to square their ideas with the moral authority of the Church?

A Prayer: Holy Spirit, form my conscience so that I may live in the truth.

TO LIVE IN LOVE NOW AND FOREVER

In this booklet, *The Way of Love*, Vol. III: Making Loving Moral Decisions, I have tried to show that while everyone wants to be loving on some level, we are often blocked by our faults and by uncertainty, often caused by selfishness.

On the basis of intuitions and reason we can determine what is loving and unloving, good and evil, but actually living in terms of the loving and good in spite of the pressure to choose selfishly, is fostered by strong belief in a God of Love.

When we know the Lord, the answer to the skeptical query, "Who's to say what's right or wrong?" becomes clear: The Lord is to say!

Knowing our tendency toward self-deception, we are happy to be part of a Church of Love. The same Church in which Christ intimately enters us out of love through his sacraments, is also the Church through which the Holy Spirit can guide us.

The original meaning of life was to image God, the Father, who is all goodness, love and holiness, by a perfect earthly life lived in union with him. After human kind's fall and the redemption, our participation in God's life takes place in union with Christ by the power of the Holy Spirit. It consists in restoring the broken image amidst terrible struggle with the powers of darkness that are without and within. We are received back into union with God in a continual cycle of fall, mercy, grace, thanksgiving and praise. Overshadowing all, we live in the promise of eternal joy as lovers of God and of his creation.

Originally created for paradise, the poor fallen human person is forever longing for happiness. How many of our vices have their deepest roots in the frantic need to grab, grasp and cling to whatever seems to promise such joy, at any cost to ourselves and others. We sell our souls to be popular—a tinsel substitute for the perfect appreciation each of us would have experienced in paradise. We strive ruthlessly to succeed, to demonstrate that we are powerful, hiding the puniness which follows the original fall. We make gods of material goods, that their glitter may distract us from our ugly, empty thoughts and schemes. And thus man becomes the victim of man.

And yet in the midst of our misery we have glimpses of the true good. God's beauty dances in his natural creations. God's goodness shines through simple, loving human gestures. And finally we fall in love with God made visible in the God-man, Jesus Christ, the Savior, who becomes total Victim in order to forgive, that henceforth no victim need feel alone and no victimizer despair.

We kneel before him: "You are the Life and the Truth, Lord: show us the Way!" And as he departs he sends us the Holy Spirit, to teach, to give, to bring virtue and witness to fruition. He forms us into Church as his mystical body. He comes to us in the Word. He is mysteriously yet intimately physically present in the sacraments. He is in the community of repentant sinners who still love the Savior and have before them the vision of the holy Mother of God and holy saints interceding.

And yet with all the truth and life and holiness, still we fall. We are like Peter, who could walk on the waters when his eyes were fixed on the figure of Christ but sank immediately when looking at himself. Mesmerized by our fantasies of redemption on earth, we grab and grasp and cling to what will not satisfy. Then, like the prodigal son tasting dust and ashes, we remember our heavenly Father. Unworthy, we come to be cleansed in the Sacrament of Reconciliation. Hidden in Christ's wounds, we join hands again with our brothers and sisters at the supper of the Lamb.

We take up again the cross of being human and we struggle, groaning in prayer, to become good—that man may not be the victim of man. And in union with Christ, with the guidance and grace of the Spirit, enfolded in the maternal embrace of Mary, we persevere in spite of everything in loving God and neighbor, perhaps more purely because we know how impure we are!

And in the end, we have been told:

"No eye has seen, no ear has heard, no mind has conceived what God has prepared for those who love him." (1 Corinthians 2:9- NIV)

VOLUME 4
A 100 DAY SPIRITUAL MARATHON

INTRODUCTION

The Way of Love: Step by Step – a 100 Day Spiritual Marathon
came about in this way: "Why don't you write a blog, Ronda?"
one dear friend asked? "Why don't you write one of those lovely
daily meditation books, Ronda?" And, finally, "Why don't you
write a blog for our web-site, ccwatershed.org., Ronda?" Since
ccwatershed is a delightful web-site, featuring new sacred music
presented by admired dear friends, I decided to pray about it.
After writing many blogs about my daily observations
concerning Catholic living, and enjoying it no end, I got a desire
to shift the format from unrelated meandering thoughts to
something more organized, more pungent, and more vital.

I wanted to write something that would deal with a passionate
concern of mine about myself and others – how is it that I, and
many of my closest friends, long and yearn to be holy, defined by
me as having nothing but love in our hearts, and yet it doesn't
happen. As well as love, we find pockets of anger (the bad kind),
anxiety, discouragement, disgruntlement… and other unloving
emotions.

Now, the absolute center of our spiritual life is Jesus' love for us
conveyed in the Holy Mass and expressed in our responses in
such wonderful prayers as the rosary, liturgy of the hours,
adoration, talking to Jesus all day and availing ourselves of
frequent confession to wash away our sins. However, all of these
graces cannot complete their work in us if we persist in a kind of
denial of our worst patterns of thought, word and deed in spite
of general prayers to be more loving.

My remedy, then, for the pockets of unloving thoughts, words, and deeds in our lives, was to write for myself and my blog-readers a 100 day book, not of sweet meditations but, instead, of challenges. I wrote it. I tested out each one on myself, with ardent prayers for God's help, in the writing and the practicing, with the result that some of my nearest and dearest thought I had improved greatly.

The Way of Love: Step by Step may be used by you, individually, as a tool but also you might want to use it in a prayer group that already exists, or you might feel led to start a group devoted to this spiritual marathon, meeting week to week for the teaching and sharing and making the steps during the week.

A few notes:

The Way of Love: Step by Step is a sequel to a series that includes these booklets: *What is Love? Overcoming Obstacles to Love and Making Loving Moral Decisions* to be published by Simon Peter Press (Johnnette Benkovic's publishing company.)

The challenges offered in the *Way of Love: Step by Step* involve primarily smaller sins, faults, and defects of character. If you are a Catholic, to overcome big mortal sins requires sacramental confession. Of course, it is very helpful for all spiritual growth to go to confession also for venial sins and defects. Those with substance abuse addictions need counseling and/or special 12 Step programs to supplement work on Way of Love: Step by Step.

Each Page of the Way of Love: Step by Step will include

a Scripture,

a challenge,

an example,

space for you to put in your own victories of love for that day, my prayer for on-going help from God to grow in the way of love and space for your prayer for help from God.

If you don't like writing, you can simply think about the challenge during the day and make mental note of your victories.

Perhaps you think the word "challenge" is a little hard sounding. Maybe confrontational on my part? Really, this word reflects that sad fact that due to original sin it usually requires effort on our part to even think of lifting our hearts to God. We prefer to remain in our own little world of controllable daily rounds.

Each week will have a theme such as gratitude, more loving conversation, trust vs. anxiety…14 themes in all. Hopefully, the insights gained and the week of practice will set up a pattern so that you will want to continue, for instance, being more grateful, not just for the week of the challenge but for the next 100 days… and why not for the rest of your life?

Warning! Sometimes if we begin to work on a sin, fault, or defect, we can become depressed. We might actually like to be angry as a sort of protest and, then, feel bored when we are more peaceful! Persistent negative feelings may be a signal that we need more than this booklet to overcome spiritual obstacles. Additional remedies could be spiritual counseling, psychological counseling, charismatic healing prayer, unbound deliverance ministry, or free self-help groups such as Emotions Anonymous or Recovery International for anger, fear; and depression. I, Dr. Ronda, am not a counselor, but if you wish to reach me concerning any questions that arises as you pursue the Way of Love you can e-mail me at <u>chervinronda@gmail.com</u>.

Another warning: don't get discouraged if you fail to meet the spiritual challenge of each day perfectly. Each failure can become the impetus to do better in this area in the future.

Let us step forth on the way of love with this Scripture as our challenge:

"You are the temple of the living God, just as God has said: I dwell with them and walk among them. I will be their God and they shall be my people. Since we have these promises, beloved, let us purify ourselves from every defilement of flesh and spirit, and in the fear of God strive to fulfill our consecration perfectly." (2 Corinthian 6:16; 7, 1)

Let us pray, dear God of love, you know my deepest desire is to have a heart filled with love for you and all those I encounter. Send the Holy Spirit to inspire and correct me – step by step.

THEME

1

THE CHALLENGE OF THANKSGIVING

(Note to Reader: At the start of each week there will be a small teaching by Dr. Ronda about the theme for those 7 days.)

Teaching:

Many spiritual writers think that the key to happiness on earth is gratitude for the gifts of God. We should not be so weighed down by the crosses of life that we have no gratitude for the gifts of God. Some saints who were forced into solitary confinement by their enemies were able still to rejoice at the sight of a tiny sliver of sky seen through a window of their prison cells.

Gratitude "opens the gift." This means that when we take everything for granted we don't see these benefits as gifts from God. We may enjoy the good thing or person, but we don't get the added joy of realizing that this good is a personal gift of God to us.

Day 1: The Challenge of Gratitude for Necessities

"It is good to give thanks to the Lord, to sing praises to Your name, O Most High." (Psalm 92:1)

Dr. Ronda's examples: Working on the challenge of thanking God all day for necessities I started out, naturally, thanking God for the most basic things such as food, clothing, and shelter. This included my wake-up tea, prune juice (smile), and instant flavored oatmeal and proceeded to my sturdy blue denim jumpers, long cotton underwear, to the good old house where I am rooming, all the way to the beautiful new chapel at Holy Apostles College and Seminary where I go to daily Mass. I soon extended thanksgiving for necessities to more banal items that for me are necessities such as toilet paper. It gave me a surprising lift to fill my thoughts which are often filled with anxious worries, instead thanksgiving prayers for the love of God expressed in these gifts.

Your examples:

My prayer: Dear God, I realize that because I don't think of how You are providing for me through the people I never see who are working hard to produce my necessities of food, shelter and clothing, I take all this for granted. May the Holy Spirit remind me moment by moment that my food, clothing, and shelter and lots more are gifts from You.

Your prayer:

Day 2: The Challenge of Gratitude for Beauty

Oh give thanks to the Lord; call upon His name; make known His deeds among the peoples! Sing to Him, sing praises to Him; tell of all His wondrous works! (Psalm 105:1-2)

Dr. Ronda's examples: The beauty I love most in creation is the ocean, the faces of beloved people, music and trees ...of supernatural beauty I love God, and Jesus, Mary, and the saints (specific paintings of them as well) and Holy Mass.

Your examples:

My prayer: Father God, creator for all beauty, I am so grateful for beauty, yet I allow the busyness caused by the desire to do my work (apostolates all) that I do not enjoy all the beauty You want for me. May the Holy Spirit open my eyes and heart to all the beauty You want to give me to cheer and exalt my spirit.

Your prayer:

Day 3: The Challenge of Thanksgiving for those who Love(d) us

"How good and holy pleasant it is for brethren to dwell together in unity!" (Psalm 133:1)

Dr. Ronda's examples: I thanked God for my parents, my twin-sister, many of my teachers, godparents, husband, mentors, children, grandchildren, priests, and so many friends of a lifetime of 74 years! Then I added thanksgiving for God's love.

Your examples:

My prayer: Holy Trinity of Love, in your image we are to love one another. On the way of love so many have tending us, bound our wounds, walked with us, taught us laughed with us. In heaven there will be such a thanksgiving, but now, day by day, step by step, may we be more grateful.

Your prayer:

Day 4: The Challenge of Gratefulness for Tech

"I have said these things to you, that in me you may have peace. In the world you will have tribulation. But take heart; I have overcome the world." (John 16:33)

Dr. Ronda's examples: I thanked God for my computer that enables me to quickly contact family and friends and hear from them, and write books and blogs such as these. I was grateful for great music on the radio from all over the world and for CDs and players, and for Catholic radio and TV and everything else I have loved on radio and TV. I thanked God for GPS so I don't get lost so much; airplanes so I can visit my distant adult children and grandchildren often and even fly to the Holy Land and walk where Jesus walked, and cell phones for quick visits and now Skype to see the faces of beloved ones. I was also grateful for older "tech" such as heating systems so that I don't have to get up at 5 AM to start a fire to warm the farmhouse, and for plumbing vs. outhouses!

Your examples:

My prayer: Jesus, when you came down to earth you left the bliss of heaven for a life full of frustrations. You didn't live in our techie era, but we need You to help us bear the crosses of tech issues as the Holy Spirit directs us to use tech for the good and also for evangelization.

Your prayer:

Day 5: The Challenge of Thanking God for our own Creation

"Before I formed you in your mother's womb, I knew you... (Jeremiah 1:5)

Dr. Ronda's examples: I thanked God for creating my innermost self and then for my body: for my good hair, for being short (I like being short because people more easily find me cute), for all the parts of my body, for my long life because of relative healthiness, for being a twin since that gave me a pattern of wanting to be very close to others. I thanked God for being a Jew (of the people of the elect – I converted at 21 and call myself a Hebrew-Catholic), for my national ancestries of Spanish, Russian, and German and all the aspects coming from those cultures that I enjoy. I thanked God for being created female, with the great gift of motherhood. I thanked God for my talents for speaking, teaching, and writing. And, especially, I was grateful for the gift of being a member of His Church.

Your examples:

My prayer: God, only You know everything in my make-up that You designed with my life on earth and in eternity in mind. Let me never take the good part for granted. Step by step, may I praise you as I use these gifts.

Your prayer:

Day 6: The Challenge of being Grateful even for Crosses

"The one who offers thanksgiving as his sacrifice glorifies me; to one who orders his way rightly I will show the salvation of God!" (Psalm 50:23)

Dr. Ronda's examples: Out of having an unusual background of atheist parents, not married, came a great witness of the miracles of my conversion; out of not fitting in at school very well came, as a teacher, the desire to make my class work easy to understand; out of sufferings of marriage and motherhood came clinging to Jesus in daily Mass and in prayer; out of not fitting in with certain Catholic groups came many graces from other movements in the Church; out of crosses on some jobs came lots of graces and benefits to students at other places. Out of the suicide of my son came trust in God's mercy and more empathy for the sufferings of all people. Out of being a widow came becoming a dedicated widow of the Church.

Your examples:

My prayer: Dear Jesus, many time in the past I felt crushed by crosses. I find that You brought good out of each of these real sufferings. Some of these goods I only realized decades later. Help me to accept my present crosses with real trust that Your plans are for the good even if the crosses are heavy. Let me walk hand in hand with you one step at a time into the future.

Your prayer:

Day 7: The Challenge of a Whole Day of Gratitude for all Blessings

"Enter his gates with thanksgiving, and his courts with praise! Give thanks to him; bless his name!" (Psalm 100:4)

Dr. Ronda's example: Since Day Seven for me fell on Thanksgiving Day, I could thank God for Thanksgiving Day. I recalled that some billionaire donated money to have a chapel for Thanksgiving in a Mall in Texas. I enjoyed the Thanksgiving hymn sung at the Mass and remembered that Eucharist means thanksgiving. I actually felt a little sadness to be leaving this theme for the next one which you will see is more challenging in certain respects.

Your examples of the challenge of thanking God all day long:

My prayer: At the end of this whole week of responding to the challenge to be grateful, dear Lord, I feel so blessed. Guardian angel, will you remind me to continue this practice every day, one step at a time, for the rest of my life? I renounce the spirit of taking things for granted and lay it at Your feet, Jesus, to take it away.

Your prayer:

THEME

2

THE CHALLENGE OF ENGAGING IN ONLY LOVING CONVERSATIONS

"Do not let any unwholesome talk come out of your mouths, but only what is helpful for building others up according to their needs, that it may benefit those who listen." (Ephesians 4:29-32)

Teaching:

A most fundamental question raised in the Scripture passage is what our real intention is in conversation. Do we enter into it prayerfully, eager to build one another up by affirming the good things you see in him or her and benefiting others by helpful ideas, looking for good advice, do we use conversation often mostly to "vent," or enjoy feeling superior to others through gossip? How about anecdotes about the doings of the "enemy" such as the "boss" or politicians? Kierkegaard, the great Danish Lutheran existentialist, wrote that "the sins of others should make us weep rather than gossip." Ridicule isn't loving either, is it, even if the person isn't present?

When we talk are our voices so low that others (especially elderly people with hearing loss) have to strain to understand us? Do we fail to show interest in others by remaining mostly silent spectators? Or, do we talk too much, dominating most conversations? Are our voices loudly annoying or raspy? On the positive side, how about telling funny jokes to lighten others up, or to change the topic from something that is not so good to something better?

Is our conversation always full of "I" and "me" instead of lovingly drawing out the thoughts, feelings, and wisdom of others?

Does the name above all names, Jesus, come up often in a day's conversations?

How about the "conversations" we rehearse in our heads? In our quiet time, who is our secret "friend," God or evil spirits? (For instance evil spirits can help us imagine vengeful, sarcastic, words we could use to 'annihilate' someone who hurt us, whereas the Holy Spirit gives us wisdom about how to help someone who needs our consoling advice.)

If a lot of this teaching fits bad things you sometimes do or think, it could be a good subject for confession.

The challenge for the first day of this theme is just to observe yourself and others in conversation and check to see whether your conversation is truly wholesome and positive or tearing down, gossipy or unloving.

Day 8: The Challenge of Observing Unloving and Loving Conversations

Dr. Ronda's examples: At table at the place where I teach, I told two edifying stories about graces people got to convert or reform. Then I bubbled over with jokes. This led to everyone lightening up from fear of exams and telling their own funny stories. Later I engaged in empathetic conversations with friends in dire circumstances. I had good fairly loving conversations at dinner but at lunch I made a big mistake that is probably a warning. I was talking about the wonderful conversion of a man from alcoholism to becoming a Catholic leader, only to find out that one of the people at the table knew this man, but hadn't known he was a former alcoholic. I think that when we try to becoming more loving with the help of the Holy Spirit, He takes the opportunity to show us dangers we never thought of. I have to be much more careful of anecdotes where someone could be identified.

Your examples:

My prayer: Come, Holy Spirit of love, take over my undisciplined tongue. Move my heart to want to use conversation to build up rather than to compensate myself for feeling hurt by demeaning others. May even the sound of my voice reflect gentle loving kindness.

Your prayer:

Day 9: The Challenge of having Loving Conversations at Work or other Places outside the Home

"And the passersby say not God bless you." (Psalm 129:8)

Dr. Ronda's examples: I like to say "God bless you" often even though sometimes people criticize me thinking I am acting as if a laywoman is trying to give priestly blessings. The above Scripture shows that saying "God bless you" is something good to do for anyone. Today I noticed that asking questions of holy people is better than "strutting my stuff." I got a lot of good advice by asking questions at work. Since I eat meals with my colleagues and students here at Holy Apostles College and Seminary I learned a lot at meals today just by talking less. I called a co-worker and apologized for getting so edgy when he was trying to teach me a tech thing. He said it was okay because he is learning patience with non-techy people from dealing with me! But I also slipped into anecdotes with good endings but with plenty of gossipy things before the end that weren't necessary to relate.

Your examples:

My prayer: Father God, you made my tongue to speak good. I am grateful for even the slips because they are teaching me how much I need to grow in the Way of Love in the realm of conversation. Please help me with the rest of this week to do better and better with Your grace.

Your prayer:

Day 10: The Challenge of Engaging in Loving Conversations with Family and Friends

"Do you see a man who is hasty in his words? There is more hope for a fool than for him." (Proverbs 29:20)

Dr. Ronda's examples: With three friends I was much lighter than usual and therefore could take in more of the loving expressions in their eyes when they were talking to me. I did express lots of hostility in talking about a friend I was mad at to someone else. Even though this mentor didn't know this person at all, I could feel how unforgiving I was from the tone of my voice. With another friend I talked better through a conflict because I was less pushy and more vulnerable about it.

Your examples:

My prayer: Sweet Mother Mary, I don't believe you would ever have spoken with personal hostility even if you were speaking prophetically about the fall of the mighty. Please be my friend and intercessor to keep me from hasty, harsh talk. Help me to see that light fun is so much better! When another friend wanted my advice about serious problems, I think that because I pray for her so much, I was able to be of help. How like you, dear Mary.

Your prayer:

Day 11: The Challenge of Avoiding Talking too Loudly, too Softly, too Much or too Little.

"When words are many, transgression is not lacking, but whoever restrains his lips is prudent". (Proverbs 10:19)

Dr. Ronda's examples: At breakfast, by speaking less hastily, I was really helpful instead of talking too much about trivia. With a friend, I got her to tell me when my voice is too loud and when it is not too soft. Since often I talk too loud partly because I don't hear too well, I realize I can think I am talking too softly when I am just right! Later in the day I started longing for more silence even though I usually find silence boring. I felt more peaceful skipping the formal lunch I had a good conversation later today with a student where I could hear the Holy Spirit, hopefully, sending advice through me to resolve a small conflict. If I hadn't listened more carefully than usual, maybe this wouldn't have happened. At a dinner I spoke well and made many points but my voice was too loud and I could see that it was because there was anger in my heart. In a car conversation I talked imprudently about matters that could be misunderstood, sigh!

Your examples:

My prayer: Dear Lord, I went to bed heavy-hearted seeing how difficult loving conversation is for me. It was such a struggle to speak with love. Help me to notice well the good examples that came with Your grace and to believe that You want to show me how to do this better step by step, day by day.

Your prayer:

Day 12: The Challenge of Avoiding Other Rude Modes of Conversation

"The tongue is set among our members, staining the whole body, setting on fire the entire course of life, and set on fire by hell."(James 3:6).

Dr. Ronda's examples: I wanted to avoid the rudeness of interrupting others. I did well part of the time, but then got excited about an issue in my class at the school and did interrupt, but because I didn't raise my voice rudely it came out less strident. I avoided rudeness of talking at table only to the ones I wanted to and ignoring a quieter person. A person called. I said I was too busy to talk but he kept on talking. I politely insisted that I had to get off the phone. I saw how it felt to others when they say they are busy but I persist in one last few sentences. It registers as my time counts and yours doesn't?

Your examples:

My prayer: Dear Holy Spirit, I challenge you to help me the rest of this week, and the rest of my life, to douse my fiery tongue so that it is a messenger of love, not of self-assertiveness.

Your prayer:

Day 13: The Challenge of Avoiding Boasting to be more Loving in Conversation

"If you have been foolish, exalting yourself ... put your hand on your mouth." (Proverbs 30: 32)

Dr. Ronda's examples: Boasting, a bad, proud, defect in my character, is only one way of being self-centered in conversation. Another bad habit can be presuming to speak for others. Another would be making statements as if I am the oracle of all wisdom. I had a faculty meeting today and I found that lowering my voice when expressing my opinion, plus humor, cut through some of the above defects. In another situation where I am usually becoming a raging lunatic, through the grace of God, I managed to be calm, soft, and vulnerable. In an important conversation initiating a project I noticed that when I was focusing on the talents of other participants in the project it felt very good but, when I began to boast I felt more insecure, not about the project but about my own progress in the "way of love."

Your examples:

My prayer: Holy Spirit, I can see how You are trying to help me to see the benefits of loving conversation vs. the defects that I am pin-pointing in myself. You also want but to be a good example for others in this area. Keep me from discouragement. Let me see even one victory of love a day as a step toward the goal.

Your prayer:

Day 14: The Challenge of Trying to Converse Lovingly one Whole Day!

Scripture: "If I speak in the tongues of men and of angels, but have not love, I am only a resounding gong or a clanging cymbal." (1 Corinthians 13:1-3)

Dr. Ronda's examples: Pondering the idea of a softer, gentler voice, I thought about how Mary didn't speak loudly to the baby Jesus. Maybe I need to speak gently to the baby Jesus in others?

I did better on this throughout the day, but I noticed that I get bored and even depressed when I only speak lightly and softly! Loud talk with overt or explicit anger could be an adrenalin rush? How terrible! Because I was working on this challenge, in a written conflict with someone on e-mail I managed to express myself lovingly instead of as defensively as I usually would.

Your examples:

My prayer: Holy Spirit, I truly believe that you show us the darkness in us not to make us quail with fear and want to give up on spiritual growth. No! You tell me to persevere and to take seriously the theme of the whole Way of Love project, step by step, even if some days it's one step forward and two steps back. When I feel depressed, from not being able to talk angrily, please fill in that void with graced love from You, the comforter. I renounce the spirit of loud, boastful, self-centered conversation and lay it at Your feet, Lord Jesus. Take it away!

Your prayer:

THEME

3

THE CHALLENGE OF LOVING FORGIVENESS VS. RESENTMENT

"Forgive us our trespasses as we forgive those who trespass against us." (Luke 11:4)

Teaching:

Today we begin theme 3 of The Way of Love: Step by Step – Loving Forgiveness vs. Resentment. Here is the teaching to introduce the challenges of this week. As Christians most of us say the Lord's prayer at least once a day. It includes the incredible challenge of forgiving everyone who has hurt us if we want to be forgiven by God ourselves. Yet how often we hear others say "that is unforgivable." And in our hearts sometimes, even if we say we forgive, we may harbor deadly resentment. "To sin is human; to forgive is divine," is a line from the English poet, Alexander Pope. Most of us know that in the case of really bad hurts to really forgive from the heart comes only with grace from God.

Refusal to forgive can be seen in ways as unloving as hate, bearing grudges, total withdrawal, to milder forms such as avoiding others who want to reconcile. In my book *Taming the Lion Within: Five Steps from Anger to Peace* (see www.rondachervin.com click on Books) I identify as one of the most common underlying reasons for anger. This is that I want to be the heroine of the drama of my life and I want others to be secondary characters or walk-ons who say and do what will enhance my role! Since they are also having the same wish and want me to be a secondary character, they will resist and I will usually feel angry every day.

Here is a story of forgiveness that should help us forgive anyone! A woman told me that her husband left her and their two children to live with another woman. He had 3 daughters with this other woman, but didn't get a divorce from her to marry the second woman. After a few years our heroine of forgiveness agreed to take her husband back for the sake of the children. Then just before the birth of their third child, the man left her again for the second woman. However, this betrayed woman found Jesus and went back to the Catholic Church. Her husband came back to Church as well. He confessed his sins and they enjoyed many years together. On his death bed the other woman called the wife and asked for her forgiveness. She gave it. The second woman and the daughters came to the funeral and they are now all close!

Saint Mother Teresa of Calcutta used to ask the dying if they wanted to go to heaven. When they said "Yes!" she would say, "First you have to forgive."

Maybe your first reaction to this is, "Yes, yes, yes… I can forgive anyone but not that one." If so, don't close your heart. Try. With God all things are possible.

During this week we will look at growing in love by forgiveness in specific areas of our lives: family, friends, bosses, co-workers, God, and lastly, forgiving ourselves.

Day 15: The Challenge of Widening the Scope of Forgiveness

"Forgive seventy time seven." (Matthew 18:22)

Today make a list of all the people you have ever known who you have been angry at whether you have forgiven them or not. (If you are writing things down vs. listing them in your mind, you might want to use initials vs. the names.)

Dr. Ronda's examples: I came up with almost forty names of people who I felt hurt by in big or smaller ways. I pondered this huge number and realized that if I feel hurt by anyone who doesn't want to be just what I want him/her to be, then I will always feel hurt.

Your examples:

My prayer: Oh, my Jesus, You who forgave your torturers during Your passion, in order to usher in the kingdom of love, help me this week. You know the stinging hurt and bitter anguish of the ways I have been wounded. Yet You demand that I forgive. So, put Your merciful heart into mine so that I may receive the balm of mercy to pour out on my enemies, as You did.

Your prayer:

Day 16: The Challenge of Forgiving Family Members

"Father, forgive them, they know not what they do." (Luke 23:24)

Dr. Ronda's examples: I have done healing exercises along these lines many times, but this time I got special new graces of understanding. I always resented that my father was not affectionate. From feeling anxious just today about a present-day father-figure who isn't a teddy bear, I suddenly realized it came from shyness, not from coldness. Then I could forgive my own father as well as this present "father-figure." I saw that my mother felt inferior as a middle child who got little affirmation and that was why she was so critical of everyone – to compensate and feel superior because of her intellect. I forgave her for being so critical of everything I said and did. I saw that my sister was critical of me partly also for the same reason my mother was. I saw that my husband couldn't overcome his poor Jewish ghetto background in the way he wished he could, and that made him jealous of my professional successes. I forgave him for that. I saw that since he was a much more sensual person by nature than I am that it was more of a temptation for him to do certain things that hurt me. I forgave him. With our now adult children I could see why they acted in ways that upset me greatly and I thanked God for how much love there is in their hearts in spite of those actions.

Your examples:

**My prayer: Oh, Jesus, so merciful, compassionate and forgiving,
thank You for these special graces today for forgiveness of family
members. When bad memories or present happenings make me
feel hurt, let me swiftly run to you for comfort and then quickly
forgive my family members.**

Your prayer:

Day 17: The Challenge of Forgiving Friends

*"Love prospers when a fault is forgiven, but dwelling on it
separates close friends." (Proverbs 17:9)*

**Dr. Ronda's examples: I realized that occasionally hurts between
friends have been totally the fault of the friend and I forgave
them. But most often these hurts have come from my wanting
desperately for someone to be something he or she couldn't be
given that person's character. So I can forgive them for not being
"perfect" but more importantly I need to choose friends more
realistically. Or mingle with sadness when they fail me, the
thought that their virtues far outweigh what they can't or won't
give me!**

Your examples:

My prayer: Oh, dear Mother Mary, I am your spiritual daughter. Please whisper in my ear what I need to know so as to be less hurt unnecessarily. With those few friends who truly were gravely at fault in how they treated me, let me forgive them from the heart as you forgave all those who hurt you and Joseph and Jesus.

Your prayer:

Day 18: Forgiving those in Authority: Teachers, Managers, the Church?

"What causes quarrels and what causes fights among you? Is it not this, that your passions are at war within you? ... You covet and cannot obtain, so you fight and quarrel." (James 4: 1-2)

Dr. Ronda's examples: Finding the above Scripture, I realized that I get so angry at anyone in a boss position because I "covet" my will in all situations. Even if I have some justice in my side of a quarrel, I often neglect to even consider that they could be right, at least partly. An example is that I get enraged because-of-the fact that since clergy choose to wear so many layers of clothing under the required vestments that they have temperature needs in the Church at variance with the congregation – they

keep it cold in the winter and crank up the A/C in the summer. Then I have to be cold or uncomfortably swathed in layers of winter clothing at long ceremonies! Instead I should understand why the priests want to wear pants for modesty under the long vestments and "forgive" them for trying to avoid being suffocatingly hot by keeping the Church cooler than I like. I can just offer up my discomfort.

Your examples:

My prayer: Sweet Jesus, have mercy on me for my self-centered desires. I have such a good life compared to most people and yet I manage to obsess about relative trifles. Open my mind and my heart to those in authority so that if I am right I can speak the truth with love, but if I am not right, I may see it, and let go of grievances.

Your prayer:

Day 19: The Challenge of Forgiving School-mates, Co-workers and Neighbors

"Blessed are the peacemakers, for they shall be called sons of God." (Matthew 5:9)

Dr. Ronda's examples: The poet Auden wrote "thou shalt love thy crooked neighbor with thy crooked heart." This means I have to forgive people who by just "being themselves" cause me annoyance and frustration. For example because a co-worker, otherwise wonderful, is lazy about some of her jobs, I have frustration in the part of my job that dove-tails with hers. Because someone is always late, I have to wait around and not do what I want to do. I forgave several such people for these faults of theirs.

A co-worker said he found it hard to forgive people for interrupting conversations with him to answer cell phones. He insisted that this is rarely necessary since there is rarely an emergency, and people do it because they want instant gratification of their need to get in touch with someone. He said we should not answer until we are alone. I had not thought of the rude, unlovingness of this practice of carrying the cell-phone around and interrupting conversations with people right next to me to answer the phone. Because of this friend's admonition, I stopped carrying the cell phone around on ring unless I really need it for work. On another point I saw that I should not do things that aren't necessary that are hard for others to forgive!

Your examples:

My prayer: Father God, since we are made for heaven, how can we help hating all the annoyances of our life on earth and being angry at those who cause them? I hear You telling me that loving forgiveness does more to prepare our souls for heaven than does efficiency in our work. Amen!

Your prayer:

Day 20: The Challenge of Forgiving Ourselves

"Therefore, if anyone is in Christ, he is a new creation. The old has passed away; behold, the new has come." (2 Corinthians 5:17)

Dr. Ronda's examples: I decided to forgive myself today for my worst sins. Even though I have confessed them, I have not always forgiven myself for them. I tried to spend a whole day not speaking in a self-deprecatory way, as I usually do, calling myself an old hag, a chatter-box, etc. I am presently taking a leave of absence from my work place and because of this challenge I took in happily all the love of people for me who say they will miss me. Some I wouldn't have thought would miss me.

Your examples:

My prayer: Dear Jesus, I do believe that You have forgiven all my sins. Thank you for the great gift of the sacrament of reconciliation (confession). I do believe that You want me to believe that in spite of my defects and faults, You find me lovable for begging You to help me moment by moment, step by step. I thank You for the love You show me through family, friends, and colleagues.

Your prayer:

Day 21: The Challenge of asking Forgiveness from those I have Hurt

"You hypocrite, first take the log out of your own eye, and then you will see clearly to take the speck out of your brother's eye." (Matthew 7:5)

Dr. Ronda's examples: I asked forgiveness from my sister who I hurt greatly in the past. In retrospect, I asked forgiveness in my heart from religious classmates I ridiculed before my conversion (I asked this in prayer since I could never find them again); for a boyfriend I rejected because he was too good and made me feel inferior; for harsh judgments of my husband and children. I asked forgiveness for harsh judgments of mentors and friends for their weaknesses. I asked forgiveness in prayer for harsh judgments of confused dissenting Catholic colleagues and priests.

Your examples:

My prayer: Holy Spirit, I am always accusing others of denial but I am often in denial of my harsh unforgiveness. Help me to feel so comforted by Your love that I will have tears of compassion for others in their failings instead of wanting to demand that they be perfect to fit my needs. I renounce the spirit of resentment and harsh judgment and lay it at Your feet, dear Jesus, for You to take away.

Your prayer:

THEME

4

THE CHALLENGE OF APPRECIATING BEAUTY

"Rejoice in the Lord always, again I say rejoice." (Philippians 4:4)

Teaching:

Kierkegaard wrote an interesting analysis of the famous scripture that heads this week's challenge. He said the most important thing in the passage is the word "again." He thought that many of us read "Rejoice in the Lord always..." and immediately think of all the reasons not to rejoice, such as the state of the world, of our finances, our family conflicts, etc. etc. So, St. Paul adds "again I say rejoice" reminding us that no matter what the reasons not to rejoice there is more to rejoice in, especially in our salvation.

I am applying this idea to the reality of beauty. Last week on the challenge of forgiveness could have been arduous. I certainly need a week to lift my soul in joy in the many forms of beauty God has given us. In our week on gratitude we had one day devoted to beauty, but now we will expand our joy in beauty.

St. Thomas Aquinas defined beauty as "the splendor of being." How is that for a beautiful definition! He also wrote that "The beauty of anything created is nothing else than a similitude of divine beauty participated in by things." About beauty in the arts Pope Benedict XVI recently said: "Art is capable of expressing, and of making visible, man's need to go beyond what he sees; it reveals his thirst and his search for the infinite."

During this week may God waft us above all our crosses and difficulties to bask in the beauty around us.

Day 22: The Challenge of Appreciating all the Beauty around you.

"And God saw all that He had made, and behold, it was very good." (Genesis 1:31)

Dr. Ronda's examples: I noticed the beauty of the sound of thunder during the night and thought about rain being beautiful in spite of it being so inconvenient. I admired everything beautiful in our Seminary chapel, especially the singing of the choir for the Immaculate Conception Mass. I rejoiced in the beauty of our celebration dinner, in how wonderful food looks when displayed with flair.

Your examples:

My prayer: Father God, a relative once told me that I was mostly either mad or sad! I felt so bad. Truly there is lots of joy in my heart, but help me to praise You more often, sincerely, for everything beautiful, along the Way of Love, Step by Step.

Your prayer:

Day 23: The Challenge of Finding Beauty in Strangers

"The alien who resides with you shall be to you as a citizen among you; you shall love the alien as yourself, for you were aliens in the land of Egypt: I am the Lord your God." (Leviticus 19:34)

Dr. Ronda's examples: For purposes of finding beauty in strangers, I stretched the above Scripture to let it refer to simply delighting in things about strangers who are different from myself. Since I was traveling, most of these examples were from the airport. Sometimes when I am at the airport I entertain myself by mild ridicule in my head of weird things like women walking in 4 inch high slender heels, etc. This time it was refreshing, instead, in the Way of Love, to look for beauty instead: the beauty of the swirling black hair of a woman, a wonderful poet-like gaunt face of a man, a fur hat that looked

great even though it was fake fur, a tall, lean red-headed man
with such an eager face, the noble face of a Hispanic priest, an
intense look of love of a mother for her teen-daughter, the
demeanor the woman at the ticket counter, full of kind interest in
solving my little problems. I stared at bright pink shoes and lots
more pink (I don't usually like pink but I tried to see into why
the people wearing it might love the bright flashiness of it.) I
enjoyed looking at Afro braids, and at a dull looking man in a
plain grey suit but with bright plaid tie. On arrival, I took the
family out to a Japanese restaurant to celebrate the beginning of
my visit. Usually the waiters and waitresses are Asian, but here
was a very round waitress with a thick Southern accent, and
with a manner full of interest in making us happy with our stay
as her restaurant that we affirmed her greatly by words and tip.

Your examples:

My prayer: Father God, how You love variety, as evidenced in
Your creation of many colored peoples and of the colors we can
use in our garb. Take away my grumbling critical spirit that
wants sameness – i.e. everyone should be a clone of me in my
tastes – so that I can have more joy in daily life.

Your prayer:

Day 24: The Challenge of Appreciating Beauty in Music and the other Arts

"And whenever the harmful spirit from God was upon Saul, David took the lyre and played it with his hand. So Saul was refreshed and was well, and the harmful spirit departed from him." (1 Samuel 16:23)

Dr. Ronda's examples: I used to love silence so much I stopped listening to music on the radio or on my CD's. In the last few years, being in a climate that is often grey during the day, I found myself getting depressed. I started listening to a wonderful Montreal Music radio station for classical music. It is called CJPX-Radio-Classique fm Montreal. Because the ads are in French, which I barely understand, I don't mind the commercials so much. I find that beautiful music lifts depression. Today, because of this challenge, I listened to new composers of the 18th century. I also loved the chant at the high Mass in the little Church I attend in North Carolina. The pastor is a former concert organist and trains the choir so it sounds as if we were in the Sistine chapel.

Your examples:

My prayer: Jesus, may I never let evil spirits bring me down from the joy and hope and can have simply by responding to beauty in music and the other arts. What a wonderful way to do spiritual warfare by letting the way the God-given talents of others praises you through melody and color inspire me.

Your prayer:

Day 25: The Challenge of Showing Appreciation of Beauty in its Lesser Forms

"Finally, brothers, whatever is ...whatever is lovely, whatever is commendable, if there is any excellence, if there is anything worthy of praise, think about these things." (Philippians 4:8)

Dr. Ronda's examples: I love neatness and order but I am less good at cleanliness of person or house. I wear drab denim jumpers that cost $5 at the thrift shop to have more money to give to the poor – this is part of my Dedicated Widow lifestyle (see www.rondachervin.com click on Widows) But today in line with this challenge I wore a nice shiny blue scarf to brighten things up. I have left, for a while, my cell-like austere room at the Seminary, with mostly pictures of Jesus, Mary and the Saints on the wall, to one daughter's log home in North Carolina that has, maybe, a million colorful objects in it. I realize that décor is related to one's values. Both my daughter and her husband love sensory things – lots of art, some by them or the grandkids. They also run the informal family "family museum" including a cedar chest from the 19th century belonging originally to my grandmother. So that would be 5 generations of use! This visit, instead of considering my daughter's house as being cluttered, I appreciated the colorful beauty of the objects on display. For good measure though, with the help of the other visiting grandmother, and one grandson, I alphabetized all the books on the shelves.

Your examples:

My prayer: Dear Mary, you were certainly austere in your life in Nazareth, but in your apparitions you are beautifully arrayed. Help me not to detract from the joy of other peoples' days by sloppiness. Help me to enjoy cleaning as a form of appreciating the beauty of the wood of furnishings, etc.

Your prayer:

Day 26: The Challenge of Appreciating the Beauty of Animals

✓ *"All you beasts, wild and tame, bless the Lord." (Daniel 3)*

Dr. Ronda example: By chance this day coincided with a problem for the tiny Australian shepherd pet of my family. He broke a leg and needed to be in a child's play pen or the lap of one of us to prevent him from putting any weight on the leg. I held him for a while and greatly admired his sad large brown eyes, bewildered by his condition, and his wonderful shaggy tan and black fur. I praised God for the joy to us of pets. The cat, who usually occupies himself playing with the now penned in doggy, chose to spend the night on my bed. He is a marmalade cat with long, glorious white and orange fur. I noticed that his

eye color and expression were quite different from that of my grey and white cat, recently given away. On the drive to Church I thought of all my favorite larger animals and praised God for their creation.

Your examples:

My prayer: Creator God, I marvel and rejoice in the variety of Your works in the animal kingdom. Please help those who rightfully protest cruel forms of animal experimentation and other atrocities. Let me take the time to enjoy petting and watching animals around me as an antidote to tendencies to work-aholism.

Your prayer:

Day 27: The Challenge of Appreciating the Beauty in the Faces of Other Persons

"So we do not lose heart. Though our outer self is wasting away, our inner self is being renewed day by day." (2 Corinthians 4:16)

Dr. Ronda's examples: "The eyes are the windows of the soul," wrote one poet. One of my daughters, also a poet, once wrote: "No one can know what it cost a person to earn his or her face." When I think of the beauty of faces I think primarily about the expression in the eyes. At Church today I looked at people's eyes who were in nearby pews. In one I found a very focused, intent, look; in another softness and sweetness. Another's eyes were especially observant. The priest's large eyes shine with sagacity and amused shrewdness. People seem to like my friendly grin.

Your examples:

My prayer: Holy Spirit, please focus me on this beauty of creation in faces and eyes, radiating the souls of others. Why isn't this beauty more important than their passing words to which I sometimes over-react defensively?

Your prayer:

Day 28: The Challenge of Appreciating Beauty in Jesus, Mary, and the Saints

"A great sign appeared in Heaven, a woman clothed with the sun and the moon at her feet, and on her head a crown of 12 stars and she was with child..." (Revelation 12-13)

Dr. Ronda's examples: Religious art had a big part in my conversion to the Catholic faith (see.www.rondachervin.com, click on free e-books for the leaflet called Saved: the Story of Ronda's Conversion). Miracles connected with art took place in spite of my, then, general dislike of classical art. My favorite paintings of Jesus are Rembrandt's Head of Christ (very Jewish – which is part of my own background) and El Greco's image in his Veronica's veil so starkly tragic of expression. I love the Cimabue old lined face of St. Francis, and Donatello's statue of a gaunt penitential Mary Magdalene. Of Mary my favorite apparition image is Our Lady of Guadalupe, but I also love the "creativity" if you will, of how she appears in the way visionaries of different nationalities would imagine her. Our Lady of Lourdes is relatively simple, but graceful and very feminine. Our Lady of Fatima more gilded. She turns up unexpectedly in different churches I visit in my travels.

Your examples:

My prayer: Our Lady of all the Apparitions, thank you for bending down to us to give us hope in this valley of tears. Thank you, Holy Spirit for inspiring artists and sculptors to give a glimpse of the heavenly beauty of our Savior, or the beauty of His love manifested on the Crucifix. I renounce the spirit of indifference to artistic beauty and lay it at Your feet, dear Jesus, to take it away.

Your prayer:

THEME

5

THE CHALLENGE OF FINDING LOVING WAYS TO GIVE ADVICE

Everyone should be quick to listen, slow to speak ... (James 1:19)

Teaching:

This theme came up because many of us give advice often, regularly, and in a way that others find annoying and even hatefully superior. You might ask people who are in contact with you often whether they want unasked for advice from anyone, even "sage" you?

An adage that carries a lot of truth is that it is better not to give advice unless asked for it. Lots of people talk into order to vent or to bond with the similar troubles of another. They don't want any advice that would involve changing themselves. Giving advice, in those cases, becomes an exercise in futility.

If you never give advice unless asked, you could spend the week observing others to see what is good and what is bad advice in terms of content, but also in terms of negative aspects in the manner of giving such advice that you observe. By contrast, you could affirm people who do ask for advice with a willingness to consider change.

I was startled when a person in Al-Anon (for relatives of alcoholics) told this story: "My alcoholic father left when I was the oldest child. At fourteen years old, I had to take care of the family while my mother was out working. Relatives came giving me advice. I wanted to say, 'Why don't you ask how you could help instead of giving me advice?'" Listening to this woman's complaint I wondered if I do that sometimes – give advice instead of help or only talk instead of feeling empathetically into the pain of the others?

A counselor suggested that it is all in the timing. It is good to listen well first to people with problems, to ponder about those problems, pray for them, and save the advice in readiness for a good time. Often this future time will be better than right away.

Day 29: Observing Loving and Unloving Advice Giving

"He will wipe away every tear." (Revelations 21:4)

Dr. Ronda's examples: I had a lot of instances today where I could practice the principles in the above teaching. I have been a widow for eighteen years but the other grandmother visiting the house where I am is a new widow. Even though I told everyone I would not give advice without being asked, I insisted that the other grandmother widow check out EWTN in England where she lives. I showed her some of the programming. At other times during the day, however, my advice was not so good even if the content was right. Suggesting that in her extreme loneliness she consider moving in with a sister, also a new widow, made no sense since she doesn't get along that well with that widow. Maybe a few years down the line the advice would be better? It seemed better when I just mentioned things that helped me like going to a grief group, instead of telling her that she should do the same. I could clearly observe that I often use quick advice to avoid the pain of empathy.

Your examples:

My prayer: Holy Spirit of love, please help me, step by step, during this long week of trying to practice loving ways to give advice. You know how much I want to help hurting people, but you also know that I enjoy being the "sage." Purify my heart.

Your prayer:

Day 30: The Challenge of Not Giving Advice Automatically

"For we do not have a high priest who is unable to sympathize with our weaknesses..." (Hebrews 4:15)

Dr. Ronda's examples: I told a friend, who has complicated problems and doesn't tell me the whole story, that I couldn't give her advice because I didn't really understand. I apologized to a woman who I gave advice to that hurt her feelings. I realized that my talking too much and without forethought had a lot to do with giving unwanted advice. I prayed to Jesus to tell me more about the people I am judging irritably or cynically. I saw that a person whose offers of help seem smothering did this because she was so hurt as a child that she always wants to make life better for others even when they don't want to be helped. Because I listened instead of talking so much, an old friend revealed that there was severe mental illness in her family tree. This explained a lot I hadn't understood, so that if I ever feel really called to give her advice, it would be better advice for my understanding more of her past.

Your examples:

My prayer: Dear Jesus, I felt discouraged when I realized how pervasive is this trait in my character of giving unwanted advice or hasty advice. I humbly come to you Prince of Peace to ask you to help me be more loving, step by step, so that I may be more truly helpful.

Your prayer:

Day 31: The Challenge of Giving Loving Advice at Work

"Do your best to present yourself to God as one approved, a workman...who correctly handles the word of truth." (2 Timothy 2:15)

Dr. Ronda's examples: In the case of two different groups of people, I am trying to work better with them. Instead of giving my advice, I prayed first and asked the kind of questions that would help them to make good decisions. In another work situation I wrote a polite, non-pressuring letter to the boss of a project asking him how he wanted me to handle a sticky issue. He wrote back right away saying it was fine and would be taken care of. This was better than writing a 2 page single spaced explanation about my side of the story ending with giving him advice about how he should handle the other party.

Your examples:

My prayer: Holy Spirit, help me to give advice and instructions, instead of with an "edge," in the best manner. Help me care more about loving relationships than getting things done my way.

Your prayer:

Day 32: The Challenge of Offering Advice in a Gentle Way

"Because he himself suffered when he was tempted, he is able to help those who are being tempted (Hebrews 2:18).

Dr. Ronda's examples: I wanted to give sarcastic advice but because of this exercise I postponed giving that advice. This was good because I found out many extenuating circumstances leading to a forgiving vs. self-righteous approach to the problem. I asked whether my self-advice is gentle. Self-talk like "You idiot, why did you get involved in that problem in the first place?" could be replaced often by humor in my such as "Well, dearie, if you chose this plan with people with these obstacles to fulfilling it, why are you surprised?...how about applying the Serenity Prayer about seeing the difference between what you can change and what you can't change???"

My prayer: Mother Mary, help me to see that when sarcastic advice wells up it is because I am frustrated in some proud plan of mine that might not really be the plan of God. Help me to pause before giving advice to see if the timing is right.

Your prayer:

Day 33: The Challenge of Loving Advice for Family and Close Friends

"Pray for one another." (James 5:16)

Dr. Ronda's examples: I spent some time with a friend I thought could use Emotions Anonymous (The 12 Step Program for those with Mental Illness). Instead of telling her to try it, I told about my good experience. This was better than trying to coerce her to engage in the program. Someone who is a non-practicing Catholic asked me to pray a novena for her son close to death. Instead of advising her to go back to Church instead of asking me, a stranger, to say a novena for him, I just said I would pray for him. I wrote a suggestion to a friend I was in conflict with in the mildest most neutral FYI type style. I prayed a lot for each of these people.

Your examples:

My prayer: Holy Spirit, you know how depressed I feel when I am not teaching people whether it is appropriate or not! Help me to truly believe that praying for others counts as much as teaching them when it is not appropriate. Let me not say what they will think of as religious clichés. <u>Let me look for what You want me to say.</u>

Your prayer:

Day 34: The Challenge of Loving Freedom enough not to try to Control others through Advice

"But the fruit of the Spirit is love, joy, peace, patience, kindness, goodness, faithfulness, gentleness, self-control…" (Galatians 5:22-23)

Dr. Ronda's examples: Al-Anon teaches that you can only control yourself, not others, but since I had a friend in what seemed to be a life or death situation I pounded in advice. It seemed futile because basically the friend doesn't want to risk what is good in her situation even though she is risking her life. I felt deflated. I tried doing penance for her instead. That felt better. Sometimes when we are working on a virtue, in this case, the virtue of letting go, God shows us how big this is by letting us try the opposite with bad results. Sigh!

Your examples:

My prayer: Holy Trinity, Holy Family, all my intercessor saints, your frustrating project is to try to sanctify me! How can I become good clay in your hands if I am so busy trying to mold others. Even if my intentions are good and loving, my method is often not so good. Please give me the trust to believe that even when I can't help, you can unsnarl even life and death situations. After all, WWII had an end.

Your prayer:

Day 35: The Challenge of Loving Silence

"Be still and know that I am God!" *(Psalm 46:10)*

Dr. Ronda's examples: I thought of this, one of my favorite Scriptures, in relation to giving advice. I saw that the more I trust in God the less I would give unwanted, repetitive advice. There are things my relatives do in a way very different than the way I would do them. My being silent and not giving unwanted advice I got to realize that they are much happier at this time of their lives than I was when I was their age. Then, I was doing it "my way" and trying to force my husband to do it "my way." Not that "my way" is wrong but that this younger couple of relatives compromise better than my husband and I did. I had a tech problem and I was very discouraged and upset. I wrote to the head of the tech administration about this. I was going to call him and consider dropping a big project, but I waited silently for him to respond to the e-mail. As soon as he got to his computer, he jumped onto to Skype to humbly tell me it was his mistake, and it is all fixed. I saw that bearing the discomfort of being silent instead of jumping on the phone got me this grace of a solution. The tech administrator said, "You don't have to worry about problems with tech people. We see problems as just something to fix."

Your examples:

My prayer: Come, Holy Spirit, on this last day devoted to the "Way of Giving Loving Advice, Step by Step", please show me how to benefit from all the fresh insights You have been giving me in this area fraught with tension for me. I renounce the spirit of fixing others by unwanted advice and lay it at Your feet, dear Jesus, to take it away.

Your prayer:

THEME

6

THE CHALLENGE OF LOVING SACRIFICE

"But when Christ appeared as a high priest of the good things to come, He entered through the greater and more perfect tabernacle, not made with hands, that is to say, not of this creation; and not through the blood of goats and calves, but through His own blood, He entered the holy place once for all, having obtained eternal redemption." (Hebrews 9:11-12)

Teaching:

Christianity is about hope but it is also about sacrifice. The very essence of Christianity is the sacrifice of Christ for us on the cross. All of us have to sacrifice just to exist. Sometimes the necessary sacrifices are easier to make than voluntary ones, but sometimes it is the opposite. For example, sometimes working to put bread on the table is easier than giving up a favorite TV program to help a child with homework. But sometimes it is easier to give up some treat for Lent than to perform necessary sacrifices for the family such as commuting on a crowded freeway. However, even penitential saints sometimes chose joy over voluntary penances. I love to think of the highly sacrificial St. John of the Cross taking his contemplative monks out for a pleasant walk in the mountains because they seemed bored. They sang as they strolled, putting religious words into the popular tunes of the day.

Even those of us who try to avoid sacrifices wouldn't want to be considered, well, simply too selfish to make sacrifices for others! Given the healthiness of a normal balance between suffering and joy in life, I find it helpful to realize that doing little sacrificial deeds of love for others is an antidote to depression. How so? Because, as Thomas Aquinas taught, we can only love ourselves loving. Sitting feeling miserable is not being loving. During this week of following a Way of Love: Step by Step through sacrifice, you may find it to be true that making little voluntary sacrifices actually lifts your spirits.

Day 36: The Challenge of Monitoring Loving Sacrifices vs. Signs of Self-Centeredness

"Be ye perfect, as your heavenly Father is perfect." (Matthew 5:48)

Dr. Ronda's examples: I was planning to just do a scorecard on sacrificial vs. self-centered things I saw during a whole day. Instead I jumped into doing more loving things myself such as: returning phone calls when not "in the mood." Disposing of dead squirrel the cat brought into the house since I was first up at a family dwelling I am visiting for Christmas vs. waiting for the men to do it. Sacrifices observed included how even though I said I would do them, my daughter helped with washing the big messy steak pans. I noticed that my son-in-law turned off the A/C so I wouldn't be so cold. At Mass I racked up all the sacrifices to make the Church so beautiful for Christmas when many non-practicing Catholics and other Christians come, but also just for us, the regulars. Even though he celebrates 4 Masses on the weekends, my Pastor makes the sacrifice to say a Saturday AM Mass in honor of Mary throughout the year. Watching the noble, very formal way He says Mass, I realized that although I don't like formality when repressed people exhibit it, when a free-spirited type like this Pastor is highly formal at the Mass, it is different. I could see how he becomes formal as a priest because he loves so much the sacred meaning of the Mass, not because he prefers formality in general. A sacrifice I made later was being in the family room having to listen to a Christmas Medley with such "shocks" as Bach was followed by a song asking Rudolf the Red Nose Reindeer to provide a "rock" Christmas.

Your examples:

My prayer: Jesus, we like to sacrifice for others in ways we choose, but only You can make us want to sacrifice for others when we are forced to by life, or by obedience, or "compelled" promptings of the Holy Spirit. This week as we struggle with following the Way of Love: Step by Step, be with us moment by moment urging us on.

Your prayer:

Day 37: The Challenge of Little Deeds of Love

"Do unto others as you would have others do unto you." (Matthew 7:12)

Dr. Ronda's examples: This is Christmas day and most of the little deeds of love were from family members to others family members in the way of personally delightful gifts. I did lots of dishes. I took out garbage sometimes even though it is a chore of the grandsons. We have a custom I modified from a traditional one: throughout Advent kids put a piece of straw in a box to line the Nativity on Christmas Eve. I adapted this successfully to each night of Advent the kids put a piece of yarn into the crèche when they do something good and then Christmas Eve we braid them into a blanket for baby Jesus. Mostly my little good deeds were biting my tongue to avoid being negative about the luxurious Christmas and instead affirming everything that was good, such as my daughter's custom of making cupcakes for Jesus' birthday and singing Happy Birthday to Him to involve the little kids in something they understand. My son-in-law, who doesn't go to Church, lit more candles around the living room as part of his way of observing Christmas. In the midst of all this came this little miracle. Before the Christmas dinner I was reading Pope Benedict's beautiful Christmas Eve sermon. It has much reference to seeing beneath the materialism the simplicity of the infant Jesus. I begged my daughter to let me read portions of it at the dinner. Since she doesn't go to Church any more I was amazed when she said, "Oh, yes. I just read it. The whole sermon was linked to on the first page of Google News!"

Your examples:

Prayer: Dear St. Mother Teresa of Calcutta, you said we should do little things with much love. We try and sometimes it comes out well, and other times we are suddenly shocked to find we have inadvertently hurt someone's feelings. Please intercede for us that our thoughts, words and deeds be truly loving in intent, wisdom, and effect.

Your prayer:

Day 38: The Challenge of Sacrifice in Prayer

"Offer up the sacrifice of praise" (Hebrews 13:15)

Dr. Ronda's examples: I think I have a mild form of ADD where I have great trouble sitting still. I am always fidgeting with my chap-stick, writing down little reminders on post-its, etc. I decided to see what it would be like if whenever I was at prayer or Mass to take care of little needs beforehand. As a result I did experience greater recollection at Mass and Liturgy of the Hours and quiet prayer.

Your examples:

My prayer: Mary, our great model for praying whole-heartedly, I can't imagine you interrupting prayer to do little unnecessary things. I picture you with serenity doing many little things with love, but then in prayer focusing your whole mind, heart and soul on God. Would you be my mother in this area of my life?

Your prayer:

Day 39: The Challenge of Bending to the Way of Others

"Love is not arrogant…" (1 Corinthians 13:4)

Dr. Ronda's examples: A relative asked if she could tell me the one thing that makes me hard to live with. Of course, since I am working on the Way of Love: Step by Step, I absolutely had to say she could. She said that I act kind of like a VIP who others should drop what they are doing to help. I would have used the older term "prima donna." She said it is not because I am arrogant exactly, but because I am so workaholic I am crazy for closure and so think everyone should help me finish my great works right away. Well, that is kind of arrogant because it presupposes that what others are doing isn't as important! So I spent the day trying to ask for favors in a more open-ended way such as "Whenever you have a moment to spare, could you possibly help me with "x." That was a sacrifice, as it turned out since it is now 2 days that one relative didn't find a minute to help me with something I was going to do for this blog! I made other small sacrifices such as cleaning a tub in the guest-bathroom that seemed just stained irrevocably but did yield slightly to brillo and what my generation called "elbow grease."

Your examples:

Prayer: Jesus, help me to accept that sacrifice is necessary in all human situations. I will never be exempt until I reach heaven. And it is because of Your sacrifice that I hope someday for that freedom from small and big suffering. Help me this week where I am visiting family to eagerly make small sacrifices for the good of family fun and fellowship, on the way of love: step by step.

Your prayer:

Day 40: The Challenge of Keeping Promises in a Timely Way

"If a man vows a vow to the Lord, or swears an oath to bind himself by a pledge, he shall not break his word. He shall do according to all that proceeds out of his mouth". (Numbers 32:5)

Dr. Ronda's examples: One of my pet peeves is people who make promises and then get angry if I remind them. Instead of doing what she or he promises, which would involve a small sacrifice, such people blame me for being a nag. It seems so unfair. To use examples from the lives of others: a husband promises to get his wife's car fixed ... fails to do so and then it breaks down on the road, or a wife promises to clean up the house but postpones this irksome task until the house looks like a pig-sty. Generally I am good at keeping promises but when I started working on this day of the Way of Love: Step by Step, the Holy Spirit seemed to smile at me and say, "How about the promises you make to God, such as prayers you mean to say daily or an hour a day minimum of quiet prayer in His presence? ... Does God get furious if you don't do it, or does He find gentle ways to urge you to keep those promises such as when you get cranky and miserable because you are too little in His presence He draws You into prayer?" As a result of this gentle admonition to me about prayer, I thought for at least this day I should find gentle, humorous ways to remind others of their promises vs. nagging or grumbling, even in my head.

Your examples:

My prayer: Oh, dear Jesus, you beg us to forgive. Sometimes I can forgive big things better than tiny things if these immediately impact my agenda. Please help me to forgive such littler things and give me wisdom to see if I can improve them without rancor.

Your prayer:

Day 41: The Challenge of Suffering with Trust

"God is for us a refuge and strength, a helper close at hand, in time of distress." (Psalm 46)

Dr. Ronda's examples: Working on this challenge in the Way of Love: Step by Step I asked myself what my present sufferings were. Mostly they involve insecurity about the future and whether the plans I have made will work or not. I realized that trust is a sacrifice. How so? It is a sacrifice of some morbid pleasure we get in being pessimistic or in obsessing over possible future negatives? In trust I sacrifice the false idea that by obsessing over things out of my control I can make them better. Instead I gently give them to God whose providence means that whatever the outcome He can bring good out of it. After pondering these ideas I did a long prayer on my mercy chaplet of just praying over and over again "Jesus, I trust in you."

Your examples:

My prayer: Father God, You have taken care of me for 74 years now. You have brought me through much greater sufferings than I now have to bear. I bring to you my fears for the future and ask You to give me the trust You deserve.

Your prayer:

Day 42: The Challenge of Offering Every Sacrifice to God for a Whole Day

"Bear one another's burdens…" (Galatians 6:2)

Dr. Ronda's examples: The alarm clock didn't wake me. I woke up late with only ½ hour max to get ready and drive 20 minutes away but I did it as a tiny sacrifice of going to Mass without my wake-up tea. Regular confessions are from 4 PM – 4:45 PM on Saturdays. Since the Church is 20 minutes away I thought of asking the priest, who is also a good friend, to hear my confession after the morning Mass. I hesitated because I feel uneasy asking any "father figure" for favors. Then I thought that if the priest choses to hear confessions only once a week it is good for him to be eager to hear confessions when people want to go during the week. It was a sacrifice to overcome my hesitancy in the fear of annoying the priest. As it turned out he was as pleasant as can be about it. I felt very happy because I find it awful when lay people are afraid of the priest concerning asking him to do things that are part of his role. I called someone who wrote a real letter for Christmas vs. one of the letters sent to 500 friends and relatives. I tried to make bread with my daughter's new bread-maker even though I was afraid of lousing it up since the directions disappeared with Christmas wrap. The sacrifice is to tackle tech stuff even if I might feel stupid. I called a friend who misses me since I will be gone for a while from being near to her. I took a little walk even though I don't like exercise that much (because it's good for me). I wrote a letter of amends to someone who might be angry at me.

Your examples:

My prayer: Thank you, Holy Spirit, for inspiring me to put this theme of making sacrifices into the Way of Love: Step by Step. I renounce the spirit of lazy self-centeredness, dear Jesus, and lay it at Your feet to take away.

Your prayer:

THEME

7

THE CHALLENGE OF BEING FRIENDLY

"A friend loves at all times..." (Proverbs 17:17)

Teaching:

In the wonderful Legion of Mary way of evangelizing, team members are told that the greatest way to win others for Christ is by making friends of them. Of course, we all know that people will listen to us if they feel we love them and be wary and distancing if they think we just want them as statistics for our own merit badges.

As well, being friendly is just a basic part of being loving. We may excuse ourselves for being withdrawn, shy, impolite or even rude on the basis that "not everyone can put a fake smiley face on all day long." Of course, insincere friendliness is not the Way of Love. However, what the Holy Spirit of love wants for each of us is that we be truly friendly as a response to the goodness, neediness, or even enmity of others. That is just Gospel! They say in 12 Step "Say what you mean, but don't say it mean!"

Of course, outward friendliness is easier for extroverts than introverts or those who are shy. Just the same, we have to overcome whatever is part of our nature or a result of wounds of the past that keeps us from being hurtful to others. Many shy people appear to others as unfriendly and even arrogant! As one pundit put it: "we need to be wounded healers not wounded, wounders!"

During this week we will go step by step exhibiting different kinds of friendliness. Being polite, I believe, is the minimum of friendliness, yet sometimes when I am in a bad mood I simply ignore others, fail to say thank you for little favors or services, and hide behind an unfriendly façade.

Let's see how it feels to be friendly in all circumstances this week such as home, the marketplace, with fellow workers, at Church.

Day 43: Monitoring my own and others' Friendliness Moment by Moment

"A man that hath friends must show himself friendly." (Proverbs 18:24)

Dr. Ronda's examples: I noticed that "night people" are often quite unfriendly and withdrawn in the morning. I am all chirpy and people who are half-asleep in the AM don't like it. I diagnosed this as the reason someone was unfriendly when I made a request. But another person was very friendly and helpful who I didn't expect to be. I sent a print out of something to two people who don't use e-mail so they could enjoy it ⁄. Usually I think, in an unfriendly manner, that if people didn't go through the hell I did to learn tech then why should I bother with snail mail. At Church there is a woman who always greets friends but also anyone who looks lonely before daily Mass. I know some of us, me included, would prefer silence before Mass but this woman is so genuine. She is in dreadful pain all the time which she offers up for everyone. I think it is sign of great friendliness that she greets people.

Your examples:

My prayer: Saints of God, when I think of you I always think you were recollected, aware of the presence of the Trinity all the time, yet I also picture you as friendly so that others knew that you loved them. Please intercede for me that I may always be both aware of God and also friendly.

Your prayer:

Day 44: The Challenge of being Polite and Helpful

"How good and pleasant it is for brethren to be together." Psalm 133:1

Dr. Ronda's examples: Someone said, since it is hard to change the worst things that can happen in life, we ought to be as good as possible about the little things. Politeness is surely one of these. I said good morning and a few words even to people who are too sleepy in the morning to initiate greetings or sometimes to respond. I tried doing helpful things – one boomeranged. I decided to bring in a huge trash bin from the road to its place near the house to help a grandson whose chore that is. On the way I fell and scrapped a knee – there is also a large bruise on my hand. Well, I can offer it up and not do those kind of helpful things again! I identified rudeness in an incident where a friend asked me which diner I wanted to go to for lunch. She started listing the advantages of a few. I barked back rudely "Hey, I am want to talk to you. I don't want to waste time fussing over which restaurant we go to." She looked hurt and said, "I just wanted you to have a treat." Mea culpa. At Mass I thought that to be polite to the Lord is to say prayers reverently not just to say them.

Your examples:

My prayer: Oh, dear Lord, once I get concrete about becoming more loving step by step, I realize so many areas of being unloving on my part. A lot come from blurting things out without thinking of their effect on another. May the Holy Spirit of love make me as loving in small things as our Blessed Mother must have been.

Your prayer:

Day 45: The Challenge of Smiling Lovingly

"A glad heart makes a cheerful face." (Proverbs 15:13)

Dr. Ronda's examples: I am known for my smile, but I realized, working on this challenge, that it is sporadic, especially if I am in a low mood. So I had to pay attention today to smiling at people I met in Church. I could see that strangers seemed pleased and surprised that I smiled at them. I also practiced smiling at myself in my thoughts and at Jesus, Mary and Joseph. In a work situation, I saw that, in some cases, smiling was related to not bearing grudges or blaming others in a situation where I wished that some others would do something they don't usually do. I gave a talk at a place I used to do ministry in and I could see that people who came appreciated my previous friendliness to them. I purposely smiled a lot at some who I didn't know too well.

Your examples:

My prayer: Oh my Jesus, Mary and Joseph, I have a picture I drew of you three smiling at me. I think of Christians I have known with many heavy crosses, who yet smiled often in a touching way to show their love for me and others. May I never consider that depressed feelings are more real than love.

Your prayer:

Day 46: The Challenge of a Loving Touch

Dr. Ronda's examples: I recalled that bumper sticker "how many hugs did you give your kid today?" Since I am with family right now, touching people is easy, but I noticed doing it that I feel good hugging them even if they don't return the gesture. I was with an old friend I hadn't seen in years. It felt good that we patted each other during very emotional sharings. The same with members of her family I hadn't seen in a long time. Some of the widows in the Church here are still having a once a month lunch with prayer and conversation. I was part of the start of it years ago. Because of this challenge I was even more outgoing than usual.

Your examples:

My prayer: Mother Mary, I believe that you were the warmest motherly woman who ever lived. My speculation is that people loved to touch you. Help us to be so truly chaste that no one will misjudge us if we reach out, especially to those who are lonely.

Your prayer:

Day 47: The Challenge of Lovingly Affirming Others

"Two are better than one, because they have a good return for their work: if one falls down, his friend can help him up. But pity the man who falls and has no one to help him up!" (Ecclesiastes 4:9-10)

Dr. Ronda's examples: I realized that a huge aspect of the Way of Love: is affirming vs. criticizing others. Even if we are correct in our critical assessments, generally people need lots of affirmation in order to persevere through this valley of tears, step by step. An example that surfaced for me was seeing again a Guatamalan charismatic leader at the parish here where I used to live and minister. Although he is an incredibly effective minister to the Hispanic community, since his English is not perfect, he was very anxious about applying for the deacon program. The Anglo-Pastor urged him on and I wrote a letter of recommendation greatly affirming him for being a dynamite preacher but also full of prudence and compassion – qualities that don't always go with being a dynamite preacher. I knew the people who run the deacon preparation program would need to know about his prudence since most non-charismatics worry that such leaders can become cult-idols. Seeing him again, one year into the program, I realized how important my affirmation of him was also for him. During the day I also made a point of affirming people for small things like their hair style or whatever.

Your examples:

My prayer: Holy Spirit of love, I have always wondered why some find it so much easier to criticize than to affirm when affirmation has such great effects. Yet, I, too, spend a lot of time criticizing others, often harshly, in my head if not in words. Help me to love to affirm others, not only verbally, but also in those inner conversations. May I always be conversing inwardly, not with devils, but with You.

Your prayer:

Day 48: Loving Phone Calls or E-mails to Distant Family and Friends

"Rejoice with them that do rejoice, and weep with them that weep." (Romans: 12:15)

Dr. Ronda's examples: I wrote an e-mail to my far away sister telling her how eager I am to see more of her after my move to Los Angeles. I wrote to very dear new friends thanking them for a year's companionship. I e-mailed a distant godchild and invited him to visit me when I am nearer during my leave of absence from the seminary. I wrote to the Watershed leaders to

thank them for this time of sharing their entries and my
gratitude for their hosting my blog.

Your examples:

My prayer: Dear Holy Family, I think you were a hearth of love
to all in your neighborhood as well as visiting families and
friends. May no one among my family and friends ever feel that
I am distancing myself from them by being "too busy" to relate.

Your prayer:

Day 49 : The Challenge of being Friendly all Day Long

"A cheerful look brings joy to the heart..." (Proverbs 15:30)

Dr. Ronda's examples: Tomorrow I leave this part of my family
in North Carolina to go to another part of my family in
California. Sometimes near to leave-taking I go into a kind of
sour-grapes mode – i.e. if I don't think you guys are so
wonderful I won't hate to leave so much. Because of this
challenge of the Way of Love, I will come against this tendency
and shower this part of my family with the love and gratitude
for them that is truly in my heart.

Your examples:

My prayer: **Thank you, Father God, for the gift of my life. Thank you for the wonderful traits of the members of my family, my husband and children passed on and here on earth, for our Pastor, and for my friends here in this part of the country. May the way I show friendliness to each of them shine forth as more than conventional patter, but real love as step by step I leave them for now. I renounce the spirit of unfriendliness and lay it at your feet, dear Jesus. Take it away!**

Your prayer:

THEME

8

THE CHALLENGE OF BEING LOVINGLY PATIENT

"For this reason, since the day we heard about you, we have not stopped praying for you.... so that you may live a life worthy of the Lord and please him in every way... being strengthened with all power according to his glorious might so that you may have great endurance and patience..." (Colossians 1:9-11)

Teaching:

Some opposites of patience would be irritability, nagging, and pushiness. One aspect of the virtue of patience is flexibility vs.

rigid insistence of everything being done on time even when this is not absolutely necessary. Impatient people, such as myself, tend, really, to value order above loving compromise with the ways of others. Whereas we are never to compromise on moral truth and behavior, impatient people tend to make orderliness and efficiency about neutral matters imperative. As if, for instance, neatness was more important than kindness.

I once read a novel by Anne Tyler about a woman married into a family that was dreamy and creative rather than practical. After years of chafing at the irrational ways of her husband and the rest of the family, she realized that providence put her in this family exactly because they had such need of a person as practical and rational as she was.

In the Myers/Briggs Personality Tests, one polarity is between those who tend to be laid-back trying to see what is best to choose as situations unfold vs. those who try to control outcomes through tight planning. Clearly, to be loving we need to relate to each circumstance of life in the most loving way, sometimes very flexibly and open-endedly, and at others with planning out of respect for the needs of others.

In a broader context, Kierkegaard insisted that all sins come from impatience. Consider: I could be violent in action or in words because I can't stand waiting for another to obey my will. I could lie in order to get what I want without painfully waiting for something to happen in the right way. I could lie because I don't have the patience to convince another to forgive me or to endure punishment and instead try to cover up my misdeeds. I could indulge in sexual sin because I don't have the trust to wait for a spouse God may send or wait for fulfillment of my greatest longings for intimacy until I can get these in a spiritual way when I am in heaven. I rage at others because I hate what is happening, refusing to patiently accept the sufferings of life that I cannot change or avoid.

Essentially loving patience comes from trust that, even if I cannot get what I want, God will provide what I really need on earth or in heaven.

Day 50: The Challenge of Observing Impatience and Patience in Ourselves and in those Around Us

"It is better to live in a desert land than with a contentious and vexing woman." (Proverbs 21:19)

Dr. Ronda's examples: A friend was supposed to meet me at a given time. She didn't show up. I called and didn't get an answer. I drove off impatiently. Ten minutes later she called. It was a misunderstanding. I exercised patient love by turning back to our meeting place to see her. A relative judged me a little harshly over an issue I thought she misunderstood. Instead of stomping off impatiently, I addressed the matter lovingly and sweetly and let it go that I couldn't bring her around to totally understanding me. We have differences where I live about neatness. Instead of cleaning up a mess but grinding my teeth impatiently, I patiently asked if some others could help me clean up. We did it together in no time. In general, I found that I could see solutions to trivial problems that came up when I didn't work up the impatience.

Your examples:

My prayer: Blessed Trinity: is the whole of creation, redemption, and salvation history, for You, one big exercise in patience? You could have been too "impatient" to create anything, instead being enfolded in your own Trinitarian happiness with each other! But, no, You willed to share Your joy with temporal creatures whose lives unfold gradually! Only through the grace of trust can we bear the length of this step by step journey. May it be, not a way of resistance, but a "way of love."

Your prayer:

Day 51: The Challenge of Overcoming Impatience Expressed in Speech

"Clothe yourselves therefore, as God's own chosen ones (His own picked representatives), [who are] purified and holy and well-beloved [by God Himself, by putting on behavior marked by] tenderhearted pity and mercy, kind feeling, a lowly opinion of yourselves, gentle ways, [and] patience [which is tireless and long-suffering, and has the power to endure whatever comes, with good temper." (Colossians 3:12)

Dr. Ronda's examples: I needed lots of patience with travel. I thought about how on 5 hour flights they don't serve free food as they used to years ago. I was annoyed about how there is no room for small valises in the overhead bins, because people rightly don't like paying $27 to check their bigger valises. I thought about all this without getting impatiently fussed up, figuring that is just the way it is going to be to keep costs down on flights. Usually I would feel a need to talk rancorously about these changes with the other passengers while waiting on line. I felt more serene not doing that number this time!

Your examples:

My prayer: Holy Spirit of Peace, help me to see how peaceless it truly is to be impatient most of the time. Let me value true peace from accepting what I cannot change.

Your prayer:

Day 52: The Challenge of Overcoming Feelings of Impatience when Frustrated

"Moreover [let us also be full of joy now!] let us exult and triumph in our troubles and rejoice in our sufferings, knowing that pressure and affliction and hardship produce patient and unswerving endurance." (Romans 5:3)

Dr. Ronda's examples: I was dying to see the new house my daughter in Los Angeles is renting and moving into within a few days and also the Church that I prayed would be in walking distance. A mile is walking distance surely, but for an oldie like me, maybe not, so I wanted to see how far it really was. We went to see the house, prior to moving in, but it was not deemed that there was time to pass the Church. I felt crest-fallen and very impatient, but I held it in and offered it up and that way prevented making the day ugly for the others on the trip. Then I got an upset stomach from something I ate – unusual for me. Since I wanted to help packing I didn't want to be running to the toilet all afternoon. My daughter gave me a prescription medicine she had around. It had the funny effect of making me go into some kind of minor amnesia for 12 hours. When informed about this, I felt frightened. It turned out all right, but I was impatient that we couldn't quite figure it out and it messed up all my packing goals. I am having to PATIENTLY await the return of normal energy since I feel groggy today, a crucial last minute packing day. I don't have much choice, but the choice is, with God's grace, to curb the impatient reaction in favor of humble resignation. I didn't know if all the cars would be needed for the move so I couldn't get to Mass. Here in Los Angeles it would take $100 in a taxi to get back and forth to Mass even though it's 3 miles away.

Your examples:

My prayer: Jesus, how slow life on earth most have been to you after the eternal/infinite/all togetherness of heaven! You chose to embrace this our slow frustrating state of being. Help us value sweet resignation over efficiency.

Your prayer:

Day 53: The Challenge of Approaching Work Goals Patiently

"By your steadfastness and patient endurance you shall win the true life of your souls." (Luke 21:19)

Dr. Ronda's examples: These examples are all about the "work" of moving. I do everything very systematically months in advance but that is not the style of my daughter and her family. So it requires patience to deal with all kinds of last minute glitches. I am reminded of some statistics that say people rate as the worst: 1. death, 2. Having to speak in public, and, 3. moving. At the moment my daughter has computer work to do, so we have to interrupt the marathon shove everything into boxes moving plans. I will just work on other things patiently instead of trying to hasten things. This morning involves putting everything into U-Haul that didn't get into the Pods. I realized that humor is good for patience. I felt a little sting that someone barked at me over a trivial remark, but then he got humorous and it was fine. I should copy that humor when in stress. Actually, I think, that is typical of men in "work" situations – they bark. They wouldn't offer profound apologizes but crack jokes to show that you are not in their bad books. I enjoy seeing how the men in the family, son-in-law, grandson, and weight lifter Marine friend moved things so swiftly and efficiently.

Your examples:

My prayer: Father God, creator of super-abundance. After the Fall we have to live with the paradox that we want many things but having many things means multifarious complications in how to organize, tend, clean, and deal with these realities. Help me to be patient in my desire for a heaven without such complications. Thank you for sending Jesus to assure us of that hope. May we be purged of the sin that impedes the kingdom on earth as it is in heaven.

Your prayer:

Day 54: The Challenge of Exercising Loving Patience in the Family

"We pray] that you may be invigorated and strengthened with all power according to the might of His glory, [to exercise] every kind of endurance and patience (perseverance and forbearance) with joy." (Colossians 1:11)

Dr. Ronda's examples: Since usually, as a dedicated widow, I live alone and very simply, I had forgotten what it's like to have a whole big family moving house! The set-backs are a proof that this spiritual marathon "Way of Love: Step by Step" is not a luxury but a necessity. Without the Holy Spirit reminding me every minute of the 3 days of packing, moving, and unpacking, that love is more important than any conflicts, I think I would have lost it. And I was but a minor player as the helping grandma! For me, the biggest part is not thinking that when everyone is at their worst what they do and say represents their "real" selves. Anyhow, the easiest part, as it turned out, was setting up the computers, so the possible week long hiatus in these blogs will not happen, after all.

Your examples:

My prayer: Jesus, if you thought of our worst selves as our real selves, you would have kept Noah's flood going until the end of the universe! Help us to forgive and forget whatever goes on under extreme stress and be happy for better days of "normal life" when our faults are a little less vivid.

Your prayer:

Day 55: The Challenge of Loving Patience with Brothers and Sisters in the Church

"Do not kick against the goad." (Acts 9:5)

Dr. Ronda's examples: Each of us can imagine the perfect parish Church we would like to be part of. Moving to a new home and checking out nearby parishes is certainly a challenge in terms of loving patience about whatever might not be either to one's taste or, worse, one's convictions. Let me start with what is great about the nearest one to me: it is 7 minutes walking distance in sunny California which means the road will not often have to deal with distracted philosopher Ronda at the wheel! It is a huge Church with 10 Saturday evening and Sunday Masses. At the 7 AM Sunday Mass the parking lot was crowded! The Pastor is magisterial. They have no talking before or during or even after the Mass but plenty of coffee and donuts even after daily Mass. On Martin Luther King day one of the two early AM Masses had more than a hundred parishioners for a partly sung Mass and Benediction! They have ample opportunities for pro-life and social justice ministry.

So, what could be wrong? To fulfill the challenge of loving patience with brothers and sisters in the Church I will not itemize these features!

Your examples:

My prayer: Dear Mary, Mother of the Church, whatever is not what your Son would want in His Church you sorrowed over. And now, from heaven, you intercede for any of us who are longing to correct certain things but have not the authority or a way. If we are patient, and there is a way, show us what to do. Meanwhile, keep us from kicking at the goad.

Your prayer:

Day 56: The Challenge of 24 hours of Loving Patience

"The gifts of the spirit are...and self-control." (Galatians 5:23)

Dr. Ronda's examples: Lots of impatience with the cold. I am planning to buy a spot heater since everyone around me likes it colder than I do, but I keep postponing it dreaming that from walking to Church, for instance, my circulation will improve. Someone told me not to make noise. I was impatient since I thought my noise was inevitable and the request of the other was whimsical. I don't like waiting for the walk sign at traffic intersections. I have to wait for the pastor of my new Church to get back from retreat before talking to him about my future ministries in his Church. The internet goes on and off because of my new location. All of these trivial difficulties made me impatient but, because of this exercise in the Way of Love: Step by Step, I checked the reaction and offered everything up for heavy prayer intentions.

Your examples:

My prayer: Father God, as I leave the theme of patience to go onto other themes, I pray that You will send the Holy Spirit to remind me of how ugly impatience really is and how beautiful and loving patience is. I renounce the spirit of impatience and lay it at Your feet, dear Jesus. Take it away.

Your prayer:

THEME

9

THE CHALLENGE OF LOVING GENEROSITY

"As for the rich in this present age, charge them not to be haughty, nor to set their hopes on the uncertainty of riches, but on God, who richly provides us with everything to enjoy. They are to do good, to be rich in good works, to be generous and ready to share, thus storing up treasure for themselves as a good foundation for the future, so that they may take hold of that which is truly life".
(1Timothy 6:17-19)

Teaching:

Generosity is such a loving Christian trait! Some people make fun of people who give money but not time or personal ministry to the poor. Some of these same mockers live way beyond the simple and austere life-style recommended by the Church. This will be a later theme. For now, I think that since money is so precious to those of us in first world countries, giving money to the needy is an excellent form of generosity. Some say, well, all those charities are frauds – half the money goes for salaries greater than what I make, etc. To this, I always teach choose a charity you trust. For me this is Missionaries of Charity run by nuns and brothers who don't even feel entitled to toilet paper! And pro-life groups I know personally. And, of course, my parish Church, where I get the infinite value of the Holy Eucharist, so I need to support all that makes that possible in terms of money for the expenses of the rectory, sacristy, parish offices, heat, A/C, etc. etc.

Generally, the really poor do not have computers and would not be reading or listening to these teachings! However, I find that the poor are often the most generous in helping others. Consider the famous example Mother Teresa used to recount of herself bring rice to a starving family only to find that they divided it with others even more starving!

But, of course, I know many people who consider giving time generously to be their ministry, in such forms as parish work, direct help to the poor and other needs of social justice, and, above all, generous time for the family. I consider it unjust for some who are heavily involved with other ministries to consider

as selfish those who don't do parish work but who take care of their families, young and elderly, plus often with single adults or both parents working outside the home or on computers out of their home offices.

The opposite of generosity is selfishness or, one might say, a certain tightness now called "entitlement" where someone is reluctant to extend him/herself both financially or with regard to time.

Day 57: Observing Generosity and Tightness of all kinds in Ourselves and those Around us.

Dr. Ronda's examples: I notice people coming early to the daily Mass to set up the coffee and snacks. My daughter here in LA spends hours talking on the phone to friends who are lonely. These same friends provide loving concern for her troubles on the phone. A god-child of mine who is disabled and home-bound, talks for hours to people in her town who come to visit her and need her excellent advice. Both my daughters generously spend time making delicious meals for the family. The parish donates food to the hungry and people donate time to help run that same ministry. I sometimes charge for my time as a speaker, writer and teacher, but very often offer this free of charge.

Your examples:

My prayer: Dear Jesus, You exhorted us to be generous. I am very generous in some ways but tight about others, especially about time when someone's needs conflict with my agenda. Please help me let go of that agenda mostly involving working for strangers, to helping others who are near.

Your prayer:

Day 58: The Challenge of Giving Money

"Whoever is generous to the poor lends to the LORD, and he will repay him for his deed." (Proverbs 19:17)

 Dr. Ronda's examples: It is my joy to give to the starving. Maybe because I am always so hungry from a diabetic condition, I hate to think of anyone hungry who could be helped by me or others I could inspire to do the same. I don't feel especially called to feed strangers myself but, as in the teaching, I look for charities that I trust. Today, after making sure all my necessities that came with my move were taken care of, I was able to send good sums to the Missionaries of Charity, pro-life, and an American priest with a parish of some 30,000 villagers of the area where his Church is a source of lunches for the kids of working mothers. It is a drug area where the priest is in danger of his life every day.

Your examples:

My prayer: Father God, thank you for the gift of abundance of resources I have always enjoyed in the United States and for work that I love. Thank you also for the gift of such joy in wisdom so that I do not need as much of physical goods as others may really do.

Your prayer:

Day 59: The Challenge of Generous Hospitality

And whoever gives one of these little ones even a cup of cold water... truly, I say to you, he will by no means lose his reward." (Matthew 10:42)

Dr. Ronda's examples: Even with take-out, dinner guests can be a big deal. My daughter had 4 friends over. Recently moved into a new home, the idea of take-out seemed like an obvious choice. She ran into a super-market with a special for Chinese New Year so we had glorious delicacies to serve. I have this little joke: "everyone talks about fulfillment, but the only time I ever see anyone looking fulfilled is eating a good meal." Sure enough what with the gourmet foods and delicious saki, etc., soon all of us looked happy as can be. In the process some guests went beyond the usual helpfulness, such as a tough Navy Seal agreeing to cut the heads off the tilapia fish and a woman baking something Chinese she had never heard of before. Of course, there is also the less fun or exciting daily hospitality. When any parents ever tells me they are afraid they aren't spiritual enough, I quote Jesus and ask them how many paper cups of water they have given the their children over the years. I like the way this part of my family also welcomes guests to stay over. I also see generosity in the business world where, for example, my daughter shares so much expertise in her training work on computers. Since I am the least good cook in my family, my hospitality is in cleaning up before, during and after. A friend once helped me understand the goodness of this by saying that cleaning before guests come she saw as a ritual of loving welcome.

Your examples:

My prayer: Dear Mother Mary of Cana, I once was told of a traditional belief that your family was part of the group called the "gleaners" who not only picked up the left-over grain in the field but also catered festive occasions. At a time when many carry heavier workloads outside the home than in the past, hospitality has become even more sacrificial. Help us women to love this traditional role and help our men to be willing to help us perform it.

Your prayer:

Day 60: Working Lovingly in a Generous, Cheerful Manner

"Each one must give as he has decided in his heart, not reluctantly or under compulsion, for God loves a cheerful giver.".(2 Corinthians 9:7)

Dr. Ronda's examples: I decided to do something to help another, but then I didn't want to drive there because it was raining and I am a poor driver and do not yet know my way around. I kind of forced myself to do it, offering it up for the goal of helping this person and it came out wonderfully. I cleaned up after a gathering. I see it as my job to clean and God gave me the love to do it cheerfully. I sorted out files from the move and felt peaceful instead of grumpy because of this step in the Way of Love. Part of my work (ministry) is running a group called Recovery, International (not 12 step). I undertook to do this by phone since I left the group for my sabbatical. I found a lot of joy in being with these old friends even though I generally don't like speaking on the phone. This was my first time here going door to door for Legion of Mary evangelization. It required some sacrifice because I like to be near food and bathrooms all the time. It felt good making the sacrifice since we met one man who was really glad to see us because he goes to the Catholic Church but his wife doesn't and we set up to see his wife sometime. He remarked honestly that since they have marital problems she would not be open to him but might be to us! A sign of how good door to door is. I was impatient with a tech person concerning new ways to do things. I apologized and made sure the phone call ended cheerfully.

Your examples:

My prayer: Dear Jesus, compared to being in heaven we can hardly think that your work as a carpenter was always delightful, but we cannot picture you ever grumbling about such sacrifices! Help us to truly follow Mother Teresa in being willing to do small things with great love.

Your prayer:

Day 61: The Challenge of Hospitality of Heart

"One gives freely, yet grows all the richer; another withholds what he should give, and only suffers want. (Proverbs 11:24)

Dr. Ronda's examples: I remember going to a lecture of the great psychologist Viktor Frankl, who had been in a concentration camp in Germany. Perhaps because of the sufferings of that time, he said that he told all his patients that they could call him any time of the night. I was so impressed that I always say the same to anyone who is in crisis. I practiced hospitality of the heart today by calling old friends even when I was tired. The daughter I am living with presently talks about feeling so much into the pain of others that it is almost too much sometimes. That kind of empathy is surely a form of generous hospitality of the heart. By contrast, a form of warding off others I have noticed is people who show by body language or tone of voice that they don't have time for you.

Your examples:

My prayer: Sacred Heart of Jesus, make our hearts like Yours! In the apparitions of the Sacred Heart You show us that Your heart is always open to us and that You feel rejected when we fail to turn to You in our sorrows. May I always hide in Your heart and may others feel that my heart is wide open to them as a conduit of Your love.

Your prayer:

Day 62: The Challenge of Loving Small Helps to Others

"… give, and it will be given to you. Good measure, pressed down, shaken together, running over, will be put into your lap. For with the measure you use it will be measured back to you." (Luke 6:38)

Dr. Ronda's examples: The head of the Legion of Mary group in my new parish is giving me rides after meetings. I plan to buy something that someone else in my home could chip in on, but I will not ask since she does so much for me. I put away food in the fridge that might otherwise spoil. I did dishes. I dragged a lot of towels from the pool area to the washing machine. I went on the telephone meeting of Emotions Anonymous so that I will improve my own control over my emotions which often are not as rational as they could be if I prayed more for grace whenever tempted to anger or anxiety.

Your examples:

My prayer: Mother Mary, I picture you as always helping others in Egypt and Nazareth. I think it is your intercession that is giving me the grace now in my new abode to really enjoy helping much more in small ways. Let me never think that only large public deeds, I can be proud of, count for the kingdom.

Your prayer:

Day 63: The Challenge of being not Tight but Lovingly Generous all Day

"In all things I have shown you that by working hard in this way we must help the weak and remember the words of the Lord Jesus, how he himself said, 'It is more blessed to give than to receive." (Acts 20:35)

Dr. Ronda's examples: My grandkids are experts at filling dishwashers since some of them are obliged to hand wash whatever doesn't get in. But I think that a pan on top of a dish could cause the dish and not the pan to be cleaned so I splay out the dishes in an orderly fashion. Instead of doing a second dishwasher I did some big pots and pans by hand out of "generosity." A category that came up today was generosity of judgment. Harsh and hasty judgments on my part are a kind of "tightness of heart." I gave away one of the books I wrote to someone who could use it. She offered to pay but I said no, no, especially since she gave me a ride.

Your examples:

My prayer: Father God, what could be more opposite to being in Your image and likeness than being "petty?" And what more like You than being lavish? Way of Love: Step by Step ... how many steps will it take for me to be more generous? I hear You reply: "It's all right. You are trying. Keep trying and never forget to ask Me to walk with you." I renounce the spirit of tightness and lay it at Your feet, Lord Jesus. Take it away.

Your prayer:

THEME

10

THE CHALLENGE OF TRUST VS. ANXIETY AND WORRY

"Perfect love casts out fear" (1 John 4:18)

Teaching:

When we read accounts in the New Testament of disciples going to martyrdom, we marvel at their fearlessness. Surely awaiting being eaten by lions or being crucified would make us feel total horror and despair. Yet the martyrs were full of trust that Jesus would help them in their torments and bring them to eternal happiness.

Many are our fears. They range from fear of being late for an appointment, fear of failing examinations, fear for our loved ones in trouble or danger, all the way to fear of terminal illness or fear of violence including, for some, the fear of violence of members of our own households; finally, fear of eternal punishment for us or loved ones.

Yet, we are taught that "fear of the Lord is the beginning of wisdom."(Psalm 111:10) Since we are weak, sinful creatures subject to all kinds of evils and sufferings, we are called to work out our salvation "in fear and trembling." (Psalm 2:11)

Even small threats to our security or welfare can trigger an immediate sense of fear. This fear can be positive when it causes us to be careful, plan well, and do whatever we can to avoid failure. Trusting in God in such situations helps, but may not remove a certain tremulous weakness.

In 12 Step Emotions Anonymous they say that that severe anxiety about being rejected or fear of falling apart shows that one's emotions are out of control and that we need to bring them to God who alone can heal us of such fears. In Theophostic Prayer Ministry, which I am studying, such anxiety is analyzed in this way. The fearful person is to try to locate the first time in childhood that he or she felt anxious. Then ask, "What was the lie the devil was telling me?" For example, the lie could be that if I was lost in a grocery store my mother would never come back. Then we are to picture, say, Jesus in that same situation holding one of our hands and guiding our mother back to us. In Unbound deliverance prayer the leader has the person in emotional turmoil make this kind of petition, "I renounce the spirit of anxiety and lay it at the feet of Jesus."

We need to avoid sinking into a quicksand of fear when challenged by situations we cannot control. We need to beg God to give us trust in His perfect love; in His provident care, even when results are disappointing or tragic. In the end, even if the worst things happen on earth, what matters most is our salvation and the salvation of those we love. We believe that God loves us and them even more than we do. When our fear becomes tortuous, we need to cast ourselves in prayer into His loving heart.

Day 64: The Challenge of Observing Anxiety vs. Trust

"Do not be anxious about anything, but in everything by prayer and supplication with thanksgiving let your requests be made known to God." (Philippians 4:6)

Dr. Ronda's examples: I noticed a cause for anxiety in myself is looking for hidden motives vs. believing what others say about what they think or feel. For example, I imagine that if someone says the slightest critical thing that they don't like me. But, when questioned, this person says, "I just made a comment. It has nothing to do with liking you. I do like you." Why shouldn't I believe that? If I bring it to God in prayer, it is easier to believe what triggers some kind of childhood wound. One friend remarked about this type of anxiety, "two-year olds think that way. They ask for reassurance any time they are criticized." I noticed that when there is any emotional insecurity in my life I get sufficiently upset to have the fantasy that I am falling apart. I saw myself obsessing about the reaction of an authority figure to me. I recalled a 12 Step method that involves writing out an anxiety and putting it in a box you call "the God box." You say "God take care of this." I made this God box and put in the name of the person I am afraid of. The fear lessened. I notice these anxieties in others around me: fear for a daughter far away and the cat's fear of a neighboring cat.

Your examples:

My prayer: Jesus, my Savior, what does "savior" mean if not that You will save me from everything that frightens me, one way or another. The worst that could happen is that the worst happens in earthly terms, and then You will gather this little wretch into Your embrace and nothing will ever hurt me again. When waves of anxiety come over me, remind me to picture You and to believe that "God alone is enough," as St. Teresa of Avila used to say.

Your prayer:

Day 65: The Challenge of Loving Trust in Jesus in your area of Greatest Anxiety

"Jesus made calm on the lake" (Mark 4:41)

Dr. Ronda's example: My greatest fear is of being alone and abandoned. When I recognized this fear, I started praying "God alone is enough" over and over again during my prayer time but also between things. It happened that the Gospel reading was about Jesus calming the storm when the disciples thought they would all drown. The Pastor quoted a spiritual writer as thinking that instead of begging Jesus to save them, they could have expressed more trust by asking Jesus to give them His peace that enabled Him not to be afraid even in a storm. "Do we try to drag Jesus into our turmoil to take it away, or, shouldn't we instead, beg Him to give us the peace to withstand turmoil?" the priest asked us. As a result of pondering this message and saying God alone is enough often, I felt much more peace.

Your example:

My prayer: Providential God, I bring to you now my worst fear. (Reader: put in the prayer your worst fear) Please quiet my soul as You calmed the storm for Jesus and the disciples. Let me not only experience surcease of anxiety, but deep peace.

Your prayer:

Day 66: The Challenge of Entrusting our Country to God

"His eyes keep watch over the nations: let rebels not rise against Him." (Psalm 66: 4?)

Dr. Ronda's examples: I prayed a rosary and mercy chaplet for an end to abortion and for the economy. I thought that if God got us past slavery and the Civil War and WWI and WWII He could save us from the horrors of the present day. I thought about the North Vietnamese, previously our enemies, and we committing atrocities there in spite of our good motives, and how "North" Vietnam is sending seminarians and nuns to study at Holy Apostles where I teach. That sure is God bringing good out of evil. I delighted in how it is that lots of good in international relations comes indirectly such as getting to know cultures of others through their foods in our restaurants starting with Chinese, Mexican, and Japanese restaurants. I put a slip of paper with USA into the God-box (described earlier).

Your examples:

My prayer: Father God, You know all the good in this country from its founding; all those who really loved You and were moral and sacrificed their lives for freedom and raised families and welcomed the "tired and the poor" from other countries and also those now praying for an end to all the evils that bedevil us. Please inspire our present and future leaders to overturn bad laws and make good laws. Review in us a love of all the good in our past history. May each of us be out of denial of any patterns that hurt our country.

Your prayer:

Day 67: Trusting God's Love in our Fears about Money and Work

"Neither death, nor life... nor things present, nor things to come, nor anything else in all creation...Nothing can separate us from the love of God in Christ Jesus, Our Lord." (Romans 8:37-39)

Dr. Ronda's examples: I have little fear about money since I have social security and a small pension and expenses I can afford. I thanked God for this security in a time when many have deep financial worries. I do worry about work a lot in the form of hating to think someday I will be too disabled or too much "a has-been" to work at my profession of teaching, writing and speaking. I put it in the God-box and then gave it to Jesus in prayer. He seemed to tell me that prayer is more important than work and I will always be able to pray, wordlessly if need be, and that can be even better. I saw that fear of not being able to work is not just because I enjoy and love my work but also the pride element.

Your examples:

My prayer: Mother Mary, I don't remember you having a "career"! Please take ~~me with both your dear hands~~ my hands in yours and laugh at these fears of mine. Take into your hands also the more rational fears about money and work of all who read this day of The Way of Love: Step by Step.

Your prayer:

Day 68: The Challenge of Trusting God's Love with our Fears about the Health and Life of ourselves and Loved Ones.

"What else have I in heaven but you? Apart from you I want nothing on earth. My body and my heart faint for joy; God is my possession forever." (Psalm 73)

Dr. Ronda's examples: Because of the suicide of my son at age 20 many years ago I don't take anyone's life for granted. If the phone rings late in the night, my heart pounds with terror, until I find out it is not serious. On the other hand, I firmly believe in the immortality of the soul which can be proven by philosophy (see my free book called Weeping with Jesus: On Grieving on my web-site: www.rondachervin.com). So I ask myself and others, wouldn't you rather be with Jesus in purgatory or heaven rather than on earth? And wouldn't you rather your loved ones be with Him? The answer is usually yes and no. We must pray that all of us persevere to the end or repent of our sins at the end. So, with this Day about trust and anxiety about sickness and death, I am putting those fears in the God-box. I am also praying for trust that the chronic problems of bad health I and others may have to endure will purge us of our sins and ready us for union with God.

Your examples:

My prayer: Mother Mary, in the depth of your soul you knew that Jesus would be resurrected, yet you must have trembled at the thought of losing His presence on earth. Intercede for us whose faith is so much less that we not hurt Jesus by disbelief in the eternal life He died to give to us.

Your prayer:

Day 69: The Challenge of Trusting in God for the Church

"You are Peter and on this rock I will build my Church, and the Gates of Hell will not prevail against it." (Matthew: 16:16-19.)

Dr. Ronda's examples: When I came into the Church at age 21 I was told, in answer to questions about evils of the past in the Church that when we say the creed we never say "I believe in Father X and Sister Y." Just the same I understand how those who have been directly victimized in some scandalous episode can feel shaken in their faith. They may think, "If Father X who says the Mass daily, didn't make it, why even try?" How sad. We don't say we will abandon the Bill of Rights because, in betrayal of these rights, we once had slavery in our country and, now, abortion! Today, in the light of this day's challenge, I lifted up to Jesus all the reasons people doubt the Church founded and graced by Him. Jesus seemed to tell me that instead of just feeling miserable, I need suffer for all betrayals within the Church with Him, in His Heart.

Your examples:

My prayer: St. Peter, you betrayed Jesus, but then repented in tears. Stop me, Jesus, from any final judgments on anyone in the Church today who has loved you but betrayed you. Intercede for me that when I betray the Lord in any way I may rush into His merciful heart. May all who feel tempted to leave the Church or who have already left the Church remain or come back to the sacraments where Jesus is pouring out His love.

Your prayer:

Day 70: The Challenge of a Whole Day of Trust in God

"Come to Me, all you who labor and are heavy-laden, and I will give you rest." (Matthew 11:28)

Dr. Ronda's examples: This day I came to see how anxiety and impatience are related. I went to a meeting hoping that someone would implement a plan of mine. Because I was so impatient to succeed I was especially anxious that I would fail. In my head, if not my actions, I was thinking as if I was the heroine of the drama of life, so that all must revolve around me. I realized how this example fit into how if we try to control things that we can't control, we lose the serenity that comes from truth in God. In fact, within that same twenty four hours someone from that meeting bumped into me in another context and was thrilled to figure out how to work with me. I had already given up out of impatience! After that, I prayed "Jesus, I trust in you" over and over. I also thought about not giving so much importance to outcomes of relatively minor matters. I recalled the charismatic adage "Walk out the door that is closing and walk in the door that is opening."

Your examples:

My prayer: I renounce the spirit of anxiety and lay it at Your feet, dear Jesus, to take away and never to return. Jesus, I trust not in me or circumstances or other people, but in You with abandonment to Your permissive will.

Your prayer:

THEME

11

THE CHALLENGE OF SIMPLICITY OF LIFE WITH MORE ROOM FOR LOVE

"Whoever has two tunics is to share with him who has none, and .... "(John 3: 11)

Teaching:

Many things are tolerated in the Church even though they are by no means part of the "way of love." Think, in the past, of slavery or killing people in duels just to avenge an insult! The Church never taught that slavery was a good but it was so interwoven

with the culture that it was only gradually that it was formally condemned starting with slave trade. I consider this to be analogous to the fact that the Church teaches that "our luxuries belong to the poor," but we don't specify an exact amount of excess that is allowable to have. This would be too complicated. Some preachers tolerate the luxurious living of their parishioners. They prefer to invite them to give more to the poor and to the Church, rather than scold them for self-indulgence. The lack of preaching on the subject in some places doesn't mean that luxury is good.

By luxury is meant having things we don't need either to survive or for our vocation. (A computer is not a luxury of the programmer or a writer. A piano is not a luxury for a pianist).

Being middle-class or upper-class is not, itself, a sin. We are to give as much away as we can in aid to the poor, choosing ways that we judge to be effective. I have personal friends who are millionaires and who live so simply that few would look at them in public and think they were rich. These people give large amounts of money for Church building, and founding of pro-life organizations. I like the fact that they dress down and drive average cars, especially because poor people in a parish can become envious if they see the pastor and other Church leaders driving an expensive looking car, even if it was a gift. Of course, as mentioned earlier in The Way of Love, volunteering time to help others is even more important than giving money.

A fascinating book on simplicity of life is *Happy Are Your Poor: The Simple Life and Spiritual Freedom* by Thomas Dubay. In this definitive study he proves that the way many people live in our so-called affluent society is totally contrary to the Gospel. It cannot be excused on the basis that "poor in Spirit" means detached from material goods and not literal simplicity of life. Poverty does not mean destitution, but it certainly doesn't mean giving small donations to the poor while hoarding.

But many middle-class and upper-class Catholics in our culture indulge not only in luxurious spending (such as having so much in our closets we cannot find the garment we are looking for) but also in waste. It is said that the garbage we throw out could feed the world. A simple practice for those following the Way of Love: Step by Step would be only buying the food we will eat each week vs. more than we can eat out of a desire to avoid ever wanting one bite more or to feel successful by buying more than enough, and then throwing out 1/3 or more of it when we feel full. It is said that a large percentage of Americans are overweight. In the past when more women were at home, it was customary to turn left-overs into stir-fries, omelets, soups, etc. It is understandable that ordering take-out vs. cooking is easier for tired people who work long hours and often, also, commute. Another wasteful practice contrary to simplicity of life is being too lazy to go through one's possessions and so buying items one already has without even keeping track.

Many readers will say, but that food we waste couldn't actually be mailed to 3rd world countries to give to the poor. My reply is that by spending less on unneeded food, clothing, gadgets, etc., we could give that money to groups that not only feed the starving but help the poor to earn money-learning trades. Mother Teresa's Missionaries of Charity, for one, use the money they get to supply village women in India with sewing machines to start making and selling clothing.

Day 71: The Challenge of Observing Myself and Others concerning Simplicity of Life

"Whoever loves money never has enough; whoever loves wealth is never satisfied." (Ecclesiastes 5:10)

Dr. Ronda's examples: In the past, when I was cooking for a family, instead of using left-overs, I used to throw out quite a lot.

I was very glad when I started to live simply because if you have less there is less to keep clean! I know of people who work at some occupation that is ethically marginal because they are afraid if they left the job they might have to live poorer. I love to see parish people working at soup-kitchens feeding the poor. In one Church where they give out vouchers for breakfast at MacDonald's I was happy to see that they allowed the poor to use the bathroom next to the chapel area to wash up. I thought Jesus was happy that while the Gospel was being read about helping the poor, our poor were actually being visibly helped since we could see them waiting for the bathroom out the glass door between us and them. I also rejoiced when in another parish we took turns watching out for the homeless staying in the basement of our Church. This went on for many winter months. The priest was the default, throughout the night, if the volunteers didn't come.

Your examples:

My prayer: Holy Spirit, thank you for inspiring me in the area of simplicity of life. Thank you that I have never been unemployed so that I have so much I can give. For the sake of having more room to love through giving, help all who read this theme in The Way of Love: Step by Step to rejoice to live more simply.

Your prayer:

Day 72: The Challenge of Simplifying Possessions

"Is not this the fast that I choose...Is it not to share your bread with the hungry?" (Isaiah 58:7)

Dr. Ronda's examples: Since, as a dedicated widow living in my daughter's house and at the seminary, all my possessions now fit in one room, this is not much of a challenge for me but, still....? I find it loving to give away some of the books I wrote when I give talks. I have to pay for those books minus a small discount. I spy the look on someone's face, who seems to wish she or he could buy the book but is hesitating probably because of the expense. And I feel joy when I just say, "if you want it, take it." I got this from an experience many years ago. Sabina Wurmbrand was the wife of Richard Wurmbrand, the famous Lutheran prisoner of the Communists who got out and gave talks all over the world. This wife was handling the book table at a talk in a Church. I came up and was fingering the book she wrote about her life. She just looked at me and said, "Take it!" I was shocked. It gave me the impetus to do the same. If you have lots more possessions than you need maybe you could think of the joy of those who buy at second hand shops when they get, say, someone's second set of china for a pittance.

Your examples:

My prayer: Holy Spirit, thank you for showering on me ideas for books to write. Thank you for inspiring publishers to get them out there. May I never hold back on giving what was given free to me by You, just to have a few more dollars in my purse.

Your prayer:

Day 73: The Challenge of Simplifying Desires for the Future

"Blessed be the poor in spirit for theirs is the kingdom of God." (Matthew 5:3)

Dr. Ronda's examples: I prayed about this and remembered that desire for prestige, power over others (even if it is spiritual not worldly power I am craving), popularity or fame – this is not simplicity of life. It is actually a form of fantasy wealth, even if it is not monetary. It is really fear of suffering and desire for ego-gratification. When I brought all this to Jesus at Eucharistic Adoration, He seemed to tell me not to plan ahead so much. I should cherish the peace that could come from not adding more projects. I could wait to add more projects until I truly am settled into my new place without have getting stressed from having too much to do. After this I got a little peace!

Your examples:

My prayer: My Jesus, may the highpoint of my future days be You, my bridegroom, at Mass and all the time I can be with the Trinity, the angels, the saints. Then may I take in all the gifts and graces you wish for me in the present day leaving the future to the providence of God.

Your prayer:

Day 74: The Challenge of Simplifying a Cluttered Lifestyle so there is more Room for Unexpected Loving Encounters and Deeds.

"Martha, Martha, you are anxious and troubled about many things, but one thing is necessary. Mary has chosen the good portion, which will not be taken away from her." (Luke 10: 42)

Dr. Ronda's examples: I like to have a clear desk, but often there is a pile of things to be done on it. Today I enjoyed a new prayer meeting that went longer than I anticipated. I enjoyed a lunch with a new friend instead of feeling pressured to get back to my desk with its pile of papers. I relaxed more during the radio blog I do with Bob and Evelyn Olson. I opened my heart to calls and e-mails from a dear friend whose spouse died suddenly. As per the message to my heart I got yesterday, I avoided taking on new projects a friend suggested. Each time I looked at the pile on the desk, I prayed with deep sighs but didn't try to diminish the pile before doing, instead, other things that are more obligatory or more personally loving.

Your examples:

My prayer: St. Martha, you became a saint in spite of the tendency to choose the active over the contemplative side of life. Teach me how you followed the admonition of Jesus. Teach me more balance so that Jesus might not be disappointed that pursuing project after project I have so little time to just sit at His feet.

Your prayer:

Day 75: The Challenge of Simplifying the Mind

"Behold the lilies of the field, how they grow. They labor not, neither spin. And yet for all that I say unto you, that even Solomon in all his royalty, was not arrayed as these." (Matthew 6:1)

Dr. Ronda's examples: Expanding the metaphor of spinning in the above Scripture, I noticed that my head is always spinning with ideas. I realized I need to simplify my mind. So, today, I forced myself not to make notes about other things in the middle of activities that need focus. I think that constantly interrupting one thing to do another or make notes to do another is kind of OCD. Another way to put it could be that multi-tasking has its place but not every minute of the day! I noticed how many of my thoughts are related to micro-managing others! I was alarmed at how hard it was for me to focus – worse than I even thought, as in wanting to leap up from writing this paragraph to turn off the spot-heater. Couldn't that wait 5 minutes? When I forced myself to stay on track it felt painful but less as if I was in bondage.

Your examples:

My prayer: Oh, Jesus, Mary and Joseph, I can't picture your heads spinning! No, never. Not that you didn't mull over problems, Mary and Joseph, but not in a frenetic way. The opposite of a cluttered head would be the simplicity of trust. Help me to pray when my head is spinning a few aspirations such as: Give me trust that whatever I am supposed to do will get done in Your time.

Your prayer:

Day 76: Simplifying Prayer to make it more Lovingly Personal

"Thou art called by name, thou art mine ... when you walk through the waters, I will be with you." (Isaiah 43:1-1)

Dr. Ronda's examples: There was a long period of time when I experienced the presence of God throughout the day and especially when I was at prayer. That was followed by a kind of "grey night of the soul" with much more distraction. I got kind of resigned to this spiritual trial. But, I realized that slowing down verbal prayer for this 100 day spiritual marathon brought much more of a sense of the presence of God, Mary, and the saints. I made it a point to look at the lovely artistic renditions of my celestial friends and to pray as slowly as possible vs. as quickly as possible. I thought of the consecration prayer I say each day that includes asking for the grace to pray as if this was the last day of my life. Lots more peace came with these efforts to make my prayer more a personal act of love.

Your examples:

My prayer: St. Teresa, my favorite woman saint, please intercede for me never to pray in that perfunctory way you chided others from doing. My beloved Trinity, Mary, and all the saints I beg you to be present when I pray so that the fire of love may be enkindled.

Your prayer:

Day 77: The Challenge of a whole day of Freedom of Spirit and Lightness of Heart

"Come to me, all who labor and are heavy laden, and I will give you rest. Take my yoke upon you, and learn from me, for I am gentle and lowly in heart, and you will find rest for your souls. For my yoke is easy, and my burden is light." (Matthew 11:28-30)

Dr. Ronda's examples: I have friends who insist on keeping Sunday as a day of rest. But, foolish I resists! As I understand it the commandment of the Sabbath is interpreted in Catholic practice as avoiding manual labor and work for pay and even that rule can be dispensed for reasons of economic necessity. Just the same, it is very good for me to drop the intellectual work and spend Sunday after Mass in quiet, pleasant, friendly activities. This day I did drop the work and spent time with 2 new friends including making my first trip to the Pacific Ocean since I arrived to stay for 8 months. The ocean is my favorite created being. Seeing it always expands my soul. God seemed to second the motion of my day of freedom of spirit and lightness by the sight of the orb of the sun changing into what looks like a huge Eucharistic host with brilliant pink clouds around it, as is often seen at the alleged apparition at Medjugorje. My friend, who had never been to Medjugorje, also saw the same vision in the clouds above the ocean.

Your examples: (If this day doesn't fall on a Sunday, pick the next possible relatively free day to complete this exercise).

My prayer: Jesus, as I finish this week of my spiritual marathon, step by step, I renounce the spirit of clutter of possessions, of schemes, of distractions and busyness and lay it at Your feet, dear Jesus. Give me, instead, a true spirit of simplicity so that more of me may be open to love.

Your prayer:

THEME

12

THE CHALLENGE OF LETTING GO OF ANGER SO AS TO BECOME LOVINGLY PEACEFUL

"My peace I give you..." (John 14:27)

Teaching:

We already had a week, the third one of the Way of Love: Step by Step, opening ourselves to loving forgiveness to overcome resentment. That week was primarily about large causes of anger. This week is more about every day irritations that seem to make peace nothing but an impossible ideal. Yet Jesus offers us peace. Think how wonderful it feels to be with a person who is genuinely peaceful. It is so soothing.

To embrace the peace of Jesus we have to expunge certain habits of anger such as refusal to accept the crosses of our workplace or our home or our parish that we cannot change. To be peaceful we have to avoid the critical spirit that comes from perfectionism. In his program Recovery International, the psychiatrist Abraham Low emphasizes the necessity of accepting the average of our own and others' behavior patterns unless we have clear authority over them as is the case with children or employees. This doesn't mean everyone is right or okay. Not at all! But, as I would put it, we should not expect ourselves or others to be perfect unless there is a major reason for conversion. That reason is rarely our displeasure. Instead of fretting and fuming, we need to employ humor or work around the obstacles caused by the faults of others. We need to think of others not so much as fallen idols but as funny little creatures. The attitude of realism brings peace. A realist expects a lot to be difficult each day with circumstances and personalities. But he or she likes to meet problems not with anger but with solutions!

A big cause of anger identified by Dr. Low is taking everything bad that happens as personally directed against oneself. Someone doesn't smile at me. What is more likely, that the person who ignored me suddenly decided to reject me or that he or she is preoccupied, busy, or had a headache? On one of our Step by Step days this week you will get a chance to practice trying to understand people's motives better instead of reacting right away with anger.

The most subtle aspect of anger that Dr. Low pinpointed is called symbolic victory. Because we feel weak and powerless in many situations, such as bad drivers on the road, we try to feel stronger and more powerful through sarcasm. Cursing or giving another driver the finger is not a real victory. It doesn't stop the other driver for unsafe practices. It is only a "symbolic" victory

– that is a fake way to feel superior. Much gossip and sarcasm has that unfruitful result. We feel superior when talking about others. We certainly don't feel more loving! By contrast, a peaceful person gives God the annoyance, pain, and sufferings caused by bad behavior of others and then peacefully waits to see if there is a grace-filled way to overcome evil with good. How much more loving than cursing drivers, would be to help train drivers in one's own family to follow the law.

To find out more about the books of Dr. Abraham Low and the free self-help groups he started to overcome anger, anxiety and depression, go to www.info@lowselfhelpsystems.org

Day 78: The Challenge of Observing Peacefulness and Anger

"Know this, my beloved brothers: let every person be quick to hear, slow to speak, slow to anger." (James 1:19)

Dr. Ronda's examples: I was pleased to be able to report that after some 17 years of being part of Recovery, International for anger, fear, and depression, I really don't go into a rage any more unless all my buttons are pushed. Since they weren't pushed, I had a really peaceful day in spite of an incident that I would have blown up into a huge crisis if I was the former me! Of course this is not just because of psychological insight and more common sense but God's grace working on my nature. My nature will always be choleric, but that doesn't mean that anger will dominate my daily life as it used to do.

Your examples:

My prayer: Thank you, Holy Spirit, for all the wisdom you have drummed into me in the last decades. Thank you for every moment of peace I wouldn't have without these graces of wisdom and pure infused liberation. Please, keep it coming!

Your prayer:

Day 79: The Challenge of Resignation vs. Rage

"Be angry but sin not; commune with your own hearts on your beds and be silent. Offer right sacrifices, and put your trust in the Lord." (Psalm 4:4-5)

Dr. Ronda's examples: This challenge reminded me of the serenity prayer – to have the wisdom to know what I can change and what I can't change. I thought of the character of a man who is kind of Stoic and not very communicative. I remembered someone writing that what women really want is to change men into women in terms of willingness to talk a lot about daily conflicts. I thought of how resignation is a relaxed state vs. the tension of anger. I reminded myself that instead of complaining I should be happy that anything goes well. Going slower vs. multi-tasking I find to be a help in overcoming irritability. I had to wait for a promised ride. I got angry, but I kept talking to myself about how trivial this was, especially since the ride was to a place where I was to give a talk on overcoming anger! The talk went very well and I was ashamed at my fantasies of giving up talks just to avoid the usual difficulties with speaking dates in terms of the arrangements. I can offer these little crosses up for the people attending the talk instead of fretfully complaining.

Your examples:

My prayer: Father God, even without original sin men and women would have been different in character in many ways. Let me accept these differences and work with them instead of going into a tizzy when the difference means I can't have things my way. Remind me to thank you for all the wonderful masculine qualities in men who help me in so many ways.

Your prayer:

Day 80: The Challenge of Understanding the Motives of Others

"The anger of man works not the justice of God." (James 1:20)

Dr. Ronda's examples: There was a man I met at a social occasion years ago. We had an argument about religion. I kind of wrote him off. Now many years afterwards I saw him again in more relaxed circumstances. He was friendly and seemed to have changed. When I "write people off" do I really understand the motives for their words or actions so well that I can think they are hopeless? In another case, I developed a theory about why a particular person was so distant. Now, meeting him again, I see that there were many other reasons, not involving rejection of me as I thought. A Catholic therapist talks about having open vs. narrow lens! A larger picture instead of one framed possibly by my own complexes? I had an immediate example. I wrote a funny poem to someone and sent it by e-mail. I didn't get a thank you or even a smiley face. I jumped to the conclusion that my poem was misread as sarcastic and that this friend now hated me. Later I found out she didn't have time to open her e-mails and when she did she was delighted with the poem.

Your examples:

My prayer: Oh my Jesus, You didn't "write off" the good thief on the cross next to Yours! Keep me from judging. Help to avoid narrow lens based on defensiveness against rejection. If I call it first, it is less painful? Send the Holy Spirit of counsel that I may understand people better in the future.

Your prayer:

Day 81: The Challenge of Excusing instead of Accusing

(If you have something against someone else) "...first go away and make peace with that person. Then come back and offer your gift (at the altar)." (Matthew 5:24)

Dr. Ronda's examples: On my way to Holy Mass this morning I thought of excusing a friend for being so indirect in his advice that I didn't even get it! I excused a man who is very hostile but doesn't realize it. I thought that probably he must have had something very wounding in his childhood to have become so angry in spite of being so devout. I excused people in the Church who don't like creative, interesting things I want to do. I realized they are right to want to be safe and if they don't know me they could think I am some wild, foolish, innovator. At a meeting someone allowed her cell-phone to ring over and over again. We are told at the beginning of the meeting to turn off our phones. I wondered why she couldn't leave it in her car if she couldn't make it turn off. I thought that perhaps she is just so anxious about others who might call that she has to see the call waiting person indicator so she could leave the meeting if it is an emergency.

Your examples:

My prayer: My Jesus, You certainly suffered from people misunderstanding Your intentions. Even though You tried to teach them to think otherwise, you offered to them the option to repent. How much more trivial are the situations I face. Even if the excuses I devise are not accurate, let me realize that it is better to wrongly excuse than to harshly accuse.

Your prayer:

Day 82: The Challenge of Loving, Gentle Speech

"Learn of me because I am meek and humble of heart and you will find rest for your souls." (Matthew 11:29)

Dr. Ronda's examples: I wrote a note to a man instead of trying to whisper loudly during Adoration. I asked someone about a potential conflict in such a soft voice that it didn't sound like a criticism. I very gently mentioned to someone that I thought something proposed was not such a good idea instead of loudly defending my point of view. I wrote a gentle e-mail to someone under great pressure.

Your examples:

My prayer: Mother Mary, there is a beautiful song about your gentleness that we sing. Why would I want to be anything but gentle? I seem to hear you telling me that gentleness comes with trust and trust comes with faith, and faith is a gift. It is a gift Jesus wants for me, so I beg you, Jesus, swath my jittery little soul with faith, trust, and gentleness.

Your prayer:

Day 83: The Challenge of Praying for Peaceful Solutions to Conflicts

"Some people make cutting remarks, but the words of the wise bring healing. (Proverbs 12:18)

Dr. Ronda's examples: I decided that after a whole week of working on peace vs. anger, I might ask for the grace to resolve a long term thorny problem. In bringing up the issue again I put it in the context of my faults only. This gave me more hope. I realized that being "right" is not as important as saving relationships. In the case of a possible conflict that doesn't have to be resolved right away I decided to employ the 12 Step principle that we don't have to solve all our problems today. Shouldn't the need to closure yield to common sense vs. frantic attempts to solve things the elements of which don't even yet exist sometimes?

Your examples:

My prayer: Holy Spirit, You are called both the spirit of counsel and the spirit of love. You show me that wisdom is better than swift but hasty, often stupid, decisions. Help me to believe that delay is not giving-up.

Your prayer:

Day 84: The Challenge of a Whole Day of Peace

"Commit thy way unto the Lord." Roll the whole burden of life upon the Lord. Leave with Jehovah not thy present fretfulness merely, but all thy cares." (Psalm 37:5)

Dr. Ronda's examples: I had to get up at 5:30 AM to do a phone Sirius radio show that was live on the East Coast. I peacefully got up and had my wake up breakfast without any "churning in the head" about how I have to stop doing things like this at my age, etc. etc. etc. I prayed to give a gentle answer to someone who asked for advice. When the computer server went down I adjusted to the hiatus without getting upset. I see that doing everything slowly including prayer is a great antidote to being stressed. At Church I offered up for two big intentions, the coldness – they don't put on heat at all in this Southern California area. I resolved to bring my long cotton underwear tomorrow. To avoid the stress of backing into a parking space, I made a detour. I noticed at a women's charismatic prayer meeting how tongues and childlike songs are peaceful and, therefore, an antidote to irritability.

Your examples:

My prayer: Father God, help me to move gently and peacefully through this last period of my life with one foot in eternity. I renounce the spirit of anger and lay it at your feet, dear Prince of Peace, to take away forever!

Your prayer:

THEME

13

THE CHALLENGE OF BEING COOPERATIVE VS. BOSSY

"A dispute arose between them about which should be reckoned the greatest, but he said to them, "Among pagans it is the kings who lord it over them, and those who have authority over them are given the title Benefactor. This must not happen with you. No; the greatest among you must behave as if he were the youngest, the leader as if he were the one who serves...here I am among you as one who serves!"(Luke 22:25)

Teaching:

There are situations where one person is clearly in charge and others have to obey. A policeman is in charge. A general is in charge of the troops. The manager of a company is in charge. The pastor of a Church is in charge. Parents are in charge of their children up until a certain age. Teachers are in charge of the classroom. Such people are not being bossy when they exercise their legitimate authority. It is loving in itself to carry the burden of such authority. Of course, it is all the more loving to exercise such authority with respect for the dignity of those who have to obey.

A bossy person is one who takes charge in situations where he or she is not in authority, sometimes over-riding the role of another who is in charge. One who is a leader in a particular situation might try to be in charge in others circumstances where this is not appropriate and this can seem like arrogance. For example, used to being a teacher, I may think that I should give little lectures in social situations, and even worse, that others should accept my teachings as if they were my students!

Come to think of it, dominating conversations is a form of bossiness. Why should I strut my stuff, instead of drawing out others with loving questions? Or, how about learning why people think differently vs. assuming I know exactly why they are so wrong-headed?

Underlying bossiness could be lack of trust in providence so that we think that unless we grab the reins the horse will go over the cliff. Bossiness could also come from thinking we are superior to others. I recall a funny old song of the sixties song that ran, "I can do anything better than you can, I can do anything better than you." Usually acting superior in one area is a compensation for feeling inferior in other areas. Bossiness certainly involves a power-grab. Once I was talking about problems in the family and a spiritual guide said humorously, "Well, Ronda, generally the grandmother isn't a very powerful figure, is she?" Gulp!

I wonder: If God is my boss, I don't have to be boss at the wrong time and place, do I?

By contrast, the loving spirit of cooperation involves the humility to see what is best in each situation vs. using it as an opportunity to take charge regardless of whether one has the gifts or expertise. For example, it is fine if a student politely raises an objection to a teacher's concept. But it is arrogant if the student adopts a tone that suggests that the teacher is an idiot and the student knows much more.

In a loving family, there is much mutual consultation about weighty decisions. No one should do anything immoral at the bidding of another person, even a parent. But where it is a matter of prudential judgments, there needs to be a tie-breaker, the father, to avoid division and finally chaos or the break-up of the family. The wife should not adopt the role of boss over the husband, constantly nay-saying his decisions, nagging him, and belittling his authority.

In church work, it is important that the team including deacons, sisters, members of the parish council, leaders of different ministries, work cooperatively under the direction of the pastor. Unless the matter involves heresy, dissent, or immoral actions, the team should not be lining up against the pastor to boss him around.

Day 85: The Challenge of Observing Cooperative vs. Bossy Behavior

"You know that the so-called rulers of the heathen lord it over them, and their great men have absolute power. But it must not be so among you. No, whoever among you wants to be great must

become the slave of all men! For the Son of Man Himself has not come to be served but to serve, and to give his life to set many others free." (Mark 10: 42-45)

Dr. Ronda's examples: I hate shopping but my daughter wanted me to go with her to get Valentine's Day decorations, so I agreed and it was fun. She appreciated that I went with her instead of giving a big lecture on luxurious spending on holidays. We arranged for a lunch visit of a new friend. My daughter mentioned that someone else usually visits on that day. I said that this would not be good because I wanted the lunch to be for sharing deeper things, not a social lunch. She said probably the other friend wouldn't come anyhow since she has cancelled many times. Instead of arguing endlessly about this, I let it go and accepted that maybe the second friend would come and maybe not and just let the Holy Spirit sort out the conversation vs. my trying to be the boss of the plan. I had a terrible computer glitch. I got very bossy threatening to leave a project because no tech person would help me right away. A friend suggested that I just act vulnerable instead and that would bring out the cooperative tendencies of the tech people better than threats. It worked.

Your examples:

My Prayer: Oh, gentle Jesus, You who could have wiped out the whole world in an instant before the crucifixion, help me not to be so bossy in tiny and larger situations where I just get frightened if I don't have the power to dominate others. Why not meekly express my needs instead?

Your prayer:

Day: 86: The Challenge of Checking Inappropriate Stances of Superiority or Authority

"Jesus knew that the Father had put all things under his power, and that he had come from God and was returning to God, so he got up from the meal, took off his outer clothing, and wrapped a towel around his waist. After that, he poured water into a basin and began to wash his disciples' feet, drying them with the towel that was wrapped around him. He came to Simon Peter, who said to him, 'Lord, are you going to wash my feet?' Jesus replied, 'You do not realize now what I am doing, but later you will understand.'"(John 13:3-8)

Dr. Ronda's examples: I watched different people in positions of authority. In some cases they seemed to bend over backwards to show that they were there to serve vs. acting superior. In others there was a tone of treating those being served as inferior because of the more powerful role of the one in authority. I noticed that when I talk more softly I feel less bossy! I saw that complaining in my head about how cold it is in Church during daily Mass is a little form of "entitlement." Going door to door with Legion of Mary, the pro who has being doing this for years said that we don't want to inundate them with arguments to refute their assertions of why they left the Church but rather show love and hand out a minimum of literature. I realized that refuting people in some situations is kind of bossy, even though it is appropriate in philosophy classrooms.

Your examples:

My prayer: Jesus, Lord but Servant, I see that even though we are all here to serve it is not right to demand service. It would have been odd if Peter had insisted that You wash His feet. Oh, help me to get it right; to be humble enough to ask for needed help but without the slightest touch of "entitlement" where I am not entitled!"

Your prayer:

Day 87: The Challenge of Offering Help in Daily Circumstances

"You have not strengthened the weak or healed the sick, or bound up the injured. You have not brought back the strays or searched for the lost." (Ezechial 34:4)

Dr. Ronda's examples: I decided at a luncheon that I didn't need to "strut my stuff," but instead draw out the other guests. Drawing out other people is a kind of helpfulness vs. seizing the stage for myself. Asking questions worked very well so that the guest of honor got plenty of time to display her great sense of humor and depth so we got to know her better. Bringing back the strays, as in the above Scripture, fits with Legion of Mary door to door finding lapsed Catholics, which I spent time doing today with a woman from our legion who had lots of experience I could learn from. I rejoiced in the wonderful help of my son-in-law with my ailing computer. He worked hours on it. I offered to pay but he refused since I am family. I helped with dishes after the luncheon.

Your examples:

My prayer: St. Francis de Sales, great teacher and great conversationalists, you moved in many circles and managed to bring those less devout into a deeper place through your geniality. Help me not to be so serious at the wrong times, and to be more serious at the right times. St. Jane of Chantal, brought up as a noble woman, in the order you founded with St. Francis de Sales you occupied yourself outside of the Mass and prayer with menial work. Help me to love to help in these small gracious ways.

Your prayer:

Day 89: The Challenge of not taking Umbrage when ones Legitimate Authority is Ignored

"I am the Lord, the God all mankind. Is anything too hard for me? Jeremiah 37:27

Dr. Ronda's examples: I saw that I take umbrage because I think if I don't make things happen they won't. This is ignoring the scripture as if it would be too hard for God to make something happen in another way if my plan is ignored. A student wrote a paper that didn't fit my assignment. It looked like she had taken a paper for another course and just inserted some of my text. I felt as if my authority was being ignored. I wanted to push my weight around on this matter. After expressing my concerns to the student, I prayed, and the Holy Spirit seemed to nudge me to just ask her to re-write the paper the correct way instead of making a big issue about it. She did what I asked and it came out fine. I prayed and prayed before dealing with another sticky situation where I have some authority and I was able to approach the other people in authority with little stress in my voice or manner but a certain firmness. I realized that I needed to accept that maybe God wanted me to do the project in another way. It felt less bossy. This matter did come out well and I felt happy using some authority but not in a domineering manner.

Your examples:

My prayer: Holy Spirit, let me learn from these experiences how to be less bossy in order to walk in the Way of Love: Step by Step. May I never take umbrage at others not accepting my authority but, instead, believe indeed that even if a project fails, You, Holy Spirit, can bring out the same goals in another way.

Your prayer:

Day 90: The Challenge of a Quiet Spirit

"The ornament of a meek and quiet spirit…is in the sight of God of great price, (1 Peter 3:3-4)

Dr. Ronda's examples: I tried for a whole day to just talk much less. It feels peaceful and kind of sweet and more like someone of 74 (I'm presently on leave and mostly teaching Distance Learning where I don't talk.) As I was waking up I decided not even to bring my silenced cell phone to Church. Let it "rest in silence" for a few hours. I welcomed the idea that cultivating a quiet spirit meant less frenetic planning for the future; more letting things unfold. The parish here in California is very large, full of spiritual helps that the elderly can benefit from. And my daughter's joyful love for me could also make it possible to be less noisy and more receptive.

Your examples:

My prayer: Sweet Mary, I am consecrated to you. I want to become more like you. That is certainly to have a quiet vs. a bossy spirit. Intercede for me that I may come to love quiet as much as talk.

Your prayer:

Day 91: The Challenge of Enjoying being more in the Background

"The Lord is my shepherd, I shall not want." (Psalm 23: 1)

Dr. Ronda's examples: I have a sense that this whole 100 Day Marathon is to usher me into the end of the race – to have made all these steps day by day in the Way of Love – that afterwards I may let my Savior carry me the rest of the way. Well, that would certainly be less bossy. I recalled how, a few years ago, when I was worrying about my future, I heard the soothing words in my heart - "Ronda, you have given so much to the Church. In the end the Church will take care of you." I realized that being more in the background would mean carrying less "baggage" in my head. It felt peaceful.

Your examples:

My prayer: Mother Mary, you were certainly a lot in the background when Jesus was doing His ministry. You didn't feel miserable about this. You were happy your Son was finally revealing Himself. Help me to enjoy watching your Son unfolding His graces through others.

Your prayer:

Day 92: The Challenge of being Cooperative All Day Long

"But the fruit of the Spirit is love, joy, peace, patience, kindness..." (Galatians 5:22)

Dr. Ronda's examples: Today I asked my family how I could help more. This might involve occasionally washing the kitchen floor, taking the lighter garbage out more, cooking for them more often. I reminded my Legion of Mary sisters and brothers that I am available as a substitute for Holy Communion services. I will also cooperate with God's grace by offering up every tiny difficulty of the day for those in spiritual, psychological and physical need. I will especially avoid all being bossy in making requests.

Your examples:

My Prayer: Mother Mary, help me to become more cooperative and less bossy. I renounce the spirit of being bossy and lay it at your feet, Lord Jesus, to take it away, forever.

Your prayer:

THEME

14

THE CHALLENGE OF SPIRITUAL WARFARE TO OVERCOME YOUR WORST DEFECT FOR THE SAKE OF LOVE

Here's your last challenge. Do you have enough trust in the Holy Spirit who brought you this far on our 100 Day Marathon to spend a week trying to overcome something that still remains as a barrier to love? Not alone, of course, with the Trinity, Mary, the angels and saints to help you?

This barrier might be something you want to work on more specifically that was already a theme but it might be something not touched on such as laziness, meanness, temptations of lust ... you name it.

Or, this is even more challenging. Ask family, close friends, your spiritual director, counselor, or members of a prayer group these questions:

1. Tell me 3 loving traits you think I have.

2. What is one characteristic you wish I could improve upon through insight and focused prayer?

(Note from Dr. Ronda: I asked the daughter I am living with these questions and in answer to #2 she said humorously but to the point: "I wish you wouldn't try to get other people to undertake spiritual challenges that could be harmful since you're not a professional counselor!" I saw her point and so regarding this challenge I advise that if you feel threatened by the step of asking others to tell you what they wish you would change, just pass over this week. You could just pray that gentle Jesus would let you know what loving traits He has helped you develop and what He would like to help you change in the future.)

Once you decide what your challenge is for this week, you will follow the same format as the other 13 weeks. You will find the Scripture. You will write a teaching. You will write the name of the challenge you think will help you for each of the seven days. You will write your examples and your prayer.

_____(Title of your Challenge)

Scripture: (You can easily find Scriptures by Google search the name of the bad trait and its opposite as in searching for Lying in Scripture. You will find many and then you can arrange them according to which one fits best the aspect of your bad trait you want to work on.)

Teaching:

Day 93: Observing _____in yourself and others

Scripture:

My examples:

My prayer:

(For the following days, entitle each day with a challenge related to one or another aspect of the flaw and its opposite.)

Day 94: _____

Scripture:

My examples:

My prayer:

Day 95:_____

Scripture:

My examples:

My prayer:

Day 96:_____

Scripture:

My examples:

My prayer:

Day 97:_____

Scripture:

My examples:

My prayer:

Day 98:_____

Scripture:

My examples:

My prayer:

Day 99:_____

Scripture:

My examples:

My prayer: (Write your prayer and end with) I renounce the spirit of _____ and lay it at Your feet Jesus to take away.

Day 100: Celebrate the Victory of the Lord in you on The Way of Love: Step by Step

"For this reason I kneel before the Father, from whom His whole family in heaven and on earth derives its name. I pray that out of His glorious riches He may strengthen you with power through His Spirit in your inner being, so that Christ may dwell in your hearts through faith. And I pray that you, being rooted and established in love, may have power, together with all the believers, to grasp how wide and long and high and deep is the love of Christ, and to know this love that surpasses knowledge-- that you may be filled to the measure of all the fullness of God. Now to Him who is able to do immeasurably more than all we ask or imagine, according to His power that is at work within us, to Him be glory in the church and in Christ Jesus throughout all generations, for ever and ever! Amen." (Ephesians 3:14-20)

Your spiritual marathon is over. You won! Even if you only got one mile ahead of where you were before you started because of running this marathon, that was a victory of grace.

Dr. Ronda's Resolutions: To pray for greater focus at Mass and other prayers. To sing and listen to joyful music more often. To make more acts of surrender. To go through life more slowly and with less talking.

Your Resolutions:

My prayer: Jesus, Mary and Joseph, help me never to stray from the Way of Love, that step by step your love may overflow from me to all those who need it.

Your prayer:

More Books By Ronda Chervin

If you enjoyed *The Way of Love* then why not check out Ronda Chervin's other books online at:

www.rondachervin.com

More copies of *The Way of Love* are available at:

www.creatspace.com/4123855